Literature, Language and Computing

Polina Eismont · Maria Khokhlova ·
Mikhail Koryshev
Editors

Literature, Language and Computing

Russian Contribution from the LiLaC-2023

Springer

Editors
Polina Eismont
St. Petersburg University
Saint-Petersburg, Russia

Maria Khokhlova
St. Petersburg University
Saint-Petersburg, Russia

Mikhail Koryshev
St. Petersburg University
Saint-Petersburg, Russia

ISBN 978-981-96-0989-5 ISBN 978-981-96-0990-1 (eBook)
https://doi.org/10.1007/978-981-96-0990-1

This Springer imprint is published by the registered company Springer Nature Singapore Pte Ltd.
The registered company address is: 152 Beach Road, #21-01/04 Gateway East, Singapore 189721, Singapore

Preface

This volume presents the collection of papers presented at the international scientific conference "Literature, Language and Computer Technologies", which was held at St. Petersburg University from November 9 to 11, 2023. The conference was held for the second time and brought together researchers who are engaged in the current problems of studying literature and language with the help of computer methods. Valeria Chernyavskaya presented a plenary talk on pragmatic trajectories of the word in the space of culture, evidentiality and the dominant nature of the corpus-based approach, which enables researchers to obtain valid and statistically significant patterns. Evgeny Kazartsev, in his plenary talk, spoke about the traditions of mathematical verse studies, focusing on the history of methods.

The participants of the conference presented their papers in five parts devoted to a wide range of interdisciplinary issues, the content of which is reflected in the proposed volume: "Quantitative Methods in Literary Studies", "Quantitative Methods in Language Studies", "Spoken Corpora: Phonetics Studies", "Communicative Interfaces" and "Corpora in Teaching and Translation".

The collection opens with an article by *Boris Kovalev*, which is devoted to the quantitative analysis of poetic works of Jorge Luis Borges and their periodization by means of thematic modelling with the BERTopic algorithm. *Alexander Grebennikov, Mikhail Koryshev, Ekaterina Ivanova* and *Tatiana Skrebtsova* describe frequency dictionary of fiction on a representative sample from the Corpus of the Russian Short Stories (1900–1930). This material is also explored in the following two papers. *Tatiana Sherstinova et al.* study sentiment across different stories and by theme and evaluate correlation between the texts' sentiment and readers' preferences. *Alexander Grebennikov* and *Tatiana Skrebtsova* describe the most common colour adjectives used in Russian literature of the early twentieth century. *Polina Maksimenko* in her article focuses on the research of Russian fanfiction and describes a project to create a database that comprises 135,000 fanfiction texts.

The volume continues with a set of papers that illustrate the use of quantitative methods in linguistic studies based on different corpora. The paper by *Anastasia Kolmogorova* and *Kristina Borisova* presents a sample of comparative sentiment and topic modelling analysis of three school textbooks describing the same events of

Russian history. A long-standing problem of automatic homographs is discussed in the paper by *Ivan Stolyarov* and *Olga Mitrofanova*, who show that BERT models can successfully solve the disambiguation problem on a relatively small training dataset of only 28 pairs of homographs. *Anatoly Baranov et al.* based on the data of historic subcorpora of Russian National Corpus demonstrate the relevant and previously undescribed changes in the inventory of Russian idioms from the nineteenth to the twenty-first century. Possessor doubling constructions in oral vernacular Russian are in the focus of *Evgenii Sokolov* and *Mariia Korolkova*'s study which show that two possessors are possible within the same structure due to semantic difference between them.

The topic of spoken corpora continues in the third part of the collection, devoted to phonetics issues, which are one of the key issues for creating communication interfaces and solving the problems of voice synthesis and analysis. *Vera Evdokimova* and *Maria Maximova* describe the results of the study on the variation of format trajectories for monophthongs in different consonant contexts in English, French, and German that may be applied in automatic speech recognition systems. A concise description of Russian discourse elements that function as a backchannel cues is present in the paper by *Denis Vasiliev* and *Elena Shamina* who prove that this kind of vocalizations contain sounds outside the phoneme inventory of the Russian language and form an integrated and inseparable part of Russian dialogue structure. The paper by *Kira Sypacheva* focuses on the frontiers of phonetics and computer science, and based on the analysis of Belfast and Newcastle dialects of English show how the acoustic analysis software may be used for dialectal speech research. *Daria Gorbunova, Kristina Zaides* and *Natalia Bogdanova-Beglarian* address the topic of spontaneous speech differences between introverts and extroverts analyzing the correlation between the frequency of vocalized hesitations and the psychotype on the data from the "One Speech Day" corpus.

The fourth part of the collection discusses the problems of creating communication interfaces. The paper by *Anna Zinina, Artemiy Kotov* and *Nikita Arinkin* examines the dual emotional reaction of Russian speakers to communication with a robot: people simultaneously feel both sympathy for the robot and distrust in its words. The communication interface created in St. Petersburg University, which helps applicants in the admission process, is described in the article by *Olga Mitrenina, Maria Ladushina* and *Anastasia Kolpashchikova*. A feature of this interface is the stylized speech of the chatbot, which addresses the applicant on behalf of the founder of the university—Peter the Great, which forced the creators to study the historical communication of the early eighteenth century and adapt the themes of the twenty-first century to it. The new Russian question-answer corpus (ruOHQA) based on the spoken interviews with the Russian speaking Holocaust survivors is presented in the paper by *Liudmila Bukreeva et al.* who suppose this corpus to be a useful source for neural network models training.

The collection is completed by the articles that consider corpora in teaching and translation. Cross-linguistic correspondences and their identification in parallel Russian and English texts are the focus of the article by *Adelya Abdulmanova, Ekaterina Vyunova and Irina Lekomtseva. Altana Bazarzhapova* describes a pilot experiment conducted in order to establish methods for translating the semantically bleached words used in everyday Russian into the Buryat language. The history of German liturgical culture is studied by *Mikhail Koryshev* and *Maria Khokhlova* by comparing a corpus of Catholic hymns and a large reference corpus. The last article of the collection by *Kira Shchukina* and *Tatiana Smirnova* deals with polycode Internet memes and pays attention to the techniques used in them.

This volume will be a useful reference for scholars in theoretical and applied linguistics, literary studies, language teaching and education.

Saint-Petersburg, Russia

Polina Eismont
Mikhail Koryshev
Maria Khokhlova

Contents

Editors and Contributors

About the Editors

Polina Eismont is an Associate Professor at Ludmila Verbitskaya Department of General Linguistics, St. Petersburg University. Her research interests include Language Acquisition and Psycholinguistics, Text Linguistics, Cognitive Linguistics, Event Structure, Music Semantics, Syntax of Nulls. She obtained her Ph.D. from St. Petersburg University in 2008. She is the author of more than 50 papers in domestic and international journals and volumes and the co-editor of two CCIS volumes "Language, Music, and Computing" (Springer Verlag, 2015, 2019) and two books—"Language, Music and Gesture: Informational Crossroads (LMGIC 2021)" (Springer Singapore, 2021) and "Literature, Language and Computing: Russian Contribution" (Springer Singapore, 2023).

Maria Khokhlova is an Associate Professor at the Department of Mathematical Linguistics, St. Petersburg University. Her research lies at the intersection of natural language processing, corpus linguistics and machine learning and was supported by grants and scholarships awarded by Russian and international foundations (RSF, DAAD, Visegrad Fund, Erasmus). She holds a Ph.D. from St. Petersburg University (2011) and was awarded the St. Petersburg Government Prize for science and teaching (2020, 2022). She is the author of more than 100 articles in domestic and international refereed journals and volumes.

Mikhail Koryshev is an Associate Professor at the Department of Comparative Studies of Languages and Cultures and the Dean of the Faculty of Philology, St. Petersburg University. His research interests focus on German language and culture, literary studies, as well as on Catholic hymnography and liturgiology. He obtained a Ph.D. in Philology from St. Petersburg University in 2005. He was a visiting lecturer in Germany, his research was supported by Erasmus and DAAD-Stiftung. He is the author of more than 60 papers in Russian and international peer-reviewed journals and book series.

Contributors

Adelya K. Abdulmanova St. Petersburg State University, Saint-Petersburg, Russia

Nikita A. Arinkin National Research Center "Kurchatov Institute", Moscow, Russia;
Moscow State Linguistic University, Moscow, Russia

A. N. Baranov Vinogradov Russian Language Institute of the Russian Academy of Sciences, Moscow, Russia

Altana Bazarzhapova St. Petersburg State University, Saint-Petersburg, Russia

Natalia Bogdanova-Beglarian St. Petersburg State University, Saint-Petersburg, Russia

Kristina Borisova HSE University, Saint-Petersburg, Russia

Liudmila Bukreeva St. Petersburg State University, Saint-Petersburg, Russia

D. O. Dobrovol'skij Vinogradov Russian Language Institute of the Russian Academy of Sciences, Moscow, Russia

Mikhail Dolgushin St. Petersburg State University, Saint-Petersburg, Russia

Vera Evdokimova St. Petersburg State University, Saint-Petersburg, Russia

Daria Gorbunova Independent Researcher, Saint-Petersburg, Russia

Alexander Grebennikov St. Petersburg State University, Saint-Petersburg, Russian Federation;
ITMO University, Saint-Petersburg, Russian Federation

Daria Guseva St. Petersburg State University, Saint-Petersburg, Russia

Ekaterina Ivanova St. Petersburg State University, Saint-Petersburg, Russian Federation

Asia Karysheva National Research University Higher School of Economics, Saint-Petersburg, Russia

Maria Khokhlova St. Petersburg State University, Saint-Petersburg, Russia

Margarita Kirina National Research University Higher School of Economics, Saint-Petersburg, Russia

K. L. Kiseleva Vinogradov Russian Language Institute of the Russian Academy of Sciences, Moscow, Russia

Anastasia Kolmogorova HSE University, Saint-Petersburg, Russia

Anastasia Kolpashchikova St. Petersburg State University, Saint-Petersburg, Russia

Evgenia Kolpashchikova National Research University Higher School of Economics, Saint-Petersburg, Russia

Mariia Korolkova St. Petersburg State University, Saint-Petersburg, Russia

Mikhail Koryshev St. Petersburg State University, Saint-Petersburg, Russian Federation

Artemiy A. Kotov National Research Center "Kurchatov Institute", Moscow, Russia;
Russian State University for the Humanities, Moscow, Russia;
Moscow State Linguistic University, Moscow, Russia

Boris V. Kovalev St. Petersburg State University, Saint-Petersburg, Russia

A. D. Kozerenko Vinogradov Russian Language Institute of the Russian Academy of Sciences, Moscow, Russia

Maria Ladushina National University of Science and Technology "MISIS", Moscow, Russia

Irina A. Lekomtseva St. Petersburg State University, Saint-Petersburg, Russia

Polina Maksimenko National Research University Higher School of Economics, Saint-Petersburg, Russia

Maria Maksimova St. Petersburg State University, Saint-Petersburg, Russia

Olga Mitrenina St. Petersburg State University, Saint-Petersburg, Russia

Olga Mitrofanova St. Petersburg State University, Saint-Petersburg, Russia

Anna Moskvina National Research University Higher School of Economics, Saint-Petersburg, Russia

Vasilisa Obotnina St. Petersburg State University, Saint-Petersburg, Russia

Ruslan Rodionov National Research University Higher School of Economics, Saint-Petersburg, Russia

Anastasia Seinova National Research University Higher School of Economics, Saint-Petersburg, Russia

Elena Shamina St. Petersburg State University, Saint-Petersburg, Russia

E. V. Sharapova Vinogradov Russian Language Institute of the Russian Academy of Sciences, Moscow, Russia

K. A. Shchukina St. Petersburg State University, Saint-Petersburg, Russia

Tatiana Sherstinova National Research University Higher School of Economics, Saint-Petersburg, Russia

Tatiana Skrebtsova St. Petersburg State University, Saint-Petersburg, Russian Federation

T. V. Smirnova St. Petersburg State University, Saint-Petersburg, Russia

Evgenii Sokolov Institute for Linguistic Studies, Russian Academy of Sciences, Saint-Petersburg, Russia

Ivan Stoliarov St. Petersburg State University, Saint-Petersburg, Russia

Kira Sypacheva St. Petersburg State University, Saint-Petersburg, Russian Federation

Daniil Vasiliev St. Petersburg State University, Saint-Petersburg, Russia

M. M. Voznesenskaja Vinogradov Russian Language Institute of the Russian Academy of Sciences, Moscow, Russia

Ekaterina K. Vyunova St. Petersburg State University, Saint-Petersburg, Russia

Kristina Zaides Independent Researcher, Saint-Petersburg, Russia

Anna A. Zinina National Research Center "Kurchatov Institute", Moscow, Russia;
Russian State University for the Humanities, Moscow, Russia;
Moscow State Linguistic University, Moscow, Russia

Quantitative Methods in Literary Studies

Jorge Luis Borges' Poetry Periodization: A Quantitative Approach

Boris V. Kovalev

Abstract The article is devoted to the problem of periodization of Borges' poetic work. Quantitative analysis demonstrates that Borges' corpus of poetry can be divided into three periods. The hypothesis is proved at the level of morphology, semantics and poetic forms. The study uses tools such as Stanza morphoanalyser and BERTopic. The obtained data allowed to define the formal, morphological and semantic characteristics of the poetic work of Borges. Besides, the author proposes to consider attributing the poetic works of Borges to three periods, instead of one or two, namely: the avant-garde, or the ultraist (1920–30s), the conservative (volumes of 1960–70s) and the synthetic (1980s).

Keywords Jorge Luis Borges · Stylometry · Borges' poetic legacy · NLP · POS-tagging

1 Introduction

Nowadays, the analysis of Borges' poetry is relevant for several reasons.

On the one hand, in modern studies much less attention is paid to Borges' poetry than to his prose. This is noticeable if one looks at the issues of the journal *Variaciones Borges*, the most authoritative journal of Borges studies published by the Borges Center at the University of Pittsburgh, over the past fifteen years. On the other hand, there are even fewer studies related to the use of quantitative and computational methods for analysing Borges' poetic texts [1].

Studies devoted to the analysis of Borges' poems can be generally divided into two groups:

1. Source studies, using the methodology of traditional close reading, exploring the history of a poetic text and its textological aspect [2, 5];
2. Poetry studies aimed at analysing the metrics and structure of the text [12].

B. V. Kovalev (✉)
St. Petersburg State University, Saint-Petersburg, Russia
e-mail: bvkovalev@yandex.ru

P. Eismont et al. (eds.), *Literature, Language and Computing*,
https://doi.org/10.1007/978-981-96-0990-1_1

The question of the classification and periodization of Borges' poetic work is often ignored by researchers. In the European and American philological tradition, the idea seems to have settled that Borges' poetic work is strictly divided into two periods. The first is the ultraist one, the period of avant-garde views of Borges. It falls in the 1920–1930s. The second period deals with the mature, or late Borges: from the second half of the 1930s until his death (1986). In modern works, this periodization is generally recognized—for example, in her study, Utrera points to it not as a unique scientific fact, but as a given. And this pattern is constantly observed.

In the Russian tradition of Borges studies, even this classification is questioned. In this sense, the article of Mezhikovskaya, which states that "for all its diversity and multi-genre, Borges's work is very integral and hardly needs to be divided into periods, with the exception of only the ultraist period, which is also distinguished rather conditionally" [9] is fundamental.

However, the question of periodization and classification of Borges' poetry work is the key to a correct understanding of the evolution of his style and his poetics.

It is also important to note that philologists rely on the "close reading" method and phenomenological scrutinizing to solve the issue of periodization. They use traditional literary methods and rely more on philological intuition and abstract sensations.

We believe that quantitative methods can be a useful tool for resolving the issue of periodization of Borges' poetic work. It can contribute to the rethinking of established dogmas and improve the understanding of the Argentine author's style and poetics.

Thus, the purpose of our study is to test the hypothesis of a binary classification of Borges' poetic work by applying a quantitative approach. Moreover, we suppose that we can distinguish not two, but three stages on the basis of the analysis of poetic forms. Finally, another purpose is to look for the evolution of the style of Borges' poetic texts, and to trace the dynamics of its changes.

Based on the criterion of poetic form, we intend to test the classification at the following levels:

1. at the morphological level;
2. at the semantic level.

In addition, it was decided to compare the data obtained using quantitative methods with the information obtained with traditional literary analysis.

To test the hypothesis at three levels, the poetic corpus of Jorge Luis Borges was annotated using NLP tools such as Stanza and BERTopic. In addition, in the case of the analysis of the form of the verse, we also used manual marking. In total, the poetic corpus of Jorge Luis Borges has 446 texts belonging to 13 volumes: *Fervor de Buenos Aires* (1923), *Luna de Enfrente* (1925), *Cuaderno San Martín* (1929), *El Hacedor* (1960), *El otro, el mismo* (1964), *Para las seis cuerdas* (1965), *Elogio de la sombra* (1969), *El oro de los tigres* (1972), *La rosa profunda* (1975), *La moneda de hierro* (1976), *Historia de la noche* (1977), *La cifra* (1981), *Los conjurados* (1985) [4]. They served as material for this study. Further, abbreviations will be used to designate volumes: *Fervor, Luna, Cuaderno, Hacedor, Otro, Cuerdas, Elogio, Oro, Rosa, Moneda, Historia, Cifra, Conjurados.*

2 Poetic Form

The form of a verse is a key criterion to determine the author's style. In this work, the poetic form is a combination of metric, strophic and general compositional features of a poetic text. Poetic form is the most important factor, because it includes many smaller criteria: rhyme, meter, number of strophes, consistency of rhyme, etc. Unlike genres, the features of the form are largely determined by linguistic characteristics. The distribution of forms in diachrony is a key indicator of the change in the author's style, it could serve as an indicator of his evolution.

In the case of Borges, this criterion is especially relevant because Borges' corpus of poetic texts can be easily divided into poetic forms. Great luck: the poetic forms of other authors, contemporaries of Borges, are much more difficult to attribute: e.g., Cesar Vallejo uses a small set of forms throughout his entire career, and at the same time these forms are difficult to differentiate.

Borges uses 11 distinct forms. Sonnet (the dominant subtype is the English sonnet), vers libre (or free verse), "traditional verse" the poetic texts that have rhyme and meter, but no formal features of sonnet or, e.g., limerick at the level of strophe or rhyming scheme), blanc verse, prose poetry, milonga, tanka, haiku, distich, double sonnet, ode.

Sonnets, free verses, blanc verses, prose poetry and traditional verses are the most frequent forms. In total, they cover over 90% of Borges' poetic texts.

Five most frequent forms are distributed among poetry volumes in chronological order in Table 1.

Table 1 The most frequent poetic forms by volume

	Vers libre	Trad poem	Prose poetry	Blank verse	Sonnet	Total
Fervor	32	0	0	0	0	32
Luna	12	3	0	0	0	15
Cuaderno	8	1	0	0	0	9
Hacedor	6	9	0	2	9	29
Otro	13	10	2	3	45	75
Cuerdas[a]	0	0	0	0	0	11
Elogio	11	2	5	1	8	27
Oro	2	2	4	13	9	31
Rosa	19	1	1	6	19	50
Moneda	4	5	0	8	19	36
Historia	7	1	6	12	4	31
Cifra	23	0	7	12	1	61
Conjurados	1	4	16	6	9	39

[a] The *Para seis cuerdas* collection consists exclusively of eleven milongas, a traditional Argentinean form, which, however, is not included in the list of the most frequent. Milongas appear at a conservative stage and at the end of Borges' life

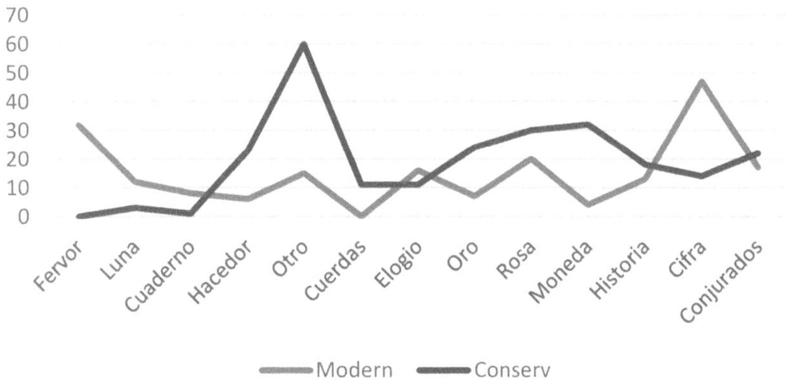

Fig. 1 Poetic forms by volumes in chronological order

In addition, the forms used by Borges are definitively divided into modernist and conservative. By modernist forms we mean those forms that, from a historical perspective, are unusual for either the Spanish or Argentinian literary tradition. Such forms appear in one or another national poetic tradition only in the twentieth century, many of them can be borrowed from non-European traditions. Modernist forms include vers libre, prose poetry, haiku, and tanka. By conservative forms we mean those forms that are familiar and frequent in the Spanish and Argentinian poetic tradition. Conservative forms are sonnet, double sonnet, traditional verse, blank verse, milonga, distich and ode.

In the graphics below, we see the frequency distribution of conservative and modern forms in diachrony (Fig. 1).

As can be seen, three periods can be easily distinguished. The first one includes the first three volumes (*Fervor, Luna, Cuaderno*). The modernist forms predominate (mainly vers libre). The ratio of conservative and modernist forms: 93% to 7%. The second period is conservative (from *Hacedor to Historia*). Conservative forms (sonnets and milongas) predominate here. An exceptional case is *Elogio*, where for 16 modernist forms there are 11 conservative ones. However, some dominance of modernist forms is explained by the fact that in the previous book *Cuerdas* there were no such forms at all, and in the next one, *Oro*, there is again a clear predominance of conservative forms (7 vs. 24). Most of the texts published in these collections were written in one relatively short period of time (3 years). But in the preface to the book *Elogio* there are prerequisites for the beginning of the synthetic stage. Borges writes in the prologue to the *Elogio*: "On these pages coexist, I think, without disagreement, the forms of prose and verse … the differences between poetry and prose seem to me accidental" [4].

The boundary lies between *Historia* and *Cifra*. In *Cifra*, there are more modernist forms than conservative ones again. At this stage, synthesis takes place: Borges turns to both old forms and new ones. The ratio of forms in the second stage: 28 and 72%, and in the third stage there is an alignment: 64 and 36%.

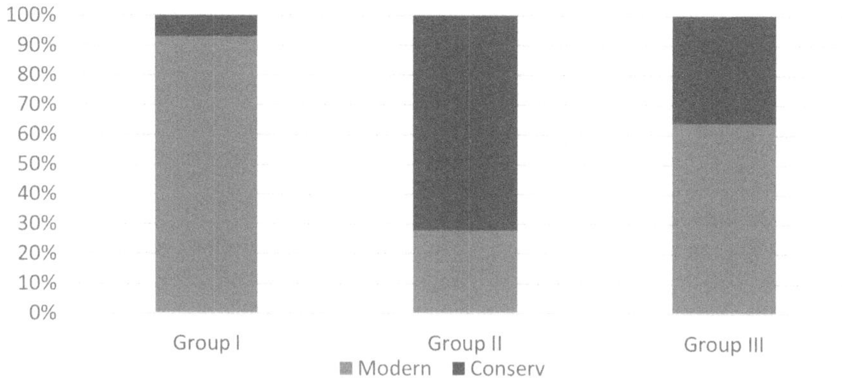

Fig. 2 Poetic forms by periods (in fractions)

The ratio of conservative and modernist forms in shares is shown in the graphs (Fig. 2).

At an early stage of his work, Borges is an ultraist. For supporters of this literary trend, metaphor and epithet are the most important elements of the text. According to the ultraists, the text should not contain random images, or meaningless adjectives. Ultraists abandon traditional Spanish forms and write mainly in vers libre. In those years, Borges is one of the most prominent representatives of ultraism; in Argentina he is actually its leader: in 1921 he writes a manifesto in which he proclaims the basic principles of Argentine ultraism.

By 1960, Borges completely rethinks his poetics. After a long break in writing poetry, he turns to traditional forms: sonnets, odes and milongas. Moreover, the aesthetic and political views of Borges are changing. He becomes a conservative. It is noteworthy that such a phenomenon as the "Latin American boom" of the 1960s coincides with the conservative period of Borges. The question of the chronological boundaries of the "boom" is still open, but one of the most famous and authoritative positions on this issue belongs to J. Martin: "It is no exaggeration to state that if the Southern continent was known for two things above all others in the 1960s, these were, first and foremost, the Cuban Revolution (although Cuba is not in South America) and its impact both on Latin America and the Third World generally, and secondly, the Boom in Latin American fiction, whose rise and fall coincided with the rise and fall of liberal perceptions of Cuba between 1959 and 1971" [8].

In the third stage, in the 1980s, Borges is the recognized patriarch of Argentinean literature. This period is a synthesis of the first and second stages. There is a decrease in the number of sonnets, a return to the poetics of verse libre and the appearance of poetry in prose. Moreover, the rethinking of the views of Borges is manifested in a variety of areas. For example, this stage is characterized by an improvement in Borges' attitude towards Gongora [2]. On the other hand, he returns to topics that interested him in the 1930s and 1940s: for example, to the concepts of P. D. Uspensky and Charles Howard Hinton [3].

Finally, analysing his poetry in the prologue to *Cifra*, Borges says that poetry is divided into the intellectual (abstract) and the verbal: "After the years, I have understood that it is forbidden for me to rehearse the magical cadence, the curious metaphore... My way is what is usually called *intellectual poetry*". This remark is self-reflexive. The early Borges is a poet of images, in maturity Borges turns to intellectual poetry, and in the latest volumes, as Borges himself notes, "his pages seek, not without uncertainty, a via media" [4].

So, on the basis of the criterion of the distribution of forms, we come to the conclusion that the poetic corpus of Borges is chronologically divided into three stages. This division is confirmed at the level of literary analysis, it fits into the general "synthetic trend" of Borges. He moves away from his earlier radical beliefs and statements and moves to a conciliatory strategy at a later stage of his work.

3 Morphological Level

At this step we carry out an automatic morphological analysis of the complete collection of Borges' poems. The pipeline, which consisted of tokenization and POS-tagging, was realized with the pre- trained neural morphoanalyser Stanza. This tool was chosen for two reasons: (1) neural network NLP systems trained on large and balanced corpora are superior in quality to statistical and rule-based ones; (2) Stanza provides a multilingual package which includes a Spanish module [11].

The set of morphological categories presented in Stanza proved superfluous for this study, therefore the analysis was conducted on enlarged groups of parts of speech: adverbs, adjectives, nouns, verbs, pronouns, numerals and auxiliares. More details on the settings and the main principles and mechanisms of the program are described in the article [7] devoted to the quantitative analysis of Borges grammar. In this article, we focus on the main trends illustrating the evolution of Borges' style at the morphological level.

Of particular interest to us is the share of parts of speech in volumes (Table 2).

An important trend should be emphasized—the decrease in the share of the adjective (from 10,2% in the first collection to 6,52% in the last; the maximum value at the first stage is 8,74% (*Luna*), the minimum value at the last stage is 6,21% (*Cifra*)) and an increase in the share of the verb in later collections (minimum value—11,81% in the volume *Cuaderno* from the first stage, maximum value—17,73% in the last collection *Conjurados*). Moreover, it turns out that the proportion of the noun also decreases.

It is noticeable on the graph that at the first stage (the first three volumes) the share of adjectives is high. In the second stage (from *Hacedor* to *Historia*) the proportion of adjectives decreases and then fluctuates, and in the third stage (from *Cifra* to *Conjurados*) it decreases again (Fig. 3). A kind of continuity is revealed: one of the main morphological tendencies of Borges' poetic texts is an increase in the share of the verbs relative to adjectives and nouns. It leads to the fact that the author's

Table 2 Part of speech frequency by volumes (in fractions)

Name	Adj.	Adv.	Nouns	Pron.	Verbs
Fervor	10,20	2,52	26,81	6,14	12,28
Luna	8,74	2,76	26,66	6,38	13,26
Cuaderno	9,47	2,30	26,66	6,86	11,81
Hacedor	9,20	2,45	25,16	8,27	12,92
Otro	8,10	2,44	28,68	7,22	12,35
Cuerdas	6,54	3,06	25,29	9,47	14,72
Elogio	7,96	2,42	24,50	8,35	14,96
Oro	7,75	3,05	25,31	7,96	14,33
Rosa	8,28	2,28	25,93	8,11	14,42
Moneda	8,36	2,27	26,31	7,35	14,25
Historia	7,69	1,88	26,09	8,18	13,88
Cifra	6,21	2,41	25,29	8,10	16,31
Conjurados	6,52	2,74	24,46	8,81	17,73

style seems to the reader to be drier and more restrained, which has been noted in philological articles [10].

Next, we tracked the distribution of parts of speech by form (Table 3).

The growth of the share of the verb coincides with the appearance in the poetics of Borges of such a form as verse in prose, in which the verb is the prevailing part of speech (16,89%). Haiku, distich and tanka are omitted, since only three texts of these forms appear in the Borges corpus. There is an opposition: sonnet versus poetry in prose.

Thus, at the morphological level, there is a continuous tendency towards a gradual (with a slowdown at the second stage) decrease in the share of adjectives and nouns and an increase in the share of the verbs. The intuitive hypothesis about the "dryness" of Borges' style at a later stage is confirmed by quantitative methods. The main factor

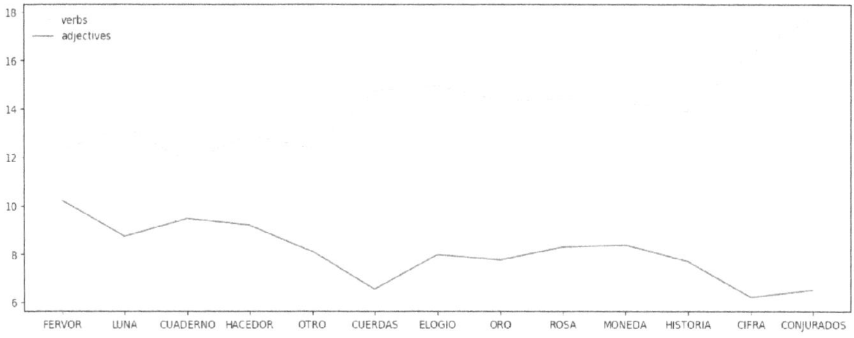

Fig. 3 Dynamics of change in the share of the verb and adjective

Table 3 Part of speech frequency by poetic forms (in fractions)

Form	Adj.	Adv.	Nouns	Pron.	Verbs
Double sonnet	10,05	3,87	24,10	9,02	16,62
Distich	4,69	9,38	25,00	10,94	18,75
Haiku	3,30	4,40	25,27	11,54	19,78
Milonga	6,25	3,24	23,72	10,34	16,18
Ode	9,66	1,38	25,00	8,45	10,34
Trad. poem	8,85	2,32	26,01	8,03	13,55
Prose poetry	6,01	2,48	26,90	8,10	16,89
Sonnet	9,10	2,90	25,30	7,89	13,89
Tanka	5,38	1,54	28,46	6,92	16,92
Vers libre	7,76	2,30	26,32	7,40	13,65
Blanc poem	8,00	2,28	26,37	7,37	13,07

in accelerating the growth of the share of the verb is the increase in the number of verses in prose as the most verbal form at the third stage.

4 Semantic Level

Stanza was also used at the stage of thematic modelling as a preprocessing tool; the pipeline consisted of tokenization and lemmatization. The thematic evolution of Borges' poetic texts is studied by implementing a topic modelling technique on the subgroups of the collection, namely the early, mature and late groups of poems. Topic modelling stems from the general notion of distributional semantics: words that occur in similar contexts have similar meanings, which makes it possible to cluster the vector representations of the words into interpretable topics.

Topic modelling was performed using the tool BERTopic. Parting from the clusterization problem as the main approach to topic modeling, BERTopic achieves higher quality of topic coherency and representation by leveraging text embedding techniques and a class-based variation of TF-IDF. The BERTopic pipeline includes creating embeddings for each document of the collection, reducing their dimensionality, clustering them and extracting topic representations [6].

In this paper we used the unsupervised setup of BERTopic, i.e. we did not state either the required number of topics or their identifiers. The model was fit on the lemmatized texts of each subgroup with the stopwords removed.

Borges's early topics are presented in Table 4.

In the early years Borges follows the doctrine of Argentine ultraism formulated by him and he avoids excessive quoting; Borges is focused on the search for national essence and he finds it in the space of the suburbs. At this time, Borges formulates the poetics of Buenos Aires and its outskirts: "He creates … the mythology of courage

Table 4 Early topics of Borges

Topic	Count	Name
0	54	0_muerte_muerte muerte_morir_muerte morir
1	53	1_venir_buscar_llegar_acompañar
2	52	2_noche_noche noche_noche naipe_naipe noche
3	46	3_hoja_tenue_caducidad_cepeda
4	43	4_calle_calle calle
5	39	5_sueño_sueño sueño_soñar_sueño soñar
6	38	6_asombro_dulce_asombro asombro_gracioso
7	34	7_cercanía_chacarita_cornisa_lejanía
8	33	8_luz_luz luz_lámpara_lámpara luz
9	33	9_vida_vida vida_vida cotidiano_cotidiano vida
10	33	10_frente_fondo_pared_fondo frente
11	32	11_libro_firmamento_pisar_libro llave
12	31	12_dejar_fecha_despecho_apagar
13	31	13_jardín_jardín jardín_manzana_recoleta
14	30	14_alto_alto alto_muro_paredón alto

and by the end of the 1920s puts in the first place the generalized figure of the "compadrito", the inhabitant of the urban outskirts" [10]. At the same time, Borges, as a number of other avant-garde artists, is looking for features of "Creolism" and "Argentinism" in the heroes of the past: both at the national level and at the family level. This explains the presence of topics "movement" (1), "street" (4), "sleep" (2), "suburbs" (7), "courtyard" (10), "garden" (13) and so on.

In addition, Borges focuses on historical figures: "Rosas" from *Fervor* is dedicated to the figure of the caudillo dictator Juan Manuel de Rosas, who ruled in the 1830–1850s and had a significant impact on the history of Argentina and the formation of gauchos as a class and cultural stereotype. "Isidoro Acevedo" from *Cuaderno* is Borges' grandfather, who heroically fought for Argentina in the wars of the mid-nineteenth century. The hero of the text "Francisco López Merino" from the same collection is a young poet who was a member of Borges's circle and committed suicide on May 20, 1928 which was a heavy blow to his comrades. Therefore, the topics of death (0), night (2) and shadow (6) play an important role.

At the second stage, the situation changed (Table 5).

The topic of sleep becomes more frequent (2), the topics "God" (6), "memory" (3) and "love" (13) appear as well. The importance of the topic of death is reduced (6). The topics of the suburbs and the streets disappear. At the same time, the topic "night" (1) is still actively used by Borges. The appearance of the topic of man (0) is due to the fact that Borges uses these words very often at this stage, since they are very productive for the formation of rhymes. However, we decided not to exclude them from the list: in this case, the formal requirements for the verse cause two

Table 5 Topics of mature period of Borges

Topic	Count	Name
0	151	0_hombre_hombre hombre_hombre hollar_hollar hombre
1	120	1_noche_noche noche_naipes_naipes noche
2	116	2_sueño_sueño sueño_sueño dormir_dormir sueño
3	112	3_memoria_memoria memoria_memorias_memoria memorias
4	104	4_sombra_sombra sombra
5	85	5_muerte_muerte muerte_muertes muerte_muertes
6	85	6_dios_dios dios
7	84	7_tierra_tierra ticrra_ticrras_tierra tierras
8	80	8_toca_jinete_quedan_di
9	80	9_luna_luna luna_moon_cometer
10	80	10_obra_by_by by_gramático
11	79	11_espada_espada espada
12	78	12_hombres_hombres hombres_men_men men
13	76	13_amor_amor amor_quererte amor_quererte

semantic blocks. This fact must also be taken into account when analysing Borges' poems.

At the third stage (Table 6), trigger words for the topics of a person (3) are again observed. In addition, the frequency of the topics of memory (from 3 to 11) and love is reduced. The topics "night", "memory" and "God", which are important for Borges in the second stage, are not in the top anymore. The topic of the night gives way to the topic of sleep (2), (9). In general, the data at this stage is heterogeneous, a synthesis of various topics and trigger words is noticeable, there is a kind of melting pot of different topics.

There are some constant combinations, but each period is characterized by a different set of topics.

The data obtained using this program correlate with the traditional idea of Borges' thematic preferences, but at the same time, BERTopic allows one to radically refine the available data and to divide the global conservative Borges stage into two parts: the mature period is more associated with the topics of memory, night and God and the late one is associated with the topic of sleep and, in general, this phase is characterized by heterogeneity.

Table 6 Late topics of borges

Topic	Count	Name
0	215	0_sur_cuyo_deja_sepa
1	92	1_penumbra_divisado_queda_esquina
2	84	2_soñado_soñado soñado_corazón_soñado fantasía
3	72	3_hombre_hombre hombre_hombre his_hombre himno
4	68	4_terrible_odio_fiel_ruiseñor
5	49	5_tierra_tierra tierra_espacio_londres
6	48	6_derecha_frente_migraciones_cercado
7	45	7_sabré_permite_evidente_basta
8	43	8_cristo_versos_jesús_israel
9	39	9_sueño_sueño sueño_insomnio_insomnio sueño
10	39	10_tantas_mil_larga_tantos
11	38	11_recuerdo_recuerdo recuerdo_nostalgia_nostalgia recuerdo
12	38	12_fe_catedrales_catedral_doctrina
13	37	13_ulises_leguas_ulises ulises_patrias

5 Conclusion

On the basis of the results of this research, we can make the following conclusions:

1. Based on the criterion of the distribution of forms, we conclude that Borges' poetic corpus can be chronologically divided into three periods. The first is ultraist, avant-garde, including the first three volumes. The dominant form is vers libre. The second is conservative, including collections of the 1960s. The dominant form is the sonnet. The third period is synthetic, it includes collections of 1980s. It starts with the volume *Cifra.* It is characterized by a variety of forms. In addition, verse plays an important role in prose, whose share increases significantly during the third period.
2. The classification based on the criterion of the distribution of forms is also confirmed at the morphological level. The main grammatical-quantitative tendency of Borges' poems is a gradual decrease in the share of adjectives and nouns and an increase in the share of the verb. The growth of the share of the verb at the last stage is especially noticeable. This is due to the increase in the share of verses in prose, since this form contains the largest share of verbs among all the most frequent forms.
3. Three periods are also distinguished at the level of semantics. Certain topics recur throughout Borges's work, but each period is characterized by a different set of the most frequent topics. At the first stage, the topics of the suburbs, the street and death turn out to be the most important, at the second—the topics "night", "God" and "memory", and at the third period—a mixture of different topics with the dominance of the topic of sleep.

4. Three-part periodization is also confirmed by facts from the history of literature. The data obtained are consistent with the general characteristics of Borges' poetics, but at the same time they clarify and correct the idea of the periodization of Borges' poetic work.

Acknowledgements The study was supported by St. Petersburg State University, project ID:94033710.

References

1. Benedict, N.: Digital approaches to the archive: multispectral imaging and the recovery of Borges's writing process in "El muerto" and "La casa de Asterión". Var. Borges (45), 153–170 (2018)
2. Betti, M.: La perla o la rosa. Góngora según Borges (in Spanish). Arte Nuevo: Revista de Estudios Áureos (8), 230–258 (2021)
3. Borges, J.L.: Relatos Scientíficos (in Spanish). Siruela, Madrid (1986)
4. Borges, J.L.: Poesía completa (in Spanish). Vintage Español, New York (2012)
5. Candelaria, B.: Variaciones sobre el poema "Rusia" (in Spanish). Var. Borges (38), 29– 48 (2014)
6. Grootendorst, M.: BERTopic: neural topic modeling with a class-based TF-IDF procedure (2022). arXiv:2203.05794
7. Kovalev, B., Gousyatskaya, P.: Quantitative grammar of poetic texts of Jorge Luis Borges: first results (in Russian). Kvantitativnaya Philologiya **2**(6), 47–58 (2023)
8. Martin, G.: Boom, Yes; 'New' Novel, no: further reflections on the optical illusions of the 1960s in Latin America. Bull. Lat. Am. Res. **2**(3), 53–63 (1984)
9. Mezhikovskaya, T.: Jorge Luis Borges (in Russian). In: Istoriya literatur Latinskoj Ameriki, vol. 5, pp. 158–193. IMLI RAN, Moscow (2005)
10. Mezhikovskaya, T.: Literatura Argentiny (in Russian). In: Istoriya literatur Latinskoj Ameriki, vol. 4, p. 385. IMLI RAN, Moscow (2004)
11. Qi, P., et al.: Stanza: A Python Natural Language Processing Toolkit for Many Human Languages. Association for Computational Linguistics (ACL) System Demonstrations, pp. 101–109 (2020)
12. Utrera, M.: Jorge Luis Borges y las analogías rítmicas: los poemas en prosa de El Hacedor (in Spanish), no. 9, pp. 582–611. Estudios de Literatura, Castilla (2022)

Validity of Lingvo-Statistical Parameters for the Corpus of Fiction

Alexander Grebennikov, Mikhail Koryshev, Ekaterina Ivanova, and Tatiana Skrebtsova

Abstract Finding variables and statistical metrics to describe rank distributions of lexemes is a relevant linguistic task. We analyze the validity of lingvo-statistical parameters (the rank mean and entropy) for describing frequency dictionary of fiction. The comparative use of the Weibull and Haustein functions as approximating ones for the values of the parameters in question is also investigated. The research draws on a representative sample from the Corpus of the Russian Short Stories (1900–1930) (total volume is more than 1,000,000 tokens). The rank mean is shown to be only a relative valid parameter for describing a large-scale corpus of fiction, while the relative validity of entropy is greatly affected by the nature of the texts analyzed. The Weibull function is proved to be the preferable one for the approximation of the parameters' growth.

Keywords Frequency dictionary · Authors' lexicography · Statistical modeling · Corpus · Stylometry

A. Grebennikov (✉) · M. Koryshev · E. Ivanova · T. Skrebtsova
St. Petersburg State University, Saint-Petersburg 199034, Russian Federation
e-mail: a.grebennikov@spbu.ru

M. Koryshev
e-mail: mkorychev@yandex.ru

E. Ivanova
e-mail: eivanova2003@mail.ru

T. Skrebtsova
e-mail: t.skrebtsova@spbu.ru

A. Grebennikov
ITMO University, Saint-Petersburg 197101, Russian Federation

P. Eismont et al. (eds.), *Literature, Language and Computing*,
https://doi.org/10.1007/978-981-96-0990-1_2

1 Introduction

Currently, quantitative linguistics is focused on finding variables and statistical metrics to describe rank distributions of lexemes (in the form of frequency dictionary), or to predict the dynamics of the statistics for those dictionaries [1]. Our previous research allowed to prove the validity of the rank mean and entropy for describing frequency dictionary of a writer, as well as to substantiate the selection of the functions for its approximation [2–4]. In the work presented, the character of the above-mentioned statistics is analyzed with the use of a much larger corpus of texts by various authors.

2 Data and Method

The research draws on the Russian Short Stories Corpus (1900–1930), an ongoing project aimed to collect, digitally process, and present the Russian literary heritage of the early twentieth century [5]. The Corpus currently contains a few thousand stories written in Russia, and later the Soviet Union, and published in literary journals or anthologies. The whole Corpus is divided into three chronological sub-corpora, their boundaries marked by significant historical events. Thus, the first sub-corpus (1900–1913) refers to the pre-war period, the second one (1914–1922) covers a series of dramatic events (WWI, the February and October revolutions, the Civil War), and the third one (1923–1930) accounts for the post-war socialist period.[1]

A sample from the Corpus was chosen as the material for the experiment (310 short stories, approximately 100 texts of any length, topic, etc., per period). Only one text by every author was allowed. The texts in all sub-corpora have been cumulatively joined by ten, and frequency dictionaries have been made for every joined portion. The total volume of the dictionaries is as follows: 24,316 tokens and 376,513 word forms for the first period; 24,617 tokens and 303,588 word forms for the second period; 30,560 tokens and 383,430 word forms for the third period; 124,081 tokens and 1,077,970 word forms for the whole sample.

At every step we have calculated the values of the rank mean (the measure of concentration):

$$r = \sum rf_r / N,$$

where r—rank, f_r—frequency for the rank, N—size of the sample;

and entropy (the measure of uncertainty):

$$H = -\sum p_i \log_2 p_i,$$

[1] For more on the project see https://russian-short-stories.ru/.

where p_i—probability, i.e., in our case, the ratio of word frequency to the size of the sample.

3 Approximation and Its Results

The obtained values for the dependencies of the rank mean and entropy on the size of the sample (approaching an upper limit) have been approximated with the use of the technique by Grigory Martynenko based on the least square method [1, 2].

The following functions have been chosen for the approximation.

The Weibull function

$$y = N_{\max} - N_{\max} e^{-cx^d};$$

and the Haustein function

$$y = \frac{N_{\max} x^{\gamma}}{x^{\gamma} + q},$$

where N—size of the dictionary, x—size of the sample, $N_{\max}$—asymptotic size of the dictionary, c, d; γ, q—parameters of distribution. The Weibull function has been widely used in linguistic research [2–4, 6–8], while the Haustein function has mainly found its application in economics and sociology [9–11].

The results obtained and the approximated maximums of the statistics in question are shown in Tables 1, 2, 3 and 4 (some omissions have been made due to the limited length of the article).

It can be seen from the tables that prognosis curves are generally close to each other, with some values of the parameters in question being equal. To prove the validity of the statistics and to select the most appropriate approximating function we should determine if the obtained theoretical maximum values are achieved on the really available text data.

Table 1 Approximation results for the pre-war period

Number of texts	Rank mean	App. with the Weibull func ($N_{\max}$ = 1506.92)	App. with the Haustein func. ($N_{\max}$ = 1607)	Entropy	App. with the Weibull func ($N_{\max}$ = 11.59)	App. with the Haustein func. ($N_{\max}$ = 11)
10	1001.43	1153.24	1151.91	10.30	10.29	10.28
40	1422.45	1353.18	1349.00	10.43	10.56	10.56
70	1396.59	1422.97	1420.40	10.69	10.68	10.68
90	1389.53	1440.01	1439.42	10.71	10.72	10.72
100	1406.92	1448.39	1449.25	10.76	10.74	10.74

Table 2 Approximation results for the period of war and revolution

Number of texts	Rank mean	App. with the Weibull func. (N_{max} = 1624,71)	App. with the Haustein func. (N_{max} = 1690)	Entropy	App. with the Weibull func. (N_{max} = 11,36)	App. with the Haustein func. (N_{max} = 12)
10	775.73	860.14	846.13	10.07	10.05	10.05
40	1589.55	1490.31	1484.60	10.71	10.70	10.70
70	1550.61	1578.29	1569.20	10.85	10.85	10.85
90	1519.71	1603.86	1601.76	10.92	10.92	10.92

Table 3 Approximation results for the post-war socialist period

Number of texts	Rank mean	App. with the Weibull func. (N_{max} = 1967.4)	App. with the Haustein func. (N_{max} = 2193)	Entropy	App. with the Weibull func. (N_{max} = 11.31)	App. with the Haustein func. (N_{max} = 11)
10	970.50	1329.62	1333.11	10.41	10.42	10.39
40	1838.33	1633.34	1631.92	11.12	11.12	11.13
70	1682.17	1729.53	1727.29	11.23	11.23	11.23
90	1694.84	1761.74	1760.28	11.23	11.25	11.25
100	1692.77	1777.14	1776.37	11.27	11.26	11.26
110	1693.40	1779.45	1778.81	11.28	11.27	11.26

Table 4 Approximation results for the whole sample

Number of texts	Rank mean	App. with the Weibull func. (N_{max} = 1542.5)	App. with the Haustein func. (N_{max} = 1562)	Entropy	App. with the Weibull func. (N_{max} = 11.37)	App. with the Haustein func. (N_{max} = 14)
10	1001.43	1110.22	1072.49	10.30	10.06	10.20
40	1422.45	1326.61	1335.77	10.43	10.54	10.54
70	1396.59	1411.21	1418.31	10.69	10.74	10.71
100	1406.92	1444.71	1448.56	10.76	10.82	10.80
130	1437.83	1461.65	1463.57	10.45	10.87	10.85
160	1439.33	1475.62	1475.91	10.62	10.91	10.89
190	1461.84	1488.72	1487.57	10.71	10.95	10.94
220	1530.37	1496.76	1494.84	10.76	10.98	10.97
250	1500.79	1504.41	1501.92	10.81	11.01	11.01
280	1521.34	1510.92	1508.12	10.88	11.04	11.04
310	1530.37	1515.67	1512.81	10.91	11.06	11.07

4 Validity Evaluation

Once we have determined the asymptotic values of the parameters in question, we are able to continue with inverse functions to calculate the size of the sample which is necessary to make for its statistic parameters to be as close to the asymptotic ones as possible. Let us calculate a sample size necessary to achieve statistic parameters differing from the asymptotic ones by 1% and by one. The results obtained are shown in Tables 5 and 6.

Table 5 Sample size (tokens) necessary to achieve maximum values of the rank mean at approximation with the Weibull and Haustein functions

Period	Sample size necessary to achieve 99% of the maximum value at approximation with the Weibull function	Sample size necessary to achieve 99% of the maximum value at approximation with the Haustein function	Sample size necessary to achieve the value differing from the maximum by one at approximation with the Weibull function	Sample size necessary to achieve the value differing from the maximum by one at approximation with the Haustein function
Pre-war	935,629	18,225,456	11,183,249	1,721,194,126
War and revolution	302,840	1,274,115	1,253,228	16,247,196
Post-war socialist	4,434,696	1.53E+09	158,457,657	5.61E+09
Whole sample	1,518,023	4,379,998	20,282,353	118,588,851

Table 6 Sample size (tokens) necessary to achieve maximum values of entropy at approximation with the Weibull and Haustein functions

Period	Sample size necessary to achieve 99% of the maximum value at approximation with the Weibull function	Sample size necessary to achieve 99% of the maximum value at approximation with the Haustein function	Sample size necessary to achieve the value differing from the maximum by one at approximation with the Weibull function	Sample size necessary to achieve the value differing from the maximum by one at approximation with the Haustein function
Pre-war	326,466,720	710,889,595	53,270,861,675	12,032,766
War and revolution	2,584,109	3.82212E+11	38,554,494	150,003,255
Post-war socialist	4,434,696	305,065	158,457,657	4,740,401
Whole sample	4,978,764	6.24805E+18	68,388,69	1.56934E+29

We should note that 320 short stories included in the experimental sample are about 30% of the whole Corpus. Therefore, the dictionary size for the whole Corpus would be more than three million tokens. It means that neither of the statistical parameters in question is absolutely valid, i.e., their asymptotic values are not possible to achieve on the really available text data.

5 Results and Conclusion

The rank mean is seen to be only a relatively valid statistical parameter (i.e., allowing 99% «scooping out»), with great variety of the necessary sample sizes among the periods. This fact proves the applicability of the validity concept when dealing with a large-scale text corpus of numerous literary works. For entropy even relative validity can be observed for one period only—the period of war and revolution.

The above results hold only for the use of the Weibill function for approximation. In the case of the Haustein function, the sample sizes necessary to achieve maximum (asymptotic) values of the rank mean and entropy seem to be abnormal.

The results obtained appear to be true as we analyze the sample albeit homogeneous in terms of the literary genre (short stories)—but very heterogeneous in terms of the topics, language, and talents of the authors, while all our previous research mainly dealt with the texts of a single writer [2–4].

References

1. Sherstinova, T., Martynenko, G.: Linguistic and stylistic parameters for the study of literary language in the corpus of Russian short stories of the first third of the 20th century. In: R. Piotrowski's Readings in Language Engineering and Applied Linguistics, Proceedings of the III International Conference on Language Engineering and Applied Linguistics (PRLEAL-2019). CEUR Workshop Proceedings, vol. 2552, pp. 105–120 (2020)
2. Grebennikov, A.O.: Issledovanie ustoychivosti leksiko-statisticheskikh kharakteristik teksta [Validity of the Statistics for Fiction]. Dis. … kand. filol. nauk. Saint Petersburg [Ph.D. (Linguistcs) Thesis] (1998). (in Russian)
3. Grebennikov, A.O.: K voprosu ob approksimatsii zavisimosti ob"ema slovarya ot ob"ema vyborki. Korpusnaya lingvistika–2017 [Approximation of the Sample Size–Vocabulary Size Dependence]. In: Korpusnaya lingvistika-2017. Trudy mezhdunarodnoj konferentsii [Corpus Linguititcs–2017. Proceedings of the International Conference]. Saint Petersburg, pp. 151–156 (2017). (in Russian)
4. Grebennikov, A.O., Assel, A.N.: Baza russkogo rasskaza XIX-XX vekov. Modeli approksimacii. [Russian Short Stories Corpus of the XIX–XX Centuies. Approximation Models]. In: Korpusnaya lingvistika-2019. Trudy mezhdunarodnoj konferentsii [Corpus Linguititcs–2017. Proceedings of the International Conference]. Saint Petersburg, pp. 379–386 (2019). (In Russian)
5. Martynenko, G.Y., Sherstinova, T.Y., Popova, T.I., Melnik, A.G., Zamirajlova, E.V.: O printsipakh sozdaniya korpusa russkogo rasskaza pervoj treti XX veka [On the Principles of Creation of the Russian Short Stories Corpus of the First Third of the 20th Century]. In: Trudy XV Mezhdunarodnoj konferentsii po komp'yuternoj i kognitivnoj lingvistike «TEL 2018» [Proceedings

of the XV International Conference on Computer and Cognitive Linguistics 'TEL 2018']. Kazan, pp. 180–197 (2018). (In Russian)
6. Sabourin, P., Bélanger, A.: La dynamique des substitutions linguistiques au Canada. Population **70**(4), 771–803 (2015)
7. Faudree, M.C., Fujimaki, A.: Exceptions to markedness universals and novel use of Weibull. Analysis in the acqisition of obstruent voicing contrasts by Japanese speakers of English. Acad. J. Educ. Res. **8**(3), 117–137 (2020). https://doi.org/10.15413/ajer.2020.0701
8. Tanaka-Ishii, K.: Statistical Universals of Language. Mathematical Chance vs. Human Choice. Springer (2021)
9. Haustein, H.-D.: Prognoseferfahren in den sozialistischen Wiertschaft. Die Wirtschaft (1970)
10. Müller, N.: Systems theories in the social sciences. In: Systems Theory in the Social Sciences. Interdisciplinary Systems Research/Interdisziplinäre Systemforschung. Birkhäuser, Basel (1976). https://doi.org/10.1007/978-3-0348-5495-5_1
11. Pu, K.: Planung und Kontrolle, Planungs- und Kontrollsysteme, Planungs- und Kontrollrechnung ; Controllingkonzepte; Unternehmungsbeispiele von, Henkel KGaA, Düsseldorf, Daimler-Benz AG, Stuttgart, Siemens AG, München, Preussag AG, Hannover. Gabler (1994)

Sentiment Analysis of Literary Texts: A Study of Theme and Readers' Preferences in Russian Short Stories from 1900 to 1930s

Tatiana Sherstinova, Anna Moskvina, Margarita Kirina, Asia Karysheva, Evgenia Kolpashchikova, Polina Maksimenko, Anastasia Seinova, and Ruslan Rodionov

Abstract This article presents an experimental analysis of Russian short stories from the early twentieth century, focusing on the sentiment of literary pieces in the context of their themes and readers' preferences toward these texts. The study utilized a corpus of 210 texts, spanning from 1900 to 1930, each manually thematically annotated by experts. Sentiment was assessed employing sentiment lexicons, specifically RuSentiLex and the Multilingual Sentiment Lexicon, across individual stories and stories grouped by theme. Additionally, an experiment aimed at identifying a correlation between the texts' sentiment and readers' preferences was conducted. Findings indicate a predominant use of words from negative lexicons in the Russian short stories of the period. An association between thematic tags and the sentiment of texts was discovered, showing that stories with positive vocabulary often

T. Sherstinova (✉) · A. Moskvina · M. Kirina · A. Karysheva · E. Kolpashchikova · P. Maksimenko · A. Seinova · R. Rodionov
National Research University Higher School of Economics, 123 Griboyedova emb., Saint-Petersburg 190068, Russia
e-mail: tsherstinova@hse.ru

A. Moskvina
e-mail: admoskvina@hse.ru

M. Kirina
e-mail: mkirina@hse.ru

A. Karysheva
e-mail: askarysheva@edu.hse.ru

E. Kolpashchikova
e-mail: eokolpaschikova@edu.hse.ru

P. Maksimenko
e-mail: pimaksimenko@edu.hse.ru

A. Seinova
e-mail: arseynova@edu.hse.ru

R. Rodionov
e-mail: rarodionov@edu.hse.ru

P. Eismont et al. (eds.), *Literature, Language and Computing*,
https://doi.org/10.1007/978-981-96-0990-1_3

correlate with themes like FUTURE, YOUTH, LEISURE, VICES, and FREEDOM. Conversely, stories with a mainly negative lexical presence commonly carry tags of DEATH, WAR, VIOLENCE, and, unexpectedly, CHILDREN. Furthermore, the study highlighted an absence of correlation between the sentiment portrayed in the texts and the reader preferences, suggesting a complex dynamic between narrative tone and reader reception.

Keywords Russian short story · Theme · Sentiment analysis · Literary texts · Readers' preferences

1 Introduction

This paper investigates the sentiment analysis of small prose literary works, examining the correlation between their thematic elements and reader preferences toward these texts. The primary objective lies in uncovering the relationship between a text's theme and its emotional tone, which is calculated based on the prevalence of emotional lexicon within the text. The aim of the study was to explore how the theme of a literary text is connected to the prevailing sentiment within the text, that is, whether the stories associated with a particular theme have a predominantly negative or positive lexicon. Recognizing that sentiment is intrinsically linked to readers' evaluations, a second experiment was undertaken to identify potential correlations between the textual sentiment and reader rating.

The task of sentiment analysis is an essential part of natural language processing, which can be implemented by various methods — using rules, dictionaries and machine learning [1]. Most often, such studies are implemented on the basis of the reviews of goods and services from the Internet, as well as posts and comments on social media, in order to assess the opinions of consumers; sentiment analysis is also actively used by sociologists and political scientists to study and evaluate public opinion or the social networks' or groups' attitudes toward a particular issue, which helps to build more effective strategies for promoting goods and services, influencing the public opinion, and holding successful election campaigns.

The application of sentiment analysis methods to literary texts does not carry such an obvious utilitarian component. However, it contributes to shedding light on the lexical features of literary texts, which, alongside with classical stylometric methods, expands the range of quantitative methods that can be used in philological analysis. The following works can be mentioned as successful examples of the application of sentiment analysis to literary works [2–6].

Since sentiment analysis is closely related to opinion mining, we decided to conduct the study with a readers' preference assessment regarding the texts under consideration and a correlation analysis of the obtained ratings with the sentiment of the texts.

2 Data and Method

2.1 Data Description

The material for the study was a sample of 210 stories by Russian authors, taken from "Subcorpus-300" of the Russian Short Stories Corpus [7]. A feature of the corpus is a systematic approach to the analysis of Russian literature, which implies the inclusion of texts by the maximum number of writers who worked in the period under study [8]. This provides a wide variety of author's styles and trends in fiction literature [9].

One more advantage of this material is the expert markup of all texts on the thematic level [10]. The search through the texts' topics is possible on the corpus website [7]. To obtain expert thematic markup, all texts of the subcorpus were read by an expert; as a result, each story received a thematic tag (one or more) that most closely matched its content [11].

The sample contains texts by both well-known and almost forgotten authors. 210 stories for the study were selected randomly, one story per writer, while taking into account the year of creation; the texts were selected in an equal proportion based on the three historical periods used when marking the corpus: (1) the pre-war period (1900–1913), (2) the period of acute social cataclysms—wars and revolutions (1914–1922), (3) the early Soviet period (1923–1930). The total volume of the text sample is 713 245 words.

The relatively small sample size of this study is determined by the fact that in order to obtain an objective reader's assessment, each of the texts was read by three experts. Thus, in order to obtain feedback on all the stories, a total of 630 texts had to be read and evaluated, which is a fairly impressive amount of expert work.

2.2 Sentiment Analysis Methods

The lexicon-based methods were used to determine the sentiment of the texts, since a preliminary analysis showed that machine learning methods, usually pre-trained on modern texts taken from the Internet, are not very well suited for studying literary texts written some 100 years ago.

As dictionaries for this study, we used: (1) RuSentiLex (RSL), which is actively used in practice [12, 13] and (2) a Russian dictionary from the Multilingual Sentiment Lexicons collection developed by the Data Science Lab [14].

Two tools were used: first—the open-source program for machine learning and data visualization Orange [15], which among other functions supports sentiment analysis, second—the SentiAPP online program [16].

One of the options for sentiment analysis available in Orange is a dictionary approach based on the sentiment vocabulary lists of the built-in Multilingual Sentiment Lexicons (MSL), in addition, it is possible to upload custom dictionaries. Our study compares the results of using MSL and RuSentiLex (RSL) dictionaries. Orange implements the calculating method first proposed in [17]. The overall sentiment of the text is calculated as follows: the number of types of negative words is subtracted from the number of types of positive words, after which the resulting value is divided by the document's length in words and multiplied by 100. Thus, the number of repetitions of each sentiment word is not taken into account, and the overall sentiment of the text depends primarily on the diversity of emotionally charged vocabulary in it and its overall length. The specifics of the algorithm's implementation [17] is that two lists are given as input: positive and negative words, each word on a new line.

SentiApp processes texts at the user request, displaying the results in two formats: as a frequency list of emotionally charged vocabulary (negative, neutral and positive), and as the total number of unique word types for each of the core rating categories.

When working with Orange, two series of calculations were carried out, first on word forms (non-lemmatized texts), then on lemmatized data; when working with the SentiApp program, only lemmatized data were used as input. Lemmatization in both cases was performed using the ru_core_news_sm model of the spaCy library [18].

2.3 Reader Preferences Assessment

Reader preferences were assessed using the data obtained from reading experiment. All participants were studentes of the philology department. Each participant was given a list of stories to read individually. After reading each of the stories, the participants assessed the extent to which they had liked the story on a ten-point scale: a score of "1" suggested that the participant in the experiment had not enjoyed the story at all, and "10" that they had liked it to an exceptional degree. At the time of reading, only the title of the story was available to the participants, the author's name was concealed in order to reduce the influence of the author's status on the respondents' assessment. Each story was assessed by three readers; in further calculations, the average rating of the text was used [19].

3 Results of Sentiment Analysis

Table 1 shows a fragment of the final table with the obtained sentiment analysis data. It contains the following data: (1) meta-information: story code (ID), its author, title, and year of creation, (2) quantitative sentiment indicators obtained using different software tools and dictionaries (an asterisk icon (*) indicates lemmatization), (3) the average reader rating that the text received as a result of the experiment.

Calculations performed in Orange according to the algorithm [17] result in sentiment values in the range of [−100; 100]. However, as can be seen from Table 1, the final values turned out to be very small in absolute value and mostly negative, which

Table 1 Sentiment and reader assessment (a fragment)

ID	Author	*Title*	Year	Tool					Avg rating
				Orange				SentiAPP	
				MSL	RSL	MSL*	RSL*	RSL*	
S001	Amfiteatrov A.V	*Kurortnyj muzh (Resort husband)*	1911	−0.19	−0.52	0.17	−2.09	0.58	6.67
S005	Auslender S.A	*Zanyatye lyudi (Busy people)*	1912	0.07	−0.47	−0.19	−3.39	0.44	6.33
S007	Avilova L. A	*Vlast' (Power)*	1906	0.28	−0.40	0.46	−1.94	0.52	6.67
S008	Baltrushajtis Yu.K	*Kapli (Drops)*	1901	−0.52	−0.40	−2.00	−3.29	0.39	8.33
S009	Bal'mont K.D	*Krik v nochi (Scream in the night)*	1908	−0.37	−0.35	−2.17	−4.03	0.25	6.00
S011	Basanin M	*Paskhal'nyj zvon (Easter bells)*	1911	0.46	0.29	2.86	2.93	1.56	8.00
S012	Bashkin V.V	*Potyanulo (Drawn)*	1910	0.13	−0.34	0.11	−2.21	0.58	4.33
S013	Belyj A	*Rasskaz No. 2 (Story No. 2)*	1902	0.10	−0.08	−0.13	−1.26	0.59	7.67
S018	Budishchev A.N	*V lesnoj izbe (In a forest hut)*	1912	0.35	−0.05	−1.53	−2.68	0.63	7.00
S020	Cenzor D.M	*Den' Kopytkina (Kopytkin's day)*	1911	0.00	0.29	1.98	0.99	1.14	8.67
S021	Chapygin A.P	*Priyutilis' (Sheltered)*	1907	−0.22	−0.28	−0.67	−1.65	0.38	5.67
S023	Chekhov Aleks.P	*Tsepi (Chains)*	1904	0.03	−0.08	−1.93	−4.53	0.39	8.67
S024	Chirikov E.N	*Obostrennye otnosheniya (Acute relationships)*	1903	−0.07	−0.49	−0.21	−3.14	0.38	9.00
S025	Doroshevich V.M	*Noch' (Night)*	1906	−0.57	−0.71	−2.74	−3.30	0.39	5.33

(continued)

Table 1 (continued)

ID	Author	*Title*	Year	Tool					Avg rating
				Orange				SentiAPP	
				MSL	RSL	MSL*	RSL*	RSL*	
S026	Dymov O	*Pisateli (Writers)*	1910	0.09	−0.41	0.40	−0.27	0.71	6.00
S027	Elpat'evskij S.YA	*Snegurochka (Snow girl)*	1904	0.11	−0.11	−0.79	−1.91	0.38	7.67
S029	Garin-Mihajlovskij N.G	*Evrejskij pogrom (Jewish pogrom)*	1901	−0.70	−0.76	−3.08	−1.87	0.62	6.67
S033	Gor'kij M	*Tyur'ma (Prison)*	1904	−0.45	−0.55	−1.43	−2.87	0.31	8.33
S035	Grin A.S	*Apel'siny (Oranges)*	1912	−0.25	−0.43	−1.64	−1.97	0.58	8.67
S037	Hasidovich V.D	*Ogon'ki (Lights)*	1906	0.18	−0.09	0.92	−0.12	0.58	5.33
S039	Yablochkov G.A	*Barrikada (Barricade)*	1913	−0.34	−0.18	−1.22	−2.36	0.41	7.67
S040	Yasinskij I.I	*Rozy (Roses)*	1913	−0.13	−0.13	−0.11	0.00	1.00	6.33
S041	Yushkevich S.S	*Dud'ka zabavlyaetsya (Dud'ka is having fun)*	1910	0.23	0.00	0.54	1.75	1.11	7.33
S043	Karmen L.O	*Za chto?! (What for?!)*	1904	−0.61	−0.22	−2.33	−2.22	0.58	7.33
S045	Kolotovkin I.F	*Budni (Workdays)*	1909	0.35	0.09	−0.40	−0.40	0.75	7.00
S046	Korolenko V.G	*Moroz (Cold)*	1901	0.08	−0.03	−0.70	−1.73	0.44	7.67
S048	Krinickij M	*Materiya (Matter)*	1906	−0.26	−0.38	−0.96	−3.19	0.40	9.00
S052	Lazarev-Gruzinskij A.S	*Nezabudki (Forget-me-nots)*	1913	−0.68	−0.31	−0.48	−2.57	0.52	7.67

(continued)

Table 1 (continued)

ID	Author	*Title*	Year	Tool					Avg rating
				Orange				SentiAPP	
				MSL	RSL	MSL*	RSL*	RSL*	
S056	Mamin-Sibiryak D.N	*Monetka (Coin)*	1910	0.24	0.10	0.75	0.19	0.77	6.67
S057	Maurin E.I	*Fikciya (Fiction)*	1909	−0.41	−0.46	−2.11	−2.91	0.53	7.33
S059	Mujzhel' V.V	*Poka (While)*	1907	−0.19	−0.24	−0.66	−1.63	0.46	6.00
S061	Nemirovich-Danchenko V.I	*Zabytyj rudnik (Forgotten mine)*	1904	−0.18	−0.21	−1.04	−1.45	0.42	9.67
S062	Nevezhin P.M	*Oblomki sem'I (Shatters of a family)*	1912	0.12	−0.22	−0.23	−3.13	0.46	7.67
S063	Nikonov B.P	*Nakanune ot"ezda (Before leaving)*	1906	0.04	−0.27	0.51	−1.52	0.72	9.00
S065	Oliger N.F	*Prud (Pond)*	1906	0.05	0.05	0.42	−1.78	0.41	7.00
S066	Opochinin E.N	*Zajcy (Hares)*	1907	−0.05	−0.45	−0.69	−1.26	0.62	7.67
S067	Ossendovskij A.M	*Lozha svyashchen-nogo almaza (Lodge of the sacred diamond)*	1913	−0.05	−0.10	−1.07	−0.75	0.87	2.67
S068	Pil'skij P.M	*Odnazhdy (Once)*	1903	−0.40	−0.57	−1.47	−3.37	0.39	7.67
S071	Remizov A.M	*Krepost' (Fortress)*	1906	0.05	−0.15	−1.30	−3.14	0.18	6.67
S072	Roslavlev A.S	*Raketa (Rocket)*	1913	−0.11	−0.51	−0.56	−1.78	0.50	6.67
S073	Sadovskoj B.A	*Muha (Fly)*	1912	0.38	−0.66	−0.46	−0.46	0.68	6.33

indicates the predominance of words with a negative connotation. In the SentiAPP column, the ratio of the absolute number of unique positive words to negative ones was calculated for each text. This is always a positive number. The lower this indicator is, the stronger the predominance of negative vocabulary in the text. In cases where this indicator exceeds 1, we can assume a "positive emotional valence" of the text. Our data show that for the Russian short story at the beginning of the twentieth century this is a rather rare occurrence. In the fragment of the sample presented in Table 1, there are only three such stories: "Paskhal'nyj zvon (Easter bells)" by M. Basanin, "Dud'ka zabavlyaetsya (Dud'ka is having fun)" by S. Yushkvich and "Den' Kopytkina (Kopytkin's day)" by D. Censor.

The average reader rating ranges from 2.67 to 9.67 out of 10 possible points; the mean of all means is 6.91, the standard deviation is 1.36, and the coefficient of variation is 0.20. On average, the statistics obtained show a fairly high consistency in the ratings given by readers.

4 Evaluation of the Results

In the course of the analysis, it was found that more diverse results in terms of meanings can be obtained using lists of emotional vocabulary derived from RSL. This is likely attributed to the larger volume of entries in its dictionaries compared to those of the Russian language presented in the MSL dictionary.

	Positive words	Negative words
MSL	1266	1684
RSL	2907	8175

Regarding the comparability of results obtained from different approaches using Orange, the relevant correlation coefficients are presented in Table 2. This table indicates that the highest level of consistency is found in lemmatized texts that have been processed with various dictionaries.

The highest value of the correlation coefficient was found for the algorithms used in Orange and SentiAPP when the RSL dictionary was applied to lemmatized texts. It was 0.8646, which indicates that these algorithms give comparable results and can be relatively interdependent.

Table 2 Correlation coefficient between sentiment values obtained using two dictionaries (MSL and RSL), with (*) and without lemmatization

MSL versus MSL*	0.68904
RSL versus RSL*	0.72337
MSL* versus RSL*	0.81758
MSL versus RSL	0.57818

Despite the absence of statistically significant differences for the data obtained using these dictionaries, it seems appropriate to significantly expand the vocabulary lists, taking into account the specifics of the Russian language of the early twentieth century and the lexical characteristics of the literary texts of this period.

5 Themes and Sentiment

Table 3 shows a list of the most frequent themes in Russian short stories of the early twentieth century [20, 21], sorted by sentiment: the lower the rank of the topic, the more positive vocabulary corresponds to it, conversely, the higher the rank, the higher the predominance of negatively colored vocabulary. Since three options for calculating the sentiment of lemmatized texts were implemented in this study and they produced slightly different results, to obtain the most objective data, it was decided to average the ranks of topics by sentiment obtained in different ways. The values of these average ranks are presented in the rightmost column of the Table 3.

The narratives predominantly using positive vocabulary were found to be those labeled with thematic tags such as FUTURE, YOUTH, LEISURE, VICES, and FREEDOM. Stories filled with dreams of a bright, unfettered future, hopes invested in youth for a better life, and the joyful emotions tied to rest, vacations, and leisurely travel unsurprisingly rank among the most lexically positive literary works. Yet, surprisingly, the theme of VICES—often associated with "negative" elements like drunkenness, greed, envy, and the like—also ranks high on the sentiment scale. These texts, at the lexical level, exhibited a relatively positive tone, presenting a paradox between the generally negative connotations of the theme and the predominantly positive tone of the vocabulary.

This discrepancy might suggest that the allure of vices is often portrayed through the prism of positive emotions or a "glamorous" lifestyle, leading to an artistic depiction rich in positively connoted words. Alternatively, the classification of stories under VICES by experts may reflect a moralistic judgment of the characters' actions, which does not necessarily dictate the use of negative vocabulary by the author. In any case, this highlights the complexity of sentiment assessment based solely on lexical analysis, as it may not accurately reflect the nuanced moral evaluations embedded within the text.

Interestingly, texts addressing family matters (tagged FAMILY) tend to skew toward the negative spectrum. Despite the societal norm of viewing the family unit positively and the generally affirmative connotations that the concept of family may evoke, Russian narratives frequently delve into the tribulations of unhappy marriages and infidelity; these constitute the primary subtopics encapsulated by this tag.

As for narratives rich in negative vocabulary, it is unsurprising that stories bearing the thematic tags DEATH, WAR, and VIOLENCE are prominent. However, an unexpected discovery was that tales centered on CHILDREN ranked third in negativity. It is important to clarify that the Corpus of Russian Short Stories does not encompass "children's and youth stories"; all texts within the corpus are crafted for

Table 3 Frequency list of topics by sentiment, ordered from positive to negative

Rank	Theme	Avg. rank
1	FUTURE	1.67
2	YOUTH	2.33
3	LEISURE	3.00
4	VICES	3.33
5	FREEDOM	5.67
6	NATURE	7.33
7	CITY	9.00
8	PROGRESS	9.33
9	LOVE	9.67
10	VIRTUES	11.33
11	FANTASY	11.33
12	DREAM (GOAL)	12.33
13	ART	13.00
14	LIFE	16.00
15	DREAM (SLEEP)	16.33
16	MONEY	16.67
17	FAMILY	18.00
18	LABOR	18.00
19	RELIGION	18.33
20	SOCIAL PROCESSES	18.33
21	REVOLUTION	21.67
22	SOCIAL GROUPS	21.67
23	PSYCHOLOGICAL STATE	22.33
24	RELATIONSHIPS	23.00
25	POLITICS	23.00
26	DEATH	24.00
27	CHILDREN	24.67
28	WAR	26.33
29	VIOLENCE	27.33

mature audiences. This finding suggests that "adult stories" about children, distinct from popular children's literature, are imbued with emotional negativity, portraying the complex and often harsh realities faced by young protagonists. Their trials are rendered even more poignant by their inherent vulnerability and the historical backdrop of their narratives. Among these tales are stories about children in adult-like roles (for instance, in F. Laskova's "Anna and Bor'ka" (1916), Bor'ka at seven talks to his mother as if he were a seasoned adult who has seen it all). Additionally, it is noteworthy that stories featuring children as key characters frequently intersect with the theme of DEATH: this theme was present in 10 out of the 27 texts reviewed.

6 Sentiment of Literary Text and Reader Assessment

The findings of the research indicate a lack of correlation between the sentiment of a literary text and the readers' evaluation of it, with the correlation coefficient not exceeding 0.025 across all applied methods. However, the influence of a story's theme on reader preference is a different matter, as evidenced byour recent publication [19]. While it cannot be categorically stated that a story's theme solely shapes the reader's impression, certain patterns have emerged. Stories tagged with VIRTUE, POLITICAL STRUGGLE, REVOLUTION, and DREAM received the highest ratings from readers, whereas those associated with tags like FANTASY, LIFE, and SOCIAL GROUPS received the lowest. These preferences may be universal and potentially identifiable in other datasets, but further investigation is required to confirm this hypothesis.

7 Conclusion

The study revealed that Russian short stories from 1900 to 1930 predominantly utilize words from negative lexicons. The fact that the dictionaries employed in the experiments contain more negative than positive terms prompts critical questions: (1) Do the dictionaries accurately capture the "emotional diversity" of the Russian literary language? and (2) Is the dominance of negative vocabulary a linguistic constant (at least for Russian)? To address the first query, it appears necessary to substantially enrich existing sentiment dictionaries with less common evaluative vocabulary found in literary texts. As for the second question, attaining a definitive answer may not be feasible in the foreseeable future.

The correlation between thematic tags and the sentiment conveyed in literary texts has revealed intriguing patterns; some are anticipated, while others are surprising and even contradictory. Notably, the positive sentiment associated with stories themed around VICES and the distinctly negative sentiment in adult narratives about CHILDREN stand out. Given the relatively small sample size, these findings should be regarded as preliminary. Nevertheless, expanding the research to include a broader corpus of literature is constrained by the necessity of expert thematic tagging of the texts. The suitability of automatic topic modeling methods for this task remains uncertain.

Another outcome of the study is the complete lack of correlation between the sentiment of the literary text and reader preferences; however, discernible trends do emerge in the ratings of texts with specific themes.

Furthermore, it is worth mentioning that the sentiment analysis methods used in the study do not account for the frequency of non-unique lemmas in the text (for instance, the sentiment impact of the word "beautiful" is counted once, irrespective of its recurrence in the text). The extent to which repeated lemmas influence the sentiment of a literary text is an issue that warrants separate investigation.

Acknowledgements The paper was prepared within the framework of the Basic Research Program at HSE University in 2023 (project "Text as big data: the modeling of convergent processes in language and speech by computational methods").

References

1. Nikolaev, I.S., Mitrenina, O.V., Lando, T.M. (eds.): Applied and Computational Linguistics, 320 p. M.: LENAND (2016)
2. Kim, E., Klinger, R.: A survey on sentiment and emotion analysis for computational literary studies. Zeitschrift für digitale Geisteswissenschaften (2019). https://arxiv.org/ftp/arxiv/papers/1808/1808.03137.pdf
3. Eric, N., Henry, S.: Character-to-character sentiment analysis in Shakespeare's plays. In: Proceedings of the 51st Annual Meeting of the Association for Computational Linguistics, pp. 479–483. Association for Computational Linguistics (2013). https://aclanthology.org/P13-2085.pdf
4. Kim, E., et al.: Investigating the relationship between literary genres and emotional plot development. In: Proceedings of the ACL Workshop on Language Technology for Cultural Heritage, Social Sciences, and Humanities, pp. 17–26. Association for Computational Linguistics (2017). https://aclanthology.org/W17-2203.pdf
5. Min, S., Park, J.: Modelling narrative structure and dynamics with networks, sentiment analysis, and topic modeling. PLoS One (T. Gross, Ed.), vol. 14, 4 December 2019
6. Saif, M.: From once upon a time to happily ever after: tracking emotions in novels and fairy tales. In: Proceedings of the ACL Workshop on Language Technology for Cultural Heritage, Social Sciences, and Humanities, Portland, OR, pp. 105–114. Association for Computational Linguistics (2011). https://dl.acm.org/doi/pdf/10.5555/2107636.2107650
7. Corpus of Russian short stories 1900–1930 [Electronic resource]. https://russian-short-stories.ru/. Accessed 14 Feb. 2023
8. Martynenko, G.Y., Sherstinova, T.Y., Popova, T.I., Melnik, A.G., Zamirajlova, E.V.: On the principles of creation of the Russian short stories corpus of the first third of the XX century [O printsipakh sozdaniya korpusa russkogo rasskaza pervoy treti XX veka]. In: Proceedings of the XV International Conference on Computer and Cognitive Linguistics 'TEL 2018'. Kazan Federal University, Kazan, pp. 180–197 (2018)
9. Sherstinova, T., Martynenko, G.: Linguistic and stylistic parameters for the study of literary language in the corpus of Russian short stories of the first third of the 20th century. In: R. Piotrowski's Readings in Language Engineering and Applied Linguistics, Proceedings of the III International Conference on Language Engineering and Applied Linguistics (PRLEAL-2019), Saint Petersburg, Russia, November 27, 2019, CEUR Workshop Proceedings, vol. 2552, pp. 105–120 (2020)
10. Skrebtsova, T.: Thematic tagging of literary fiction: the case of early 20th century Russian short stories. In: Proceedings of the International Conference "Internet and Modern Society" IMS-2020. CEUR Workshop Proceedings, vol. 2813, pp. 265–276 (2020)
11. Skrebtsova, T.G.: Dynamics of Russian short stories themes at the beginning of the 20th century. In: Philosophy and the Humanities in the Information Society, no. 3, pp. 45–60 (2020)
12. Chetviorkin, I., Loukachevitch, N.: Extraction of Russian sentiment lexicon for product meta-domain. In: Proceedings of COLING 2012: Technical Papers, pp. 593–610 (2012)
13. Lukashevich, N.V., Levchik, A.V.: Dictionary of evaluative words of the Russian language [Electronic resource]. http://www.labinform.ru/pub/rusentilex/rusentilex_2017.txt. Accessed 3 Oct. 2023
14. MSL—Multilingual Sentiment Lexicons. https://sites.google.com/site/datascienceslab/projects/multilingualsentiment

15. Orange. Sentiment Analysis. https://orangedatamining.com/widget-catalog/text-mining/sentimentanalysis/
16. Sozontova, Y.: SentiAPP (2020). https://yussoz.shinyapps.io/SentiAPP/
17. Hu, M., Liu, B.: Mining opinion features in customer reviews. In: Proceedings of AAAI Conference on Artificial Intelligence, vol. 4, pp. 755–760 (2004)
18. SpaCy models for Russian. https://spacy.io/models/ru
19. Sherstinova, T.Y., Kolpashchikova E.O., Seinova, A.R., Maksimenko, P.I., Rodionov, R.A.: The Russian story 1900–1930 and its perception by the reader: the experience of a quantitative analysis of the evaluation of a literary text. Čelovek: obraz i suŝnost'. Gumanitarnyje aspekty, vol. 2, no. 54, pp. 164–184. INION RAN, Moscow (2023). https://doi.org/10.31249/chel/2023.02.09
20. Sherstinova, T., Skrebtsova, T.: Russian literature around the October revolution: a quantitative exploratory study of literary themes and narrative structure in Russian short stories of 1900–1930. In: Proceedings of the International Conference "Internet and Modern Society" IMS-2020. CEUR Workshop Proceedings, vol. 2813, pp. 117–128
21. Sherstinova, T., Kirina, M.: Normalization issues in digital literary studies: spelling, literary themes and biographical description of writers. In: International Conference on Digital Transformation and Global Society, pp. 332–346. Springer International Publishing, Cham

Over the Rainbow: Colour Terms in Russian Literature of the Early Twentieth Century

Tatiana Skrebtsova and Alexander Grebennikov

Abstract In the paper, we analyse the rankings of the most common colour adjectives used in Russian literature of the early twentieth century and explore the degree of variation over particular periods and authors. Our study draws on the Russian Short Story Corpus (1900–1930) which includes a few thousand short stories produced by hundreds of writers who lived in Russia (and later, in the Soviet Union) at the time. Another source is the frequency dictionaries compiled earlier from the short stories by four prominent Russian writers. Additionally, we use data on colour term rankings in the Silver Age poetry. The analysis of the use of colour terms in the short stories has revealed that although the individual differences may range high, on the average, the intra-group rankings remain largely unaffected by the changing political context. However, the latter can contribute to the activation of the whole group, moving its members up the list in the overall rank distribution. A comparison of the colour term rankings in the poetry and prose written by the same author has shown significant differences which may be attributable to the literary genre.

Keywords Russian literature · Short stories · Colour terms · Frequency rank · Rank distribution

1 Introduction

Over the last half a century, colour terms have been a topic of extensive cross-linguistic research due to a remarkable variation in the number of basic colours as well as in the way boundaries between them are drawn in different languages. Thus,

T. Skrebtsova · A. Grebennikov (✉)
St. Petersburg State University, Saint-Petersburg 199034, Russian Federation
e-mail: a.grebennikov@spbu.ru

T. Skrebtsova
e-mail: t.skrebtsova@spbu.ru

A. Grebennikov
ITMO University, Saint-Petersburg 197101, Russian Federation

P. Eismont et al. (eds.), *Literature, Language and Computing*,
https://doi.org/10.1007/978-981-96-0990-1_4

in Russian, *light blue* (*goluboj*) and *dark blue* (*sinij*) can be distinguished, with a single counterpart *blue* in English.[1]

Another noteworthy aspect is the use of colour terms. Obviously enough, such names of spectral colours as *orange* and *violet* (as well as their Russian equivalents *oranzhevyj* and *fioletovyj*) are much less frequent than, say, *red* or *green* (the Russian *krasnyj* and *zelenyj* respectively) regardless of style or register. Still, in general, the relative frequencies of colour terms are far from being settled once and for all, as will be shown in this paper.

The present study aims to analyse the rankings of the most common colour adjectives used in the Russian prose of the early twentieth century, with a focus on the degree of variation for particular periods and authors. Its major source is the Russian Short Story Corpus (1900–1930) which contains a few thousand short stories produced by hundreds of writers who lived in Russia (and later, in the Soviet Union) at the time.[2] The opening decades of the twentieth century were a tumultuous period marked by a series of dramatic political events (Russo-Japanese war, World War I, February and October revolutions, the Civil War) that had radically changed the course of Russian history and made an impact on Russian literature and language.

More specifically, a sample from this Corpus was used containing 310 stories by 300 writers. The sample was divided into three timespans with reference to major historic milestones: (1) the period immediately preceding WWI (1900–1913), (2) the period encompassing WWI, the February and October revolutions and the Civil War (1914–1922), and (3) the early Soviet period (1923–1930). For each of these periods and the whole sample, word frequency lists were made. Previous studies have revealed significant differences in the frequency ranks of numerous words and lexical groups over the three periods [1, 2]. In this paper, we aim to find out whether the rankings of colour terms have been affected by the extralinguistic context, and if yes, to what extent.

Another data source is frequency dictionaries compiled earlier from short stories by particular authors, namely Anton Chekhov, Leonid Andreev, Alexander Kuprin, and Ivan Bunin [3–6]. Importantly, these writers also produced most of their works roughly at the beginning of the twentieth century. These frequency dictionaries enable us to look into individual preferences in the use of colour terms and set them against the average rank distribution obtained from the Corpus.

For a broader perspective, we map the results of our study on the findings obtained by Margolis [7] in his research into the colour terms frequencies in Russian poetry over the past three centuries. The genre-related differences are illustrated, in particular, by the rankings of colour terms in Ivan Bunin's poetry as opposed to his short stories.

Altogether, this set of comparisons is meant to reveal the degree to which different factors may affect the rank distribution of colour terms.

---

[1] In the domain of spectral colours, the Russian *goluboj* corresponds to the English *blue*, and *sinij* to *indigo*. In what follows, however, we will use the names *light blue* and *dark blue* respectively.

[2] For details of the project see https://russian-short-stories.ru/.

2 Data and Method

Drawing on the sample from the Russian Short Stories Corpus, four word frequency lists were made, i.e. one for each of the three above-mentioned historical periods and one for the whole sample. They total 24,316 lexemes and 376,513 wordforms for the pre-war period; 24,617 lexemes and 303,588 wordforms for the period of wars and revolutions; 30,560 lexemes and 383,430 wordforms for the Soviet period; and 124,081 lexemes and 1,077,970 wordforms for the whole sample. The word lists are arranged in descending order, the most frequent lexeme being assigned the 1st rank.

Frequency dictionaries compiled from the short stories by the four prominent Russian writers are organized along the same lines. Their size is approximately equal to that of a frequency list for a single period. Thus, Alexander Kuprin's frequency dictionary contains 21,263 lexemes and 288,260 wordforms.

The research by Margolis [7] draws on the Russian National Corpus whose data seem representative of both individual poetic language and general stylistic trends.

Our study focusses on eight Russian adjectives of colour, namely *belyj* (*white*), *chernyj* (*black*), *seryj* (*grey*), *krasnyj* (red), *zheltyj* (*yellow*), *zelenyj* (*green*), *sinij* (*dark blue*), and *goluboj* (*light blue*). In selecting them, we relied on the frequency of their occurrence. These lexemes have proved the most frequent in our data. Five of them denote colours of the rainbow. The remaining two rainbow colours, i.e. *oranzhevyj* (*orange*) and *fioletovyj* (*violet*), were dropped on account of their low occurrence. Colours *white, black*, and *grey* were added to the five rainbow colours listed above. Altogether, they can be called basic colours, cf. [8]. Additional data on other lexemes are provided whenever they can help back up observations and explanations.

In studying all rank distributions, we are primarily concerned with the 'relative' rankings of colour terms, as if the latter were cut out of the total distribution and handled as a group. Thus, we will say, for instance, that *belyj* (*white*) holds the 1st rank (being the colour term nearest to the top), *chernyj* (*black*) holds the 2nd rank (because it comes next), etc. In some cases, though, we will be referring to their 'absolute' rankings in the overall distribution.

For the sake of convenience, we will begin with the individual writers' frequency dictionaries.

3 Colour Term Rankings in Writers' Frequency Dictionaries

A comparison among the frequency dictionaries of short stories by the four Russian writers shows noticeable variation in the use of colour terms (Table 1). Significantly, the top position is occupied by either *white* or *black*. In the next section, we will see that statistically (across 300 writers) *white* is more common. However, individual preferences are less predictable. The 3rd rank is invariably filled by *red*, the 4th rank

Table 1 Rankings of colour terms in the short stories by Chekhov, Andreev, Kuprin, and Bunin

	Anton Chekhov	Leonid Andreev	Alexander Kuprin	Ivan Bunin
belyj (white)	1	2	1	2
chernyj (black)	2	1	2	1
krasnyj (red)	3	3	3	3
seryj (grey)	5	4	5	4
sinij (dark blue)	7	6	8	7
zheltyj (yellow)	9[a]	5	6/7	6
zelenyj (green)	4	7	4	5
goluboj (light blue)	8	8	6/7	8

is shared by *grey* and *green* (the former will be shown to maintain this rank in the Russian Short Stories Corpus throughout all periods).

The varying ranks once again illustrate the uniqueness of the writers' personalities and vision of the world. In a previous study [9], we looked at 50 most frequent content words in the short stories by each of the authors. The results were found indicative of the writers' favourite topics and emotions. Thus, Bunin's stories are known to focus on nature (cf. *wind, sky, field, garden, sea, wood, sun*), whereas Chekhov, by contrast, used to concentrate rather on humans and social relations (cf. *wife, husband, necessary, doctor, word*). Short stories by Leonid Andreev are marked by a preoccupation with tragic situations and feelings (cf. *death, black, dark*).

Returning to colour terms, we should note that the distance between the two top adjectives in the overall rank distribution is also relevant. Thus, the gap between the most frequent terms *white* and *black* is significantly wider in the stories by Chekhov (219 vs. 336) than in those by Kuprin (97 vs. 101). Similarly, the frequency difference between the top-ranking colour adjectives *black* and *white* is larger in the stories by Andreev (95 vs. 135) than in those by Bunin (60 vs. 64). Thus, Bunin and Kuprin used both adjectives more or less on a par. Finally, Chekhov can be said to have used colour terms much less frequently than the other writers as their absolute rankings are much lower (with *reddish brown* the only exception—see above).

4 Colour Term Rankings in Russian Short Stories Corpus

The data provided below (Table 2) show an absolute consistency across the three periods and the whole sample. While there is an insignificant variation in ranks 6–8, the upper five ranks are filled by the same adjectives. This looks rather surprising, given (a) the remarkable differences in colour preferences of individual authors[3] (see

[3] Incidentally, the Russian Short Stories Corpus contains stories by all the four writers.

above), and (b) a perceptible change in the use of other lexical groups over the three periods, cf. [1].

It is noteworthy that *white* maintains the leading position on the list. The absolute rankings of *white* and *black* for the three periods are 125 versus 129, 111 versus 123, and 99 versus 107 respectively. On the frequency list for the whole sample, though, black stands next to white (117 vs. 116), so the dominance of white eventually comes down to a minimum. *Dark blue* consistently holds the 5th rank which it never reaches in the dictionaries of individual authors (see Table 1).

Considering the overall distribution, one may also note that the positions of all colour adjectives in question went up in the Soviet period as compared to the pre-war time (Table 3). Except for *white* and *black*, the rise amounts to more than 100 ranks, and in some cases, 200 and even 300 ranks.

The above data indicate that quite often the major leap is from the second to the third period. Naturally, the upward movement of *red* can easily be accounted for by sociopolitical factors, it being the colour of blood and Red Army banners. But what about the other colours? Before venturing an explanation for the fact, let us provide statistics on other, less frequent, colour adjectives (Table 4).

As can be seen from Table 4, the trend is similar for less common adjectives, which calls for an explanation. We hypothesize that the growing use of colour terms may be

Table 2 Rankings of colour terms in the Russian Short Stories Corpus

	1900–1913	1914–1922	1923–1930	1900–1930
belyj (white)	1	1	1	1
chernyj (black)	2	2	2	2
krasnyj (red)	3	3	3	3
seryj (grey)	4	4	4	4
sinij (dark blue)	5	5	5	5
zheltyj (yellow)	6	6	6/7	6
zelenyj (green)	7/8	7	6/7	7
goluboj (light blue)	7/8	8	8	8

Table 3 Rankings of colour terms in the overall distribution (Russian Short Stories Corpus)

	1900–1913	1914–1922	1923–1930
belyj (white)	125	111	99
chernyj (black)	129	103	107
krasnyj (red)	297	212	139
seryj (grey)	344	328	224
sinij (dark blue)	356	362	246
zheltyj (yellow)	485	551	369
zelenyj (green)	687	643	370
goluboj (light blue)	685	688	465

Table 4 Rankings of other colour adjectives in the overall distribution (Russian Short Stories Corpus)

	1900–1913	1914–1922	1923–1930
ryzhij (reddish brown)	1451	1237	519
buryj (greyish brown)	4666	2101	2199
korichnevyj (brown)	6765	1178	1654
lilovyj (lilac)	6795	2553	2905
oranzhevyj (orange)	19,694	8662	6530

Table 5 Rankings of selected nouns in the overall distribution (Russian Short Stories Corpus)

	1900–1913	1914–1922	1923–1930
loshad' (horse)	314	250	193
kon' (horse)	3046	859	347
korova (cow)	1916	1179	553
sobaka (dog)	613	461	290
les (wood)	252	124	165
pole (field)	826	577	391
kust (bush)	755	543	411
trava (grass)	614	422	399

a corollary of the changing themes of short stories which, in turn, were triggered by sociopolitical transformations. A study into the dominating themes of the Russian short stories [10] has revealed that the period from 1914 onwards saw an increase in the number of stories about war (WWI, the Civil War). On the other hand, the land reform implemented after the October revolution (1917) sparked an interest in the life of the Soviet peasantry and gave rise to short stories about it. In both cases, the action of the stories normally takes place outdoors, in the countryside with its variety of colours. *Brown* is the colour of the earth, tree trunks, and some animals, *green* is the colour of grass, summer leaves, *blue* is the colour of a clear sky, etc. It might be added that the names of domestic animals and natural objects also show a definite upward trend (Table 5). This fact seems to corroborate our conjecture.

5 Colour Term Rankings in the Russian Poetry of the Early Twentieth Century

In this section, we focus on the problem of whether colour term rankings can be genre-dependent. We set our findings against the data on Russian poetry of the early twentieth century (also known as Silver Age poetry) provided in [7].

The Silver Age poetry in this study is represented by 15 authors, including, among others, Alexander Blok, Anna Akhmatova, Sergey Esenin, Vladimir Mayakovsky,

Table 6 Rankings of colour terms in Ivan Bunin's short stories and poems

	Short stories	Poems
chernyj (black)	1	2
belyj (white)	2	1
krasnyj (red)	3	6
seryj (grey)	4	7
zelenyj (green)	5	3/4
zheltyj (yellow)	6	8
sinij (dark blue)	7	5
goluboj (light blue)	8	3/4

Marina Tsvetaeva, and Boris Pasternak. The rank distributions of colour terms were compiled on the basis of their poetic works contained in the Russian National Corpus.

The results clearly demonstrate that individual variation is much higher in poetry than in short stories, so that even *white* or *black* is not necessarily on top of the list. Thus, of all colours, Mayakovsky most often used *red*, while Esenin preferred *dark blue*. However, on the average, the rank distribution of colour terms in the Silver Age poetry follows the pattern found in the Russian Short Stories Corpus, i.e. *white—black—red—dark blue*. *Grey* was not taken into consideration in [7]; therefore its position in the hierarchy remains unclear. Remarkably, the cited distribution also holds for the poetry of the second half of the twentieth century, but not for that of the eighteenth or nineteenth centuries.

An interesting case in point is writings by Ivan Bunin who left a considerable legacy both of poetry and prose. The rankings of colour terms in his short stories were provided above, in Table 1. Now we set them against the rankings based on Bunin's poems and obtained from the Russian National Corpus (Table 6).

The differences are quite noticeable. Unexpectedly, in Bunin's poetry *green* and *light blue* hold superior positions to those of *red* and *grey*. The overall rearrangement of colour terms may be due both to the specific form and content of poetic texts. In particular, it is clear that in poetry, as opposed to prose, phonological and prosodic factors, among other things, are at work and have to be accounted for.

This is a convincing example (albeit the only one) of variation in the use of colour terms in the poetic and prosaic texts by the same writer. Unfortunately, most Silver Age authors tended to 'specialize' either in poetry or prose, so we lack other data to check whether indeed the literary genre can affect colour term rankings. Still, this seems a promising idea for future research.

6 Conclusion

In this research, we have studied the absolute and relative rankings of colour terms in Russian literature of the early twentieth century from the following viewpoints:

individual differences;
individual differences versus the average distribution;
the impact of the sociopolitical situation;
genre-dependent differences.

We have found that although individual differences may get a high rank, the average intra-group distribution remains largely unaffected by the changing political context. However, the latter may contribute to the activation of the whole group, moving its members up the list in the overall rank distribution. An interesting aspect of the problem is whether colour term rankings may depend on the literary genre. Unfortunately, apart from the works by Ivan Bunin, we have no data either to prove or refute the hypothesis.

References

1. Skrebtsova, T.G., Grebennikov, A.O., Sherstinova, T.Y.: Dinamika leksicheskogo sostava russkoy hudozhestvennoy prozy (na materiale chastotnyh slovarey korpusa russkih rasskazov 1900–1930). Kompyuternaya lingvistika i intellektualnye tekhnologii: Materialy ezhegodnoy nauchnoy konferencii «Dialog». 2021. [The dynamics of vocabulary in Russian prose (based on frequency dictionaries of the Corpus of Russian short stories 1900–1930)] Computational Linguistics and Intellectual Technologies. Papers from the Annual International Conference “Dialogue” (2021)], issue 20, pp. 646–659. (in Russian).
2. Grebennikov, A.O., Marusenko, N.M., Skrebtsova, T.G.: Mapping word frequencies in fiction on sociopolitical context: the case of early 20th century Russian short stories. Terra Lingüística **14**(1), 21–30 (2023)
3. Chastotnyy slovar rasskazov A.P. Chekhova [Frequency dictionary of short stories by Anton Chekhov]. Comp. A.O. Grebennikov; ed. G. Ya. Martynenko. SPb.: SpbGU (1999). (in Russian)
4. Chastotnyy slovar rasskazov L.N. Andreeva [Frequency dictionary of short stories by Leonid Andreev]. Comp. A.O. Grebennikov; ed. G. Ya. Martynenko. SPb.: SpbGU (2003). (in Russian)
5. Chastotnyy slovar rasskazov A.I. Kuprina [Frequency dictionary of short stories by Alexander Kuprin]. Comp. A.O. Grebennikov; ed. G. Ya. Martynenko. SPb.: SpbGU (2006). (in Russian)
6. Chastotnyy slovar rasskazov I.A. Bunina [Frequency dictionary of short stories by Ivan Bunin]. Comp. A.O. Grebennikov; ed. G. Ya. Martynenko. SPb.: SpbGU (2011). (in Russian)
7. Margolis, Y.: Ot Pushkina do poetov XXI veka. Sopostavitelnyy analiz poeticheskogo yazyka v cifrovuyu epohu [From Pushkin to 21st Century Poets: A Comparative Analysis of Poetic Language in the Digital Era]. LRC Publishing House, Moscow (2022). (in Russian)
8. Berlin, B., Kay, P.: Basic Color Terms: Their Universality and Evolution. California University Press, Berkeley (1969)
9. Grebennikov, A.O., Skrebtsova, T.G.: Yazykovaya kartina mira v russkom rasskaze nachala XX veka [Linguistic picture of the world in the Russian story of the early XX century]. Philos. Hum.Ities Inf. Soc. (3), 82–92 (2019)
10. Skrebtsova, T.: Thematic tagging of literary fiction: the case of early 20th century Russian short stories. In Proceedings of International Conference “Internet and Modern Society” (St. Petersburg, 17–20 June, 2020). CEUR Workshop Proceedings, vol. 2813, pp. 265–276 (2021)

Russian-Language Electronic Fanfiction Database: Creation Principles and Quantitative Metadata Analysis

Polina Maksimenko

Abstract The paper is devoted to the research of fanfiction texts written and published in Russian. The study consists of creating and analyzing an electronic database which contains more than 135,000 fanfiction texts and metadata from the largest Russian-language fanfiction archive "Kniga Fanfikov" (*ficbook.net*). The data were retrieved through the web-scraping method and processed using Python. The database can subsequently be used for linguistic, literary, cultural, and sociological analysis, as well as implemented as a training sample for machine learning models.

Keywords Fanfiction · Electronical database · Online mass literature · Statistics · Tags · Frequency word lists

1 Introduction

Nowadays, fanfiction is one of the most rapidly developing types of online literature. Every day, tens of thousands of texts created by fans based on their favorite works appear on online platforms. Nevertheless, Russian-language fanfiction remains relatively understudied, presumably because fan texts were initially regarded as a marginal phenomenon, a "low manifestation of paraliterature" that did not deserve serious attention [1]. Later, researchers began to view fanfiction as a product of contemporary mass (particularly fandom) culture and literature, reflecting their characteristics [2]. M. Leavenworth defines fanfiction as a phenomenon of amateur mass literature that is based on the use, expansion, or reinterpretation of the fiction world created in any popular work, usually literary, cinematic, or dramatic [3].

In addition to the secondary nature of the text in relation to the original work (also known as canon), important features of fanfiction as a literary phenomenon include its creation within fan communities (fandoms) and adherence to their standards, the voluntary nature of writing, and a greater focus on characters rather than the fictional world [4].

P. Maksimenko (✉)
National Research University Higher School of Economics, Saint-Petersburg, Russia
e-mail: pimaksimenko@edu.hse.ru

P. Eismont et al. (eds.), *Literature, Language and Computing*,
https://doi.org/10.1007/978-981-96-0990-1_5

Russian-language studies on fanfiction usually rely on the close-reading method [5, 6], while another approach involving the creation of corpora and electronic databases, including large-scale samples, demonstrates its effectiveness [7–9].

2 Data Source

The most popular specialized resource for publishing fanfiction in Russia *Kniga Fanfikov*, or *Ficbook* (*ficbook.net*) [10] was chosen as the data source for creating the electronic database. It contains over 4 million fan texts within more than 25,000 fandoms. The internal organization of the portal involves dividing fandoms into nine categories (based on the type of original work): "Anime and Manga", "Books", "Cartoons", "Games", "Movies and TV shows", "Celebrities", "Comics", "Musicals", "Originals", and "Other". The largest category is "Celebrities", which includes around 1 million works and over 10,000 fandoms. It is followed in popularity by the categories "Anime and Manga" and "Movies and TV shows". The most popular fandoms include the South Korean pop group *Bangtan Boys* (*BTS*), the *Harry Potter* books and movies, the anime *Naruto* and *Fairy Tail*, and the video game *Genshin Impact*. It should be noted that *Ficbook* allows the publication of *originals*—author's texts that do not rely on any existing work or borrow characters, elements of fictional worlds, or events. Originals are often considered a branch of fanfiction as they have similar structures, genres, and characters [11]. The portal also allows users to publish translations of fan texts originally written in foreign languages.

The resource offers users an extensive system of tags that characterize the size, writing status, age rating, genre (or orientation), characters, and thematics of the work.[1] Each fan text is preceded by a brief description containing the title, the author's nickname, a link to their profile, information on all the listed parameters, and an annotation (author's comment).

3 Methods

The electronic database was created using *web scraping*—a technology that involves automatically extracting data from the Internet, typically for subsequent storage in a file system, extraction, and analysis [14]. The main advantage of this technology is its speed, high performance, and suitability for collecting and processing large volumes of data.

To apply this method to the material from the *Ficbook* website, a web scraper was developed - an automated program that sends requests to the web server of the resource and extracts information through data parsing [ibid.]. The web scraper was implemented as a Python script using the *Selenium* library, which is an API

[1] Detailed definitions of existing classifications of fanfiction texts can be found in articles [12, 13].

WebDriver functioning as a web browser [15]. It is used to load web pages, extract data from them, search for elements, and interact with them. The texts of the works were saved as files in *.txt* format, while the extracted metadata was presented as a data frame.

4 Electronic Database Description

The obtained electronic database contains 136,257 texts created by 27,792 authors within 3,411 fandoms. The fan texts were published from June 2009 to January 2013.[2]

134,615 works are written in the Russian language, which accounts for over 98% of the total number of texts, while translations make up only 1.2% of the electronic database (1,642 texts). In addition, the electronic database contains metadata about all the texts, including the title of the fanfiction, a link to the web page where the work is posted, the author's nickname, and a link to their profile on the *Ficbook* platform. It also includes a description preceding the text, information about the fandom, genre, and rating assigned to the work, as well as information about the characters (pairings) and assigned tags. It is important to note that all the fan texts included in the electronic database are marked as "Completed" (as of 22 May 2023).

5 Quantitative Analysis of Metadata

5.1 Fandom

Let us consider the distribution of texts in the electronic database by fandoms.

Approximately 28.5% of the sample consists of originals. Originals can be seen as both a way for aspiring authors to promote themselves on fanfiction platforms and as a departure from borrowing characters and plot elements from other stories [11]. Nevertheless, considering the relatively large number of original works on the fanfiction platform, it is possible to speak of the demand for fan communities as platforms for publishing original texts that are not fully derived from fan culture.

Among the list of the top 25 most popular fandoms, 11 belong to the "Anime and Manga" category (*Katekyo Hitman Reborn!*, *Naruto*, *Fairy Tail*, *Bleach*, etc.), and there are also 3 fandoms of Korean music groups (*Super Junior*, *SHINee*, *EXO–K/M*). This indicates a pronounced interest of fan writers in Asian art and culture. In the "Movies and TV shows" category, the most numerous fandoms are *Sherlock (BBC)*, *Supernatural*, *Boarding School* (*Zakrytaya Shkola*), and *The Vampire Diaries*. Interestingly, the *Harry Potter* fandom is not as popular in the analyzed sample

[2] The size of the database is limited due to the resource's request limit during web scraping.

compared to the current information on *Ficbook*: among the most popular fandoms in the electronic database, it ranks only 8th, with 2,596 fan texts (about 2% of the sample).

It should be noted that the number of fandoms on the platform has significantly increased over the past decade. Despite the fact that many new fan communities have a larger number of texts, some fandoms that emerged between the 2000s and 2010s remain popular and continue to be updated with new publications. Among them, notable fandoms include *Harry Potter*, *Naruto*, *Fairy Tail*, *The Avengers*, *Supernatural*, *Sherlock (BBC)*, and others.

5.2 Genre

Genre in fanfiction characterizes the presence and features of the romantic storyline described in the text. Thus, *gen* implies the absence or insignificance of romantic relationships in the work. *Het* marks the description of heterosexual relationships, *slash* (*femslash*) denotes homosexual relationships. *Mixed* orientation indicates the presence of multiple equivalent romantic storylines of different orientations. *Ficbook* also introduces the genre *article*, which defines a journalistic text about fandom or writing art [10].

The distribution of texts in the sample by genre is presented in Table 1. Although more than 42% of works belong to the gen genre, the majority of works focus on describing romantic (and/or sexual) relationships, accounting for approximately 57%. Statistical data confirms the observation that fan texts describe homosexual relationships more often than heterosexual ones. At the same time, relationships between men (slash) attract fan writers around 16 times more than relationships between women (femslash). The obtained data indicate that slash indeed prevails among fan texts containing a romantic storyline, which supports research hypotheses about the attractiveness of slash as an alternative to conventional gender roles [16–18]. Nevertheless, the sample can be considered balanced in terms of the ratio of the three main genres: gen, slash, and het. Therefore, it can be assumed that the distribution of texts by genre varies within different fan communities.

Table 1 Distribution of genres in the electronic fanfiction database

Genre	Number of texts	Percent (%)
gen	57,800	42,42
slash	41,671	30,58
het	28,993	21,28
mixed	4577	3,36
femslash	2568	1,88
article	508	0,37
other types of relationships	140	0,10

For instance, in the *Sherlock (BBC)* fandom, slash works account for ~49.5% of all texts, gen—for ~35.7%, het—for ~10.5%. This fact can be explained by fans perceiving and interpreting the friendship between the main characters of the original works Sherlock Holmes and John Watson as homosexual relationships (the so-called *Starsky and Hutch syndrome* [16]). In the *Harry Potter* fandom, a different distribution of genres can be observed: around 40% of texts belong to het, ~35% to gen, and only about 26% to slash. The reasons for such distribution can be attributed to the presence of both male and female canonical characters in primary and secondary roles, as well as the significance of describing heterosexual relationships in the original works, which play a remarkable role in the development of the plot and characters.

5.3 Rating

Notwithstanding the stereotype of fanfiction as erotic works [19], more than three-quarters of the texts do not contain any description of sexual interactions, and the most numerous ratings is *G* (~45% of works), which often does not imply the presence of a romantic storyline. In addition, only about 12% of fanfictions contain detailed graphic descriptions of erotica or violence, with less than 1% falling into the category of extremely violent works (*NC-21*). This distribution may indicate that fan authors are more focused on interpreting events and the personalities of canon characters, as well as on the emotional aspect of character relationships, rather than on erotic interactions between them (Table 2).

Let us turn to the analysis of the correlation between rating and the orientation of fanfiction works (Fig. 1).

More than two-thirds of G-rated texts belong to gen, while slash dominates for higher-rated fanfictions (R, NC-17, NC-21). Works about relationships between characters of different genders account for 16 to 27% for each rating. Moreover, statistical data confirms the hypothesis put forward by M. McCardle [20]. It is the pairing that determines the orientation of the work and largely influences age restrictions and ratings: gen and het are opposed to slash (femslash), as heterosexual relationships (unlike homosexual ones) are considered acceptable in society and therefore suitable for readers of any age. Indeed, for publicly accessible texts with ratings G and PG-13, the number of het and gen works significantly exceeds the number of slash and

Table 2 Distribution of ratings in the electronic fanfiction database

Rating	Number of texts	Percent (%)
G	61,153	44,9
PG-13	41,912	30,8
R	16,591	12,2
NC-17	15,443	11,3
NC-21	1158	0,8

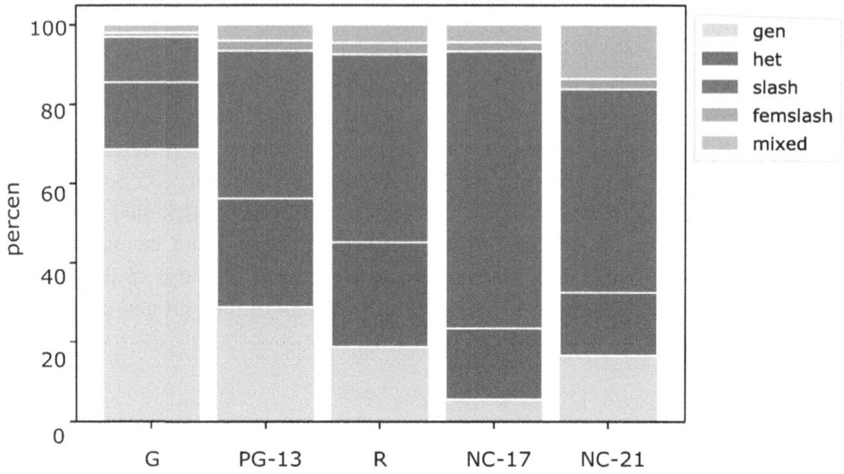

Fig. 1 Distribution of fanfiction texts of different genres and ratings

femslash works (~84.8% versus ~12.4% and ~56% versus ~39.7%, respectively). The reverse trend, also predicted by McCardle, is observed for ratings NC-17 and NC-21: the number of slash and femslash works exceeds the number of gen and het works by ~48.6% and ~21.2%, respectively. For the R rating, the distribution is relatively even: het and gen account for about 45%, while slash and femslash account for about 50%.

5.4 *Theme Tags*

Considering the category of tags assigned to works by authors based on genre features, content, mood, and text structure (Table 3), it is important to mention that the system of "genres" in fanfiction was created by the fan writers themselves and focused on the emotional, rather than literary component of the texts, so one work can combine several genres [12]. Unique genre designations for fan texts were created largely because conventional literary forms (short story, novel, poem) are unable to reflect the peculiarities inherent in fanfiction [13]. At the same time, some fanfiction genres are based on traditional literary genres and reinterpret them, such as romance, drama, comedy [12].

About one-third of the texts have the genre tag *romance*, which corresponds to the data that more than half of the works describe romantic relationships between characters. In addition, the popularity of the romantic storyline indicates a desire for fan writers to create ideal relationships for their favorite characters [6]. Interestingly, *angst* is almost as common, reflecting the anxious and depressive mood of the stories, which can be seen as the opposite of the positively colored genre of *romance*.

Table 3 Tags assigned to the largest number of fan texts

Tag	Number of texts	Percent (%)
romance (omantic)	46,234	33,93
angst	40,325	29,59
OOC (Out Of Character)	36,957	27,12
POV (povestvovanie ot pervogo litsa)	32,293	23,70
everyday life (povsednevnost)	30,772	22,58
drama	26,447	19,41
humor	23,992	17,61
psychology	22,884	16,79
poetry (stihi)	18,284	13,42
main character death (smert osnovnykh personazhei)	18,140	13,31
philosophy	15,128	11,10
AU (Alternative Universe)	15,026	11,03
explicit language (netsenzurnaya leksika)	12,392	9,09
fluff	11,401	8,37
songfic	10,322	7,58
hurt/comfort	10,230	7,51
ER (Established Relationship)	9049	6,64
fantasy	8866	6,51
banter (styob)	8623	6,33
dark	8380	6,15
mysticism (mistica)	7739	5,68
violence (nasilie)	7716	5,66
OFC (original female character)	6089	4,47
PWP (Porn Without Plot)	5862	4,30
elements of het	5446	4,00
experiment	5153	3,78
underage	4679	3,43
action	4501	3,30
sexual assault (iznasilovanie)	3916	2,87
OMC (original male character)	3669	2,69

From another perspective, *angst* can be interpreted as an emotional component of describing a romantic storyline and can be combined with the tag *romance*—in the database, both tags have 4146 works. Another interpretation of the popularity of the genre *angst* suggests a strong influence of canon on fan texts, if the original work gave significant importance to the emotional experiences of the characters [ibid]. The explanations provided are also relevant for justifying the frequency of the genre *drama*, which is similar to *angst*.

The presence of tags such as *main character death*, *dark*, and *violence* may indicate that authors look at a canon that includes descriptions of cruel and tragic moments. The noted interest of fan writers in describing "heavy" events is characteristic of fan fiction: paradoxically, readers of fan texts strive to experience suffering along with the characters [18]. The thing is, one of the functions of reading fan fiction is the shock effect, often associated with a high level of *bodily realism* in storytelling, which is indicated by the mentioned tags, as well as tags like *explicit language*, *PWP*, *sexual assault* [ibid.].

The popularity of tags such as *OOC* and *AU*, which imply significant changes in the personalities and characteristics of canonical characters and the transfer of characters to circumstances different from the original, indicates the desire of fan fiction authors to create new interpretations of their favorite characters' personalities and events in their lives that correspond to their individual fan representation. Moreover, based on the frequency of the tag *first-person narrative*, one can judge the identification of the fan writer with the main character of the fan text, which can be both a canonical character and an author-introduced character (*OFC*, *OMC*). Often, this is how the fan writer fulfills their desire to present themselves as a participant in the narrative.

Regarding text organization, the most used form is poetry. Moreover, almost 60% (10,815 out of 18,284) of texts with this tag belong to the category of originals, which confirms the functionality of fan fiction resources as a tool for promoting one's own creative work, including work unrelated to fan culture. Another popular tag related to the text format is *songfic*, which attracts fan writers, presumably because of the opportunity to create a special atmosphere or emphasize what is between the lines in the text using lines from a musical composition [13].

6 Texts Processing

All 136,257 fanfiction texts included in the electronic database were tokenized and lemmatized using the *NLTK* library and the morphological analyzer *pymorphy2* both implemented in Python [21, 22].

The total size of the sample was 505,391,801 tokens, with an average text size of 3,709 tokens. More than 57% of the electronic database consists of texts shorter than 1,000 tokens, with about three-quarters of the texts being shorter than 2,000 tokens. Meanwhile, texts longer than 10,000 tokens account for only about 8% of the sample. Additionally, 55,080 works (~40%) are tagged as *drabble*, which characterizes a short excerpt often describing a single idea, scene, or character in detail.

From the given data, it can be concluded that the majority of fan texts focus on describing one or several scenes and are close to short literary forms such as short stories and novellas.

It is important to note that the processing performed will allow the use of the electronic database for linguistic analysis and the identification of language features in texts, for example, within one or several fandoms or for comparing fan works from a diachronic perspective.

7 Conclusion

Currently, fanfiction occupies an important place among contemporary online literary phenomena and attracts increasing interest not only from authors and readers but also from researchers in various scientific fields. Fan texts are successful due to the *multifunctionality, intensity, and freedom* of the writing and reading experience [18]. In addition, fanfiction has been and remains one of the ways for consumers of culture (fans) to interact with media content and contribute to convergence culture [23].

The result of this work is the creation of a Russian-language electronic fanfiction database, which includes over 135,000 texts and data about them. Based on quantitative analysis of the obtained information, conclusions were drawn about the extensive development of fanfiction in the Russian-speaking environment over the past 15 years, thanks to the emergence of new fandoms and the expansion of existing ones. Statistical analysis confirms the significance of the romantic component in fan texts and the predominant orientation toward homosexual relationships, which is largely dependent on the specifics of the original work. Many fanfictions are characterized by a heightened degree of *bodily realism*, which makes readers experience a shock effect that is an integral part of the reading experience. However, a large portion of works does not contain descriptions of erotic scenes, thus disproving the stereotypical perception of fanfiction as predominantly pornographic texts. A significant aspect of interacting with fan texts for both fan writers and readers is relating oneself to a favorite character or embodying one's own image within the framework of individual canon interpretation.

The prospects of this research include expanding the electronic database, using its materials for training machine learning models (e.g., text classification task), comparing fan texts with other types (genres) of literature, and studying specific phenomena within the fanfiction phenomenon.

Acknowledgements The paper was prepared within the framework of the Basic Research Program at HSE University in 2023 (project "Text as big data: the modeling of convergent processes in language and speech by computational methods").

References

1. Prasolova, K.A.: Fanfikshn: literaturnyj fenomen konca XX–nachala XXI veka (tvorchestvo poklonnikov J. K. Rowling): dis. ... cand. philol. sciences. Kaliningrad (2009) (in Russian)
2. Chetina, E.M., Klyujkova, E.A.: Fandomy i fanfiki: kreativnye praktiki na virtual'nyh platformah. Vestnik Permskogo Universiteta, iss. **3**(31), pp. 95–104 (2015) (in Russian)
3. Leavenworth, M.L.: A Truth universally acknowledged?: Pride and prejudice and mind- reading fans. Storyworlds: A journal of narrative studies, **7**(2), pp. 93–110. Lincoln (2015)
4. Coppa, F.: The Fanfiction Reader: Folk Tales for the Digital Age. University of Michigan Press (2017)
5. Popova, S.N.: Lingvostilistika fanfikshn (na materiale angloyazychnyh sajtov, posvyashchyonnyh tvorchestvu J. R. R. Tolkina): dis. cand. philol. sciences. Moscow (2009) (in Russian)

6. Korobko, M.A.: Zhanr v fanfikshn: zakonomernosti ispolzovaniya (na materialah fandomov «Sherlock», «Merlin», «Sverhestestvennoe»). Uchenye zapiski Orlovskogo gosudarstvennogo universiteta, 6 (69), pp. 154–157 (2015) (in Russian)
7. Milli, S., Bamman, D.: Beyond canonical texts: A computational analysis of fanfiction. In: Proceedings of the 2016 Conference on Empirical Methods in Natural Language Processing, pp. 2048–2053 (2016)
8. Sindoni, M.G.: I really have no idea what non-fandom people do with their lives. A multimodal and corpus-based analysis of fanfiction. Lingue e Linguaggi, **13**, pp. 277–300 (2015)
9. Evans, S.A.: Where No One Has Gone Before: A Meta-Dataset of the World's Largest Fanfiction Repository. In: Proceedings of the 2017 CHI Conference on Human Factors in Computing Systems, pp. 6106–6110 (2017)
10. Kniga Fanfikov. https://ficbook.net/. Accessed 22 May 2023
11. Zhilyaeva, A.I., Lazareva, A.S., Kurguzova, N.V.: Oridzhinal: mezhdu fanfikshn i literaturoj. In: Perspektivy nauki—59. Kazan': Roketa Soyuz. pp. 186–191 (2017) (in Russian)
12. Antipina, Yu.V.: Zhanrovye osobennosti fanatskoj prozy (na primere fanfikshena po tvorchestvu brat'ev Strugackih). Vestnik CHelGU, No **13**, 21–25 (2011). (in Russian)
13. Shatrova, E.D., Lasitsa, L.A.: K probleme opredeleniya zhanrov proizvedenij fanfiction. Vestnik OGU, 1 (201), pp. 41–48 (2017) (in Russian)
14. Mitchell, R.: Web Scraping with Python. O'Reilly Media Inc., CA, Sebastopol (2018)
15. The Selenium Browser Automation Project 4.0: Documentation. https://www.selenium.dev/documentation/. Accessed 10 July 2023
16. Bacon-Smith, C.: Enterprising women: Television fandom and the creation of popular myth. Philadelphia (1992)
17. Russ, J.: Pornography by women, for women, with love. Magic mommas, trembling sisters, Puritans and perverts: Feminist essays, pp. 79–99. Trumansburg, N.Y. (1985)
18. Samutina, N.: Velikie chitate'nicy: fanfiction kak forma literaturnogo opyta. Sociologicheskoe obozrenie, **12**(3), pp. 137–191 (2013) (in Russian)
19. Caputo, K.: The new pornography: The rise of fanfic. (2016)
20. McCardle, M.: Fan Fiction, Fandom, and Fanfare: What's All the Fuss. Boston (2003)
21. NLTK 3.2.5 Documentation. https://nltk.readthedocs.io/en/latest/. Accessed 10 July 2023
22. Pymorphy 2 0.9.1. Documentation. https://pymorphy2.readthedocs.io/en/stable/user/. Accessed 10 July 2023.
23. Jenkins, H.: Convergence Culture Where Old and New Media Collide. New York University Press, N.Y. (2006)

Quantitative Methods in Language Studies

History of Russia in the 17th–18th Centuries in School Textbooks of Different Years Through the Prism of Sentiment and Topic Modeling Analysis

Anastasia Kolmogorova and Kristina Borisova

Abstract The article discusses the results of an analysis of sentiment and thematic emphases in the texts of Russian history textbooks published at different times: in 1971, 1995, and 2014. We consider those chapters of the textbooks which describe the events of the 17th–eighteenth centuries, one of the most unstable periods in the country's history. The results obtained with the help of sentiment analysis and topic modeling algorithms prove that depending on the time of the textbook publication, institutional authors model different emotional assessments, their sources (facts or opinions), and dominant lexical and semantic rows (themes) while speaking about the same periods of Russian history.

Keywords Topic modeling · Sentiment analysis · Academic texts · Russian history · Hierarchical text clusterization

1 Introduction

The article explores the problem of the NLP methodology relevance for discourse analysis of the institutional bias in school books on the history of Russia in different periods.

From the perspective of discourse analysts, the text of a school textbook is an extremely interesting object of study. It forms the basis on which many subsequent ideological and political discourses would be built later [1]. The textbook is usually written in two optics: it reflects the picture of the world of institutional authors living their lives at the current stage of society development, and it is intended to project the same worldview to the cognitive system of a new generation of citizens—schoolchildren. This problem has been repeatedly discussed in European discourse studies [2], which presume that school textbook content is deeply influenced by

A. Kolmogorova (✉) · K. Borisova
HSE University, Saint-Petersburg, Russia
e-mail: akolmogorova@hse.ru

P. Eismont et al. (eds.), *Literature, Language and Computing*,
https://doi.org/10.1007/978-981-96-0990-1_6

three factors: state standards, author's perspective, and consumer preference [3, 92]. The importance of the former stems from the fact that the data described in a school textbook is always a kind of legitimate knowledge conveyed by institutional narrators. And more often than not, it is the opinion of groups whose views are shared by the current government that has the greatest influence on the content of the curriculum. This is the so-called politics of official knowledge [4], documented in many countries.

Author's attitude is also very important for textual representation of a historical world picture, because the institutional author is at the same time a member of the society of a certain period: he lives "in the moment" of his epoch, and he shares the contemporary concepts of the scientific community to which he belongs. Finally, he retrieves and interprets historical information in such a way that it elicits the acceptance of its potential consumers – teachers and students.

It is important to note that the modeling of schoolchildren's historical world picture is carried out by subtle textual tools: nuancing at the level of emotional tonality, the arrangement and alignment of thematic focal points. Similar to the term "key word of the moment" [5], which exists in modern political linguistics, in the aspect of texts of school textbooks one may speak of "key characters of the moment" and "key accents of the moment".

The use of digital textual processing tools, such as Sentiment Analysis and Topic Modeling, helps to capture this subtle shift in the textual representation and attitude manifestations.

In this publication, we propose to discuss the application of these methods to a corpus of school textbooks from three time periods: 1971, 1995, and 2014. The focus is on the description of the difficult period for Russia between the seventeenth and eighteenth centuries. Turning-point epochs in the country's history are a kind of litmus paper for seeing a specific mindset of the era in which they are interpreted.

Here is how V.O. Kluchevsky wrote about this historical period in the famous Course of Russian History [6]:

> The custom on which the state order under the old dynasty was held has been shaken, the tradition, which guided the creators and protectors of this order, has been interrupted. When people stop acting out of habit, let go of the thread of tradition, they begin to think intensely and fidgetily, and thinking makes them suspicious and hesitant, makes them timidly try different ways of action. This timidity was also characteristic of the Moscow statesmen of the seventeenth century. In them, the abundance of new concepts, the fruit of hard experience and intense reflection were combined with a shaky political progress, with the changeability of direction, a sign of unused to their position. Aware of disproportion between available funds and the tasks on the line, they first seek new funds in the old domestic national sources, straining the forces of the people, repairing and rebuilding or restoring the order bequeathed by ancestors. But, noticing the exhaustion of domestic sources, they rush hastily to the side, attract foreign forces to help their own exhausted, and then again fall into a fearful reflection, whether they have not gone too far in dodging their native antiquity, whether it is not possible to do without foreign help. These trends, replacing one another, in the second half of the seventeenth century go side by side for a while, and by the end of it collide, make a series of political and church upheavals, and in the eighteenth century merge into the Peter the Great Reform, which forcibly drove them into a single direction leading them to one goal. Here is a general outline of the course of the internal life of the Moscow state from the end of the Troubles to the end of the eighteenth century.

Because of its importance and, at the same time, its contradictory nature, this era can be an interesting object for discursive modeling in the texts of school textbooks of different years.

To be clear in representing our ideas, we intend to adhere to the following logic: in Sect. 2 we consider existing works that have already applied methods of computer processing to school textbooks in order to identify their implicit content categories; Sect. 3 focuses on the general corpus description and research methodology; in Sect. 4 we detail, first, the results of applying the Topic Modeling algorithm to the data and, second, two models of Sentiment Analysis; in Conclusion we sum up the main tendencies we have noticed and draw some perspective of using the same methodology in further researches.

2 Related Papers

While Sentiment Analysis paradigm is now very solicited in different fields, it privileged post in social networks or all kind of reviews, but the academic texts tonality is still a rare object of observation. Apparently, there is some stereotype that school academic texts strive for emotional neutrality and impassivity in presenting some basic knowledge about the world, which will then form the basis of a person's worldview. However, according to the European tradition of discourse analysis [7–10], it is the school textbooks that are a powerful tool for shaping the young generation's picture of the world. Within the framework of this toolkit, institutional authors create subjective affectively colored images of events, set thematic and value accents, legitimizing the existing social and political order.

As for using instruments of automatic text processing for the analysis of school texts, one of the first diachronic studies in this field is proposed by Marino [11]: the author examines the sentiment of 66 psychology textbooks published over the past eleven decades and concludes that the emotional tonality of the books studied has become increasingly negative.

Having worked with a large corpus of texts, Iliev et colleagues [12] make a more general conclusion: with time the number of positive words in texts regularly produced by people decreases and all texts slide to negative tonality.

Russian researchers from Kazan Federal University [13] after having analyzed two series of textbooks (from the 5th to the 11th grade) on history and social studies conclude that negative vocabulary prevails in history textbooks. It is important that the proportion of evaluative vocabulary in high school textbooks is lower than in middle school textbooks.

In pandemic times, with the explosion of distance learning technologies, the problem of covert emotional mechanisms "hidden" in academic texts became extremely relevant [14].

In our work, we make our observations of schoolbooks texts sentiment taking into account two factors: time of schoolbook publication and a historical period depicted in it. Moreover, not only do we measure positive and negative sentiment, but also distinguish its source (fact or opinion). To go further, we apply to our subcorpora an algorithm of Topic Modeling searching to compare focus shifts in texts published in different time slots.

3 Data and Methodology

For the analysis we used the texts of three textbooks on the history of Russia in the 17th–18th centuries:

I. Nechkina M.V., Leibengrub P.S. History of the USSR. Textbook for the 7th Grade. M.: Prosveshcheniye, 1971;
II. Yurganov A. L., Katsva L. A. History of Russia. Experimental Textbook for the 8th Grade of Secondary Schools. M.: Miros, 1995;
III. Danilov A. A.: Textbook of Russian History. The End of the 17th–18th Centuries. M.: Prosveshcheniye, 2014.[1]

The choice of these textbooks is due to the fact that they belong to one of the three important political periods for Russian society (Soviet period, post-perestroika, modern times), during which different ideologies dominated.

For the analysis convenience, each of the three textbooks was divided into five parts, allocated according to the division of textbooks into chapters and corresponding to the key periods of Russian history in the 17th–eighteenth centuries:

- ”The Time of Troubles”;
- ”The seventeenth century”;
- ”The Age of Peter”;
- ”1725–1762 (The Age of palace coups)”;
- ”The Age of Catherina”.

The result of this procedure was a corpus of fifteen texts, each belonging to one of five chapters. Accordingly, there were three texts in each chapter section. A further comparison of the textbooks will be conducted precisely in accordance with these sections.

Text preprocessing was conducted as follows:

1. All information not directly related to the text was manually removed from the textbooks: metadata, images and captions, titles and subtitles, content, page numbers, punctuation marks and any characters that are not letters;
2. All capital letters were replaced by lowercase letters;
3. The texts were tokenized and lemmatized by the MyStem program in the “pymystem” module for the Python language;
4. We also removed stop words for the Russian language. Their list was expanded with the most frequent names of historical figures in the text. In addition, the

[1] Hereinafter in the text, the sources will be cited under these numbers.

words "all" and "year" were additionally deleted, because they turned out to be highly frequent in most of the topics highlighted in the analysis;
5. We identified the most frequent collocations, and united their parts by an underscore (e.g., boris_godunov).

Preprocessed texts were submitted to the analytic procedure supported by such tools as Topic Modeling, Sentiment Analysis and Hierarchical Clustering.

Topic Modeling is a general name for methods and algorithms that aim to identify the hidden thematic structure in a text [15, 405]. The main tool of Topic Modeling is measuring the distance between words, that is, how often they occur together. Due to its simplicity and interpretability, the method based on Latent Dirichlet Allocation algorithm has gained the greatest popularity among the methods of Topic Modeling analysis. Its distinctive feature is that it assumes the presence of the same themes in all texts of the corpus, but in different proportions [16].

In recent years, Topical Modeling has been actively used in discourse studies [17, 18] because topics identified through Topical Modeling can provide important information for measuring discourse [19, 20]. In the current study, Topic Modeling was performed in the R programming language using the ggplot and Structural Topic Modeling (STM) packages.

4 Results and Discussion

4.1 Topic Modeling of Textual Fragments from Schoolbooks on the History of Russia

Topic Modeling involves selecting the number of topics manually. To determine the best number of topics to analyze a selected corpus, several models were trained, each using a different number of topics. The decision was made based on the diagnostic analysis provided in the STM package. The authors of the package propose to use Held-Out Likelihood and Residuals as the two main metrics. As can be seen from Fig. 1, the number of topics in which the likelihood function retains quite high values, while the residuals have a low level, is seven. Therefore, it is this number of topics that was chosen for further analysis as the most optimal.

One of the features of the STM package is that, in addition to the list of the most frequent words, it provides other textual metrics, the most significant of which is FREX (FRequency and EXclusivity). It represents the harmonic weighted average of a word's rank in terms of its exclusivity and frequency.

For each individual topic, the words are arranged in descending order of FREX. For example, for the second topic, the word *bourgeois* is more frequent and exclusive than the word *revolution* (Table 1). It was the FREX metric that was used in the selection of topic names, combined with a closer look at the most revealing passages in the chapters.

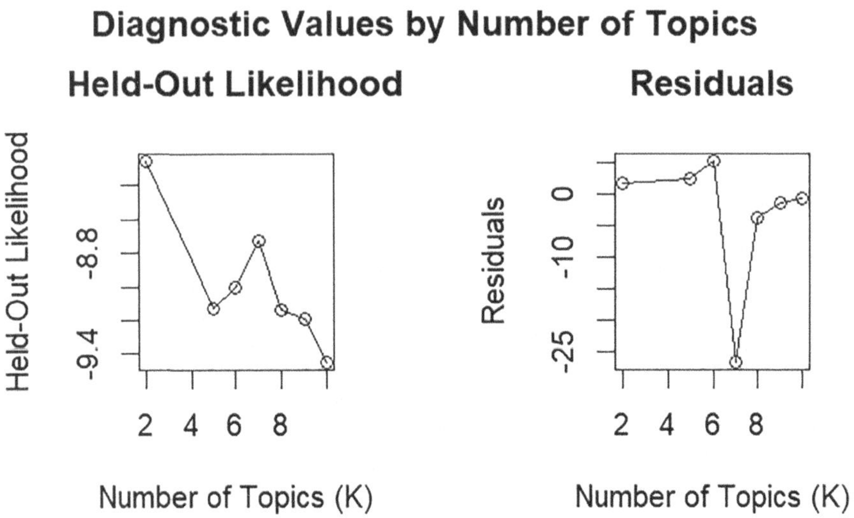

Fig. 1 Diagnostic values by number of topics

Table 1 Topics and terms

Topic number	Topic name	Top-10 of terms ranged, accordingly to FREX metric	Topic weight in topical structure of all corpus
1	Peasant wars	Krest'yanskiy, nakaz, ideya, prosveshchennyy, krepostnoy, deputat, pomeshchik, vystuplenie, khodkevich, etap	0.16
2	Industrialization and conquests	Burzhuaznyy, baltiyskiy, klass, bereg, more, ogon', kapitalisticheskiy, evropa, revolyutsiya, morskoy	0.13
3	Legislative and ecclesiastical reforms	Vek, sobor, tserkovnyy, zemskiy, ulozhenie, patriarkh, smuta, prikaz, tolpa, duma	0.13
4	The troubles	Samozvanets, tsarevich, polyak, smolensk, nagoy, moskvich, slukh, polyakov, opolchenie, uglich	0.15
5	Ukrainian question	Gnet, ukrainskiy, produkt, ukraina, pan, vosstavat', panskiy, turetskiy, panov, rynok	0.12
6	The beginning of Peter's reign, reforms and conquests	Strelets, narva, preobrazhenskiy, posol'stvo, tsarevna, streletskiy, korabl', reforma, lefort, poteshnyy	0.13
7	Palace coups	Imperatritsa, sovet, verkhovnik, konditsiya, perevorot, gertsog, verkhovnyy, taynyy, imperator, proekt	0.19

The distribution of topics (Fig. 2) shows the greatest differences in the 1971 textbook in comparison with the other two.

While the chapter devoted to the Troubles in the other two textbooks is marked by topic 4 (99.97% in the 1995 textbook and 99.96% in 2014), which actually reflects the Trouble Times, in the 1971 textbook the emphasis is shifted to the peasant wars (topic 1). In this chapter of the Soviet textbook, the people seem to become the protagonist, since it is from their point of view that the events in the book are examined: the textbook describes in detail the harshness of peasant life and emphasizes the peasant's dependence on the landlord-oppressor. This can be seen, for example, by looking at the right-hand context of the regular expressions "serfs*" and "peasants*":

…the peasants at that time were a vast majority of the working people, fed everyone, clothed everyone;

the serf worked the allotment and fed himself with his own labor; it was to the serf's advantage, otherwise he would have had to give food to his free laborer;

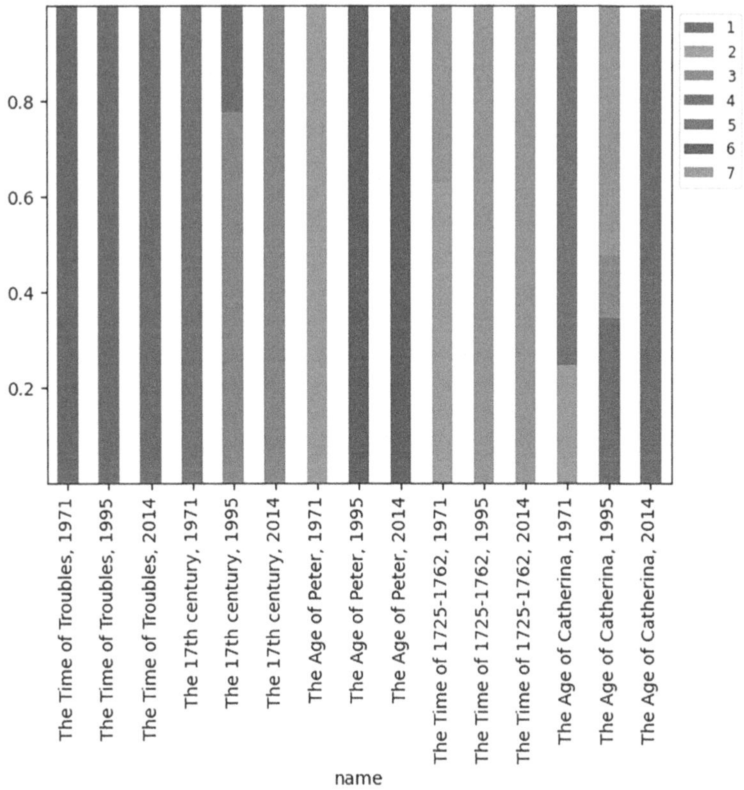

Fig. 2 Distribution of topics across the texts of three school books on the history of Russia (5 historical topics are taken from each book: The Time of Troubles (Smuta), The seventeenth century (17 vek), The Age of Peter (Jepoha Petra), The Time of 1725–1762 (1725–1762 gody), The Age of Catherina (Jepoha Ekateriny)

The serf was forced to work for the landlord free of charge;

The serf did not willingly serve the servitude and pay the tribute: the landlord had the right to force him to do so;

The serf worked under duress. The landlord punished him with rods and sticks, and dispensed with him as he wished [I].

The predominance in the Soviet textbook of topics which are not common to the other two texts is also evident in the chapter covering the events of the seventeenth century.

Thus, the results of Topic Modeling show that in the textbook of 1971 the main topic is topic 5, which tells about the fate of the Ukrainian and Belarusian lands. In contrast, in the rest of the textbooks in this chapter topic 3 ("Legislative and church reforms") clearly dominates—99.97% in the textbook by Danilov (2014) and 77.63% in the book by Yurganov and Katsva (1995). The cosine distance between 1995, 2014 textbook chapters is 0.96. When comparing the vector of the chapter from Nechkina and Leibengrub's textbook of 1971 with the chapters in Danilov and Yurganov and Katsva's textbooks, the cosine distance is 0.0034 and 0.000004, respectively.

The study of the textbook texts about the seventeenth-century events reveals that the topic of church schism is really not the key one in the textbook of 1971: only a small paragraph is devoted to Nikon's church reform, where the institution of the church has exclusively negative connotations as a means of influencing the masses. The textbook interprets the church reform itself solely as "a means of strengthening the feudal order".

Otherwise, the protection of the Ukrainian and Belarusian people from the Polish invaders is one of the topical centers of the chapter in 1971, which is reflected by the results of Topic Modeling (Fig. 2). Thus, much is said about the suffering of the Ukrainian and Belarusian people under the oppression of the Polish nobles (*…the Polish law allowed him (the landowner) to cut off the ears and nose of the peasant as a punishment, to brand his face*; *The national oppression of the Polish landowners was also heavy. They mocked at the language, at the customs of the Ukrainian and Belarusian population* [I]). The Russian people are interpreted as the defender of the oppressed peoples, and the fact that Ukraine became a part of Russian territory is seen as an event of exceptional importance for both peoples, as evidenced by the context of the use of the lemma *people*.

The Russian people sympathized with the struggle of the Ukrainians and Belarusians Against Poland;

Great was the historical significance of the unification of the Russian and Ukrainian peoples in a single Russian state;

The Ukrainian people were delivered from the national and religious oppression of Poland [I].

If we turn to the third historical subject, namely the era of Peter, the graph with the results of Topic Modeling shows (Fig. 2) that in 1971 the textbook is dominated by topic 2 ("Industrialization and Conquests"). In post-Soviet textbooks, however, topic 6 ("The Beginning of Peter's Reign, Reforms and Conquests") occupies the largest share. This topic's weight is 99.89% in the 1995 textbook and 99.88%—in the 2014 textbook.

In contrast to the 1971 textbook, these two later textbooks focus more on Sophia's regency, Peter's conflict with the Streltsy, and the development of the Tsar's personality, such as his friendship with Lefort, in whose house Peter began his acquaintance with European values and *modus vivendi*.

The next chapter deals with the period of 1725–1762. In the fourth section, touching upon the period of the palace coups, there are far fewer differences between the Soviet textbook and the other two. But the word clouds analysis, for example, shows that for the textbook by Nechkin and Leibengrub the name of *Elizabeth* is missing among the names important for the era. Its relative frequency in the 1971 text is 0.0015, while in the 1995 and 2014 textbooks it is 0.006 and 0.005, respectively. The point is that the Soviet textbook gives important, but not significant, attention to the events that took place during the struggle for the throne, since the textbook authors are of the opinion that coups were meaningless because they did not change the social order (*Palace coups were so simple and easy to carry out back then. And that is understandable: after all, they did not and could not change the class essence of the noble state*). At the same time, the motif of the class struggle and the need for radical change is vividly expressed in the Soviet textbook: topic 2 (Industrialization and Conquests) occupies 62.83% of this chapter.

Finally, considering the epoch of Catherine II, we reveal that in all three books much is said about peasants: topic 1 (Peasant War) takes 34.73% in Yurganov and Katsva's textbook and 99.19% in Danilov's textbook. In the 1971 textbook, the main motif is the oppression of the peasantry by the "dictatorship of the nobility". The chapter denounces the serf system (*It was not without reason that the nobility called the reign of Catherina II (1762–1796) their'golden age'. For them it was indeed a golden age, when the privileges of the landlords and serf oppression reached their greatest development*), and emphasizes the inevitable changes that later destroyed the noble system (*But this power and prosperity of noble Russia was undermined from within. Serfdom hindered the development of industry and agriculture* [I]). The importance of the theme of change for this chapter is evidenced by the results of Topic Modeling: topic 2 ("Industrialization and Conquests") occupies 24.42% of it. In addition, topic 5 ("The Ukrainian Question") is highly significant in the Soviet textbook. Although this event is mentioned in all three textbooks, it is in the textbook by Nechkina and Leibengrub that it is evaluated as an event of exceptional importance for the country and its future (*The working masses of Ukraine, Belarus, Lithuania and Latvia began to fight together with the Russian people against their common oppressors-the landlords and, later, the capitalists* [I]).

It should be noted that the chapter says practically nothing about Catherina II herself. Whereas the other two textbooks talk extensively, though not unequivocally positively, about her reforms, and Catherina herself is called a representative of enlightened monarchy, the Soviet textbook says nothing about the reform activities of the empress. On the contrary, the context in which her name is used shows that in the Soviet textbook she is presented exclusively as a champion of the nobility and serf system (for example, in the book she is called "*oppressor of the peasants*" [Ibid.]) as well as an opponent of any changes. A completely opposite image is drawn by the

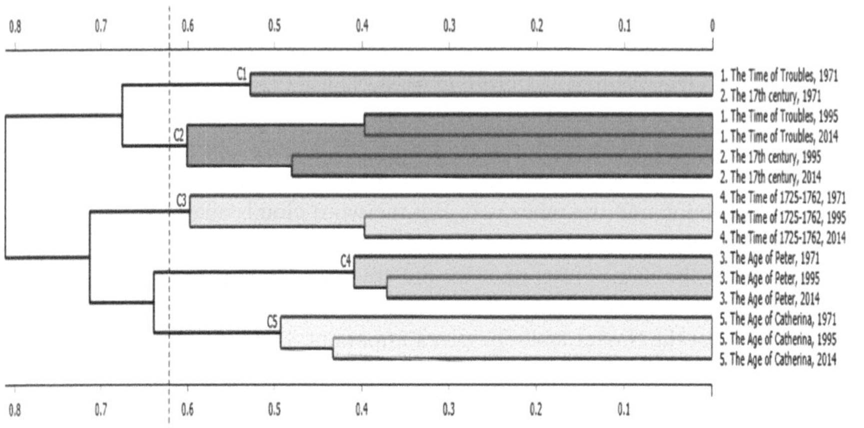

Fig. 3 Hierarchical clusterization of historical texts from 3 textbooks

authors of the 1995 textbook, which presents Catherina as a reformer and enlightened ruler.

Catherina really dreamed of a state capable of ensuring the welfare of her subjects;

Catherina saw in serfdom'an obnoxious and cruel yoke', an'intolerable situation for the human race', fraught with serious upheavals for the state [II].

Topic Modeling also shows that in 1995 the era of Catherina's reign is reflected more broadly: there is clearly more about Catherina's reforms (topic 3) and palace intrigues (topic 7). The most recent of the textbooks analyzed, however, presents an image that incorporates features of the descriptions from the other two textbooks: like in the Soviet textbook, it notes Catherina's reliance on the court.

The cluster analysis shows (Fig. 3) that most of the chapters are quite clearly divided into appropriate clusters.

For example, we can distinguish the eras of Catherina and Peter and the period of the palace coups. The exception is the topics relating to the events of the seventeenth century. They are distributed not so much by the events touched upon in them, as by the textbooks themselves. Thus, the diagram (Fig. 3) shows that the topics from the textbooks of 1995 and 2014 belong to the same group, while the 1971 textbook is separated into its own cluster.

4.2 *Sentiment Analysis of Textual Fragments from Schoolbooks on the History of Russia*

At the next step we performed Sentiment Analysis using the new Russian sentiment lexicon—RuSentiLex. The lexicon entries are classified according to four sentiment categories (positive, negative, neutral, and positive/negative) and three sources of sentiment (opinion, emotion, or fact). Hence, the lexicon consists of emotional words that convey negative/positive opinion (excellent) or negative/positive emotion (sadness) and factual words with negative or positive connotations such as cancer, unemployment, etc. [13].

To avoid noisy data, for homonyms, we manually selected meanings that are more specific for the corpus of history textbooks. For example, among the meanings of the word "revolution" ("революция"), we chose the one denoting a coup d'état.

For the analysis, we did two kinds of calculations. In the first case, we counted the sentiment itself. We excluded words with positive/negative sentiment from the lexicon and then encoded words that were presented both in the lexicon and our corpus depending on their sentiment with the following values: -1 (negative), 1 (positive), 0 (neutral). Then we obtained an arithmetic mean for each vector. In the second case, we tried to find out the main source of polarity. For that, we deleted all neutral words as they presented the vast majority of the words in the corpus. Then in the same way we encoded opinionated and emotional words as -1 and factual ones as 1 and calculated an arithmetic mean for each vector.

As it is shown (Fig. 4), we can see that the conclusion made by [13] that the history textbooks are characterized by rather negative tonality is confirmed by our research: from the entire analyzed corpus only one chapter has a positive sentiment ("The Age of Peter", 2014). It is also noticeable that the 1995 textbook does not achieve as low a sentiment in any of its chapters as the 1971 and 2014 textbooks. At the same time, the chapters of the Soviet textbook ("The Age of Catherina", "The 17th Century", and "The Time of Troubles") have the lowest sentiment in comparison with the other texts.

Also, according to the graph (Fig. 4), the chapters on the epoch of Peter the Great have a more positive sentiment relative to the rest of the texts in the corpus. At the

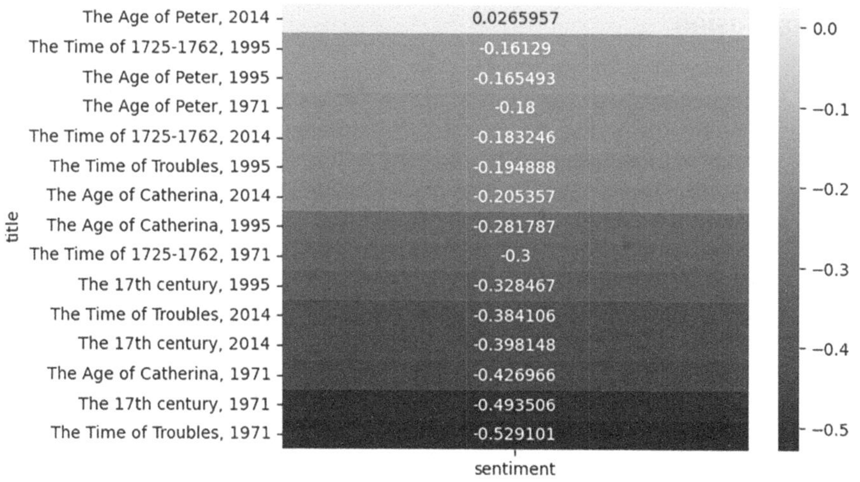

Fig. 4 Sentiment of texts in three textbooks

same time, the chapters on the Time of Troubles and the seventeenth century as a whole are more likely to have a negative tone. For example, in Danilov's textbook, the chapters describing the events of the seventeenth century have a more negative sentiment than those devoted to the eighteenth century. In general, a similar situation is characteristic of the textbook by Nechkina and Leibengrub (1971). However, in the case of this textbook, the era of Catherina is marked by a lower level of sentiment than the same chapter in the other textbooks. The distribution of chapters in Yurganov and Katsva's textbook is also noteworthy: it is the only book in which the period of the Troubles has a more positive sentiment than the chapter on the Catherinian era. In addition, the Time of Troubles in this textbook has a more positive tone than in the textbooks of other periods.

When comparing the values in Table 2, it is clearly visible that of the three textbooks, the 1971 Soviet textbook is the only one where factual vocabulary predominates in certain chapters: "The Time of Troubles" (51.91%), "The Time of 1725–1762" (52.17%), "The Age of Catherina" (54.92%). The largest percentage of evaluative vocabulary is in chapters "The seventeenth century" (67.08%) and "The Time of 1725–1762" (65.71%) from the textbook of 1995 by Yurganov and Katsva. The chapters in the newest Russian textbook 2014, however, have average scores relative to the other chapters analyzed. The most likely reason for this distribution is that the 1971 textbook focuses on personalities less than the other textbooks. The later textbooks, especially dated 1995 [II], give more details, that are frequently represented by emotive verbal means: *The young tsar, pious to a fanaticism, submitted in everything to his mother's will*; *Under Anna Ioannovna Biron was a handsome young man, physically very strong; However, Elizabeth did not allow the ladies of high society to compete with her in the splendor of their toilets.*

5 Conclusion

Based on the analysis, we can draw some conclusions about the peculiarities of historical pictures of the world transmitted by different textbooks. Thus, each of them represents patriotic values in its own way.

Obviously, the discourse of the Soviet textbook was strongly influenced by communist ideology, and the narrative itself was used primarily as an instrument of political legitimization. Elements such as emphasizing the horrors of feudal oppression, explicit condemnation of class inequality, and support for popular uprisings, as well as the textbook's characteristic motif of the need for change, are aimed at constructing a negative image of the past to justify the social and political changes that occurred in the state. The textbook offers an unambiguous interpretation of the events, emphasized by the predominance of factual vocabulary in most chapters.

The collapse of communist ideology leads to the fact that in later textbooks (1995, 2014) the focus of the narrative is rather shifted to the rulers. The authors of these

Table 2 Distribution of sources for sentiment in texts

Text title	Fact	Opinion
The Time of Troubles_1971	**51.91**	48.09
The 17th century_1971	42.13	57.87
The Age of Peter _1971	37.27	**62.73**
The Time of 1725–1762_1971	**52.17**	47.83
The Age of Catherina_1971	**54.92**	45.08
The Time of Troubles _1995	42.01	57.99
The 17th century_1995	32.92	**67.08**
The Age of Peter_1995	48.73	51.27
The Time of 1725–1762_1995	34.29	**65.71**
The Age of Catherina_1995	38.34	**61.66**
The Time of Troubles _2014	39.10	**60.90**
The 17th century_2014	39.31	**60.69**
The Age of Peter_2014	41.84	58.16
The Time of 1725–1762_2014	41.86	58.14
The Age of Catherina_2014	49.39	50.61

textbooks do not tend to discredit the rulers by creating their unambiguously negative images. On the contrary, they try to tell us about their failures as well as their achievements, which is more in line with a plurality of opinions.

Despite some similarities, there are also differences between Russian textbooks. For example, the authors of the 1995 textbook attempt to depict the tsars and emperors from a more "human" perspective, painting their psychologically detailed portraits. This approach affects the factuality of the narrative, as this edition has the lowest level of factuality compared to the other books analyzed. Nevertheless, this attribute points to the freedom of narration and expression inherent to the period in which the textbook was published (the 1990s): laws restricting the narrative in historical textbooks in a certain way had not been introduced yet. The picture of the world fostered by such a textbook is not as concrete and unambiguous as in the Soviet textbook, but it rather contributes to the development of the child's own opinion on the historical situation, since the textbook talks about both positive and negative aspects of the historical periods in question. In the 2014 textbook, on the other hand, the narrative is more concrete and factual. The picture of the world created by this textbook is somewhat more unambiguous than in the case of the 1995 textbook, but it is not as rigidly ideological as the Soviet textbook. The identified specifics of academic texts require a separate interpretation both from the perspective of the political processes taking place in the country during the time periods when the textbooks were published, and from the perspective of internal trends in Soviet/post-Soviet historical scholarship. However, it is necessary to say that the use of computer methods of textual data processing becomes an effective source of hypothesis formulation and a guiding vector of information systematization in the discourse analysis of academic texts.

Acknowledgements This article is an output of the research project "Text as Big Data: modeling of convergent processes in language and speech by digital methods" implemented as part of the Basic Research Program at the National Research University Higher School of Economics (HSE University) in 2025.

References

1. Dijk, T.A.: Ideology: a multidisciplinary approach. Sage, London (1998)
2. Citron, S. : Le mythe national: L'histoire de France en question. Ed. ouvrières: Etudes et doc. intern, Paris (1987)
3. Elbih, R.: You are what you read: textbooks and the lopsided dialectic. Counterpoints, 89–123 (2018)
4. Apple, M.W.: The politics of official knowledge: does a national curriculum make sense? Discourse: Stud. Cult. Polit.Educ. **1**(14), 1–16 (1993)
5. Shmeleva, T.V.: Klyuchevye slova tekushchego momenta [Keywords of the moment]. Collegium, **1**, 33–41 (1993) (in Russian)
6. Kluchevsky, V.O.: The course of the history of Russia (1998)
7. Pavlick, J.: Reproducing patriotism: an exploration of 'freedom' in US history textbooks. Discourse Soc. **5**(30), 482–502 (2019)
8. Dubois, J., Legris, P. (dir.): Disciplines scolaires et cultures politiques. Des modèles nationaux en mutation depuis 1945. Rennes, Presses universitaires de Rennes (2018)
9. Dubois, J.: Garibaldi dans les manuels scolaires d'histoire en Italie: les usages pédagogiques et politiques. In: Dubois, J., Legris, P. (dir.) Disciplines scolaires et cultures politiques. Des modèles nationaux en mutation depuis 1945, Rennes, Presses universitaires de Rennes, pp. 81–91 (2018)
10. Konkka, O.: Le dictateur ou le chef de la nation victorieuse ? L'évolution de la présantation de Joseph Staline dans les manuels scolaires d'histoire de la Russie postsoviétique In: Dubois, J., Legris, P. (dir.) Disciplines scolaires et cultures politiques. Des modèles nationaux en mutation depuis 1945, Rennes, Presses universitaires de Rennes, pp. 105–120 (2018)
11. Marino, M.P.: High school world history textbooks: an analysis of content focus and chronological approaches. Hist. Teach. **3**(44), 421–446 (2011)
12. Iliev, R., Hoover, J., Dehghani, M., Axelrod, R.: Linguistic positivity in historical texts reflects dynamic environmental and psychological factors. Proc. Natl. Acad. Sci. USA **113**(49), E7871–E7879 (2016)
13. Loukachevitch, N., Levchik, A.: Creating a general Russian Sentiment Lexicon. Eur. Lang. Resour. Assoc. 1171–1176 (2016)
14. Solovyev, V., Solnyshkina, M., Gafiyatova E., McNamara, D., Ivanov, V.: Sentiment in academic texts. In: 2019 24th Conference of Open Innovations Association (FRUCT), Moscow, Russia, pp. 408–414 (2019). https://doi.org/10.23919/FRUCT.2019.8711900
15. Osmanoglu, U.O., Atak, K., Caglar, H., Kayhan, T.C.: Can, sentiment analysis for distance education course materials: a machine learning approach. J. Educ. Technol. Online Learn. **3**(1), 31–48 (2020)
16. Törnberg, A., Törnberg, P.: Combining CDA and topic modeling. Discourse Soc. **4**(27), 401–422 (2016)
17. Blei, D.M.: Probabilistic topic models. Commun. ACM **4**(55), 77–84 (2012)
18. Elgesem, D., Steskal, L., Diakopoulos, N.: Structure and content of the discourse on climate change in the blogosphere: the big picture. Environ. Commun. **9**, 169–188 (2015)

19. Obadimu, A., Khaund, T., Mead, E., Marcoux, T., Agarwal, N.: Developing a socio-computational approach to examine toxicity propagation and regulation in COVID-19 discourse on YouTube. Inform. Process. Manag. **58**, 102660 (2021). https://doi.org/10.1016/j.ipm.2021.102660
20. Jo, W.: Possibility of discourse analysis using topic modeling. J. Asian Sociol. **3**(48), 321–342 (2019)

Disambiguation of Russian Homographs with Transformers

Ivan Stoliarov and Olga Mitrofanova

Abstract The purpose of this work was to test BERT transformer-based models for homograph disambiguation in Russian—a long-standing issue in Text-To-Speech systems. The paper presents different types of Russian homographs and offers an in-depth analysis of existing methods for their disambiguation. A dataset of contexts from the Russian National Corpus for 28 homograph pairs was created and manually annotated. Three BERT models for the Russian language were selected and tested in two experiments. The results have shown that these models could achieve and outperform SOTA results in disambiguating homographs of all types on a relatively small training dataset. The pretrained models could also be used to disambiguate new pairs of intraparadigmatic homographs absent from the original dataset.

Keywords Russian homographs · Homograph disambiguation · Text-to-Speech · BERT

1 Introduction

Speech synthesis is among the most rapidly developing areas of speech technologies and natural language processing (NLP). The expansion of NLP technologies in conversational artificial intelligence increases the importance of text-to-speech (TTS) models and algorithms. TTS refers to conversion of orthographic text into audible speech. It is a multi-stage process which includes linguistic processing and transcription of the incoming text required for further speech generation. The tasks of this stage include segmenting sentences, deciphering special symbols (№, %) and contractions (*i t.d.* 'etc.', *km/ch* 'km/h'), homograph detection and disambiguation.

I. Stoliarov (✉) · O. Mitrofanova
St. Petersburg State University, Saint-Petersburg, Russia
e-mail: stoliarov.iv@gmail.com

O. Mitrofanova
e-mail: o.mitrofanova@spbu.ru

P. Eismont et al. (eds.), *Literature, Language and Computing*,
https://doi.org/10.1007/978-981-96-0990-1_7

Homographs are properly defined as words of the same or different parts of speech, which have identical spelling, but differ in pronunciation and meaning, for example, *zámok* 'castle' – *zamók* 'lock', *múka* 'pain' – *muká* 'flour', etc. [1]. We consider homography as one of the manifestations of ambiguity, which forms an immanent property of natural language. In search of a reliable solution for the problem of homograph disambiguation in Russian we should take into account lexical-semantic ambiguity resolution, morphological and syntactic disambiguation, cf. [2–7].

Homograph disambiguation in synthesis systems involves selecting one of the possible options for the homograph and generating an appropriate transcription. Obviously, misreading the homograph (e.g., *zámok* 'castle' instead of *zamók* 'lock' in the sentence *Zamok otnesli v masterskuyu* 'The lock was taken to the workshop') makes it difficult to perceive the synthesized speech and thus impairs the quality of synthesis.

Our study is aimed at improving homograph disambiguation quality in Russian. To achieve the goal, we propose an experimental dataset including contexts for Russian homographs, provide a detailed description of major classes of homographs and introduce a novel approach for homograph disambiguation based on contextualized BERT embeddings.

2 Homographs in Russian

In Russian, homography is associated with different stress in words that are spelled the same way, e.g. *átlas* 'atlas' – *atlás* 'satin', *rúki* 'hands' (pl, nom/acc) – *rukí* 'hand' (sg, gen), as well as with the practice of writing the letter '*e*' in place of the letter '*yo*', e.g. *vse* 'everybody' – *vsyo* 'all', *mel* 'chalk' – *myol* 'swept' (past, sg, masc). In some cases, both of these factors are involved: *béreg* '(river)bank' – *beryóg* 'protected' (past, sg, masc), *zhený* 'wife' (sg, gen) – *zhyóny* 'wives' (pl, nom).

Based on the lexical and grammatical correlations in homograph pairs, the following types of homographs can be distinguished [7–9]:

- **Lexical (morphosyntactically congruent) homographs**—pairs of words that belong to separate lexemes and whose morphosyntactic values are identical, e.g. *zámok* 'castle' – *zamók* 'lock', *bronírovat'* 'to reserve' – *bronirovát'* 'to armour'.
- **Intraparadigmatic** homographs – homographic wordforms belonging to the same lexeme, e.g. *zhený* 'wife' *(sg, gen)* – *zhyóny* 'wives' (pl, nom), *várite* '(you) cook' (ind, pres, 2 pers, pl) – *varíte* 'cook!' (imper, pl).
- **Mixed (morphosyntactically incongruent) homographs**—homographs that belong to separate lexemes and whose morphosyntactic values are different. Homographs of this type can be divided into two categories. The first category includes pairs of words belonging to the same part of speech and differing in grammatical categories, e.g. *úha* 'ear' (masc, sg, gen) – *uhá* 'fish soup' (fem, sg, nom). The homographs in the second category belong to different parts of speech

Table 1 Types of homographs and their features

Type of homographs	Different lexical meaning	Different morpho-syntactic values
Lexical	+	–
Intraparadigmatic	–	+
Mixed	+	+

(e.g. a verb and a noun), which automatically results in a difference in grammatical meaning: *pótom* 'sweat' (noun, sg, instr) – *potóm* 'then' (adv), *béreg* '(river) bank' (noun, sg, nom/acc) – *beryóg* 'protected' (verb, past, sg, masc).

Features representing different types of homographs are summarized in Table 1.

3 Methods for Homograph Disambiguation

Various methods for homograph disambiguation have been proposed in theoretical research focusing on homographs and in actual speech synthesis systems. All approaches agree that correct interpretation of the context surrounding a homograph is crucial, but there are different ways of treating this issue. For example, rule-based methods involve manually compiling a set of rules that allow one to choose the correct way of reading a homograph depending on context neighbors. This approach was used, in particular, by B. Lobanov and colleagues in the Multifon system [10]. There are methods which are based on contextual analysis performed on syntactic and semantic levels, or complex analysis of the nearest environment of a homograph or of the whole sentence. Thus, the research carried out by O. Khomitsevich and colleagues describes a similar mechanism of homograph disambiguation in the VitalVoice synthesis system developed by the Speech Technology Centre [11]. Finally, machine learning techniques can also be applied to disambiguate homographs. As an example, the model proposed in the work of K. Gorman and colleagues can be referred to in this respect: for each pair of homographs, a multinomial classifier was created to which a set of features was fed (word context features, POS tags, capitalization feature) [12].

In 2021, M. Nikolis and V. Klimkov proposed to use contextual word embeddings which are produced by transformer models of BERT family (Bidirectional Encoder Representations from Transformers) [13]. Word embeddings from BERT are inherently context-sensitive: they encode information about lexical meaning and morphosyntactic values of the target word depending on its context. M. Nikolis and V. Klimkov tested two BERT models for English language and achieved state-of-the-art (SOTA) accuracy of 99.1% on the English homographs.

This paper presents the results of our attempt to adapt the experiment by M. Nikolis and V. Klimkov to disambiguate Russian homographs.

4 Dataset for Homograph Disambiguation

As far as we know, there is no specialized Russian dataset for training homograph disambiguation models, because homographs are usually considered together with homonyms in WSI/WSD tasks (cf. datasets for Dialogue Evaluation, especially RUSSE2018 [14]). In view of this, we decided to collect and manually annotate data to fill in the existing gap. We used contexts from general fiction and newspaper articles presented in the Russian National Corpus [15]. Each context is represented by one sentence containing the target word (homograph). Our dataset included the following groups of homographs:

- **Lexical homographs**—4 homograph pairs: *átlas* 'atlas' – *atlás* 'satin', *zámok* 'castle' – *zamók* 'lock', *múka* 'pain' – *muká* 'flour, *hlópok* 'cotton' – *hlopók* 'clap'. For each pair, we selected 100 contexts (50 corresponding to one homograph and 50 to the other), in which homographs are represented in different wordforms: *zámok – zamók* (sg, nom/acc), *zámka – zamká* (sg, gen), ..., *zámki – zamkí* (pl, nom/acc), ...
- **Intraparadigmatic homographs**—3 subgroups, each of which included 4 homograph pairs belonging to the same accent type (see Table 2). 30 contexts were selected for each pair, so each subgroup consisted of 120 contexts in total. This is the only case in which the labels are based on the set of grammatical categories (sg gen vs pl nom/acc) conveyed by different accents in the wordforms rather than on the pronunciation variants of a homograph (see Table 2). Different types of correlations among intraparadigmatic homographs are described, for example, by Kaliszan [16].

Table 2 Subgroups of intraparadigmatic homographs

Subgroup I (masc) sg gen versus pl nom/acc	Subgroup II (fem) sg gen versus pl nom/acc	Subgroup III (neut) sg gen versus pl nom/acc
véchera 'evening' – *vecherá* 'evenings'	*golový* 'head' – *gólovy* 'heads'	*mésta* 'place' – *mestá* 'places'
góroda 'city' – *gorodá* 'cities'	*gorý* 'mountain' – *góry* 'mountains'	*mórya* 'sea' – *moryá* 'seas'
óstrova 'island' – *ostrová* 'islands'	*rukí* 'hand' – *rúki* 'hands'	*pólya* 'field' – *polyá* 'fields'
póezda 'train' – *poezdá* 'trains'	*straný* 'country' – *strány* 'countries'	*slóva* 'word' – *slová* 'words'

Table 3 New pairs of homographs for experiment II

Subgroup of intraparadigmatic homographs	New pair of homographs
I (masc.)	*ádresa* 'address' (sg, gen) – *adresá* 'addresses' (pl, nom/acc)
II (fem.)	*igrý* 'game' (sg, gen) – ígry 'games' (pl, nom/acc)
III (neutr.)	*sérdca* 'heart' (sg, gen) – *serdcá* 'hearts' (pl, nom/acc)

- **Mixed homographs (nouns)**—4 pairs of nouns: *bélka* 'squirrel' (sg, nom) – *belká* 'protein' (sg, gen), *víski* 'whiskey' (sg, nom) – *viskí* 'temples' (pl, nom/acc), *góre* 'sorrow' (sg, nom/acc) – *goré* 'mountain' (sg, loc), *dúsha* 'shower' (sg, gen) – *dushá* 'soul' (sg, nom). For each pair, we collected 100 contexts.
- **Mixed homographs (verbs)**—4 pairs of verbs: *výkupat'* 'to bathe' – *vykupát'* 'to ransom', *výchitat'* 'find by reading' – *vychitát'* 'to substract', *razrézat'* 'to cut up' (perf) – *razrezát'* 'to cut up' (imperf), *sbégat'* 'to run for smth' – *sbegát'* 'to run away'. For each pair, we selected 100 contexts containing different conjugated forms of these verbs (*výkupayu – vykupáyu, výkupaesh' – vykupáesh', ..., výkupal – vykupál, ...*).
- **Mixed homographs (different POS)**—4 pairs of words belonging to different parts of speech: *béreg* '(river)bank' (noun, sg, nom/acc) – *beryóg* 'protected' (verb, past, sg, masc), *vésti* 'news' (noun, pl, nom/acc) – *vestí* 'to lead' (verb, inf), *znákom* 'sign' (noun, sg, instr) – *znakóm* 'familiar' (adj, sg, masc), *pótom* 'sweat' (noun, sg, instr) – *potóm* 'then' (adv). 100 contexts were selected for each pair.

In total, our dataset included 1960 contexts for 28 homograph pairs of different types.

In addition, in Experiment II we also tested 20 new contexts for each subgroup of intraparadigmatic homographs. These contexts included pairs of homographs that represented the same grammatical correlation (and the same accent type) but were not present among the data on which the model was trained (cf. Table 3).

5 Baseline Results of Homograph Disambiguation

First of all, we undertook to test existing solutions for homograph disambiguation on our dataset. The following models were selected for disambiguating different groups of homographs:

- **RuWordNet thesaurus** for lexical homographs (group 1). RuWordNet is a thesaurus of the Russian language which contains synsets (sets of synonyms) for nouns, verbs and adjectives and establishes different semantic relations between synsets of the same part of speech (hyponym – hypernym, instance – class, etc.)

[17]. Therefore, RuWordNet can be used to disambiguate lexical homonyms and homographs [18].
- **RNN Morph** for homographs from groups 2, 3, 5. RNN Morph is a morphological analyzer (POS tagger) for Russian and English languages which is based on neural networks and dictionary-lookup systems (pymorphy2, NLTK) and showed the best results on the MorphoRuEval-2017 competition [18]. We used the RNN Morph to disambiguate homographs that differ in morphosyntactic categories and are expected to be tagged differently.
- **SpaCy** for mixed verbal homographs from the group 4. SpaCy is an open-source software library for NLP. We used a Russian language model from spaCy (*ru_core_news_md*) which tagged verbs from group 4 with their aspect (perfective/imperfective) as it is a grammatical category that makes a difference between them [20].

The results of these models on different homograph groups from our dataset are shown in Table 4. As can be seen from the table, baseline models fail to achieve acceptable results and, from our observations, often give preference simply to the most frequent option, e.g. *átlas* 'atlas' instead of *atlás* 'satin' (in case of RuWordNet); or the tag 'verb' instead of 'noun' for *vésti* 'news'– *vestí* 'to lead' (in case of RNN Morph), etc.

Table 4 Baseline accuracies

Group of homographs	RuWordNet	RNN Morph	SpaCy
1. Lexical	62%	–	–
2. Intraparadigmatic	–	78%	–
3. Mixed (nouns)	–	78%	–
4. Mixed (verbs)	–	–	49%
5. Mixed (different POS)	–	81%	–

Table 5 Results of experiment I

Type of homographs	RuBert-base-cased (%)	RuBert-base (Sber) (%)	RuBert-base large (%)
1. Lexical	98	**99**	**99**
2. Intraparadigmatic	96	**99**	96
3. Mixed (nouns)	98	**100**	99
4. Mixed (verbs)	85	88	**95**
5. Mixed (different POS)	98	98	**99**
Average	95.0	96.8	**97.6**

6 Model Description

In our experiments, we used contextualized embeddings produced by the following pre-trained BERT models for Russian:

- **RuBert-base** (12-layer, 768-hidden, 12-heads, 180 M parameters) from the library DeepPavlov represents the target word as a vector of 768 dimensions [21]. The model was trained on Russian Wikipedia and news data.
- **RuBert-base finetune** (12-layer, 768-hidden, 12-heads, 180 M parameters) also produces word embeddings of 768 dimensions [22]. This model was trained by SberDevices team.
- **RuBert-large finetune** (24-layer, 1024-hidden, 16-heads, 430 M parameters) generates vectors of greater dimensions (1024) [23]. This model was also trained by SberDevices team.

The experimental scheme was identical for all the three models. After the dataset was loaded, each sentence with a homograph was tokenized and special tokens were added to it: [CLS] at the beginning and [SEP] at the end. After the tokenized sentence was processed by a BERT model, an embedding corresponding to the token homograph was extracted from the last (12th or 24th) layer. It was the way we formed a new dataset: the objects (X) were vectors of 768 dimensions (768 features) and the target variables (Y) were pronunciation variants (as mentioned above, in the case of intraparadigmatic homographs we used a set of grammatical categories as target variables). The resulting dataset was split into training and test data with the ratio of 4:1. We used logistic regression with L2 regularization for embedding classification task. We evaluated the model by calculating accuracy (percentage of correctly classified examples). Accuracy is calculated by the formula:

$$Accuracy = \frac{TP + TN}{TP + FP + FN + TN} * 100\%,$$

where *TP* is the number of true positives, i.e. correct predictions for class I; *TN* stands for the number of true negatives, i.e. correct predictions for class II; *FP* and *FN*, respectively, for the number of false positives and false negatives (wrong predictions).

Table 6 Results of experiment II

Subgroup of intraparadigmatic homographs	Accuracy on the test data (%)	Accuracy on the new data (%)
I (masc.)	94.0	**92.5**
II (fem.)	95.0	**100.0**
III (neutr.)	100.0	**97.5**

7 Experiments and Results

7.1 Experiment I. Disambiguating Homographs of Different Types

The experiments have shown that BERT models could achieve at least 95% accuracy in disambiguating different groups of homographs. The best average result (97.6%) was obtained by the model RuBert-large finetune, but it could be seen that some groups of homographs (1–3) were better handled by the model RuBert-base finetune. It may also be noted that verbal homographs from group 4 constituted the greatest difficulty for all the three models (85%, 88%, and 95%, respectively) (Table 5).

7.2 Experiment II. Disambiguation of Intraparadigmatic Homographs Absent in the Original Dataset

Each model trained on a subgroup of intraparadigmatic homographs was fed with new contexts including a pair of homographs representing the same grammatical correlation (and the same accent type) but absent from the original dataset. The results we obtained (cf. Table 6) indicate that the trained model is capable of predicting grammatical categories (in our case *sg, gen* vs. *pl, nom/acc*) for new homographs and, consequently, their accent type which makes it possible to disambiguate them.

8 Discussion

The experiments show that the proposed approach could achieve and outperform SOTA results for homograph disambiguation. It was also demonstrated that a relatively small dataset (100 sentences) was sufficient to train a classifier for this task, provided both pronunciation variants of a homograph are equally represented. Another advantage of our model is its universality: we used the same algorithm to disambiguate all types of homographs regardless of their distinctive features (lexical and/or morphosyntactic), without any supplementary resources being necessary.

Finally, we showed in Experiment II that the trained model could also disambiguate new pairs of intraparadigmatic homographs which were absent from training data.

However, the proposed approach has some limitations. Since BERT encodes all kinds of contextual information (lexical, grammatical, etc.) in one embedding for the token of interest (homograph), we could not easily figure out from the results which contextual features played a crucial role in disambiguation or, on the contrary, which ones proved to be insignificant.

One may also notice that verbal homographs (group 4) still pose a challenge for a disambiguation system. This seems to be due to the specificity of the verb aspect and the necessity to analyze distant syntactic relations. For example, in the sentence *Ona* ***razrezala*** *ego nozhikom na sloistye kuski, dostavala vilki, hleb* 'She cut it [some cabbage] into flaky pieces with a knife, pulled out forks and bread', the homograph *razrezala* is an imperfective verb; therefore the stress has fall on the third syllable (*razrezála*). The information about the verb aspect of *razrezala* could be extracted from the word *dostavala*, also an imperfective verb, which shows that one puts the emphasis on the process of both actions rather than on their results (normally expressed by perfective aspect). However, our model does not seem to take into account the word dostavala because of the great distance between two verbs.

As described in Sect. 4, the context of each homograph was limited to one sentence, though one may fairly assume that this breadth of context is not sufficient in some cases. Indeed, we encountered a few sentences which did not contain enough lexical and/or grammatical features for homograph disambiguation. Let us examine the sentence *Proletariat* ***zamkov*** *ne priznaet* 'Proletarians do not accept any castles/ locks'. It seems to us that both meanings ('castles' and 'locks') could be appropriate in this sentence. It is the broader context that makes it possible to figure out that 'locks' (*zamkóv*) is correct: *Zahodi! Otkryto vsegda! Proletariat* ***zamkov*** *ne priznaet. Dver' zaskripela, i na poroge malen'koj komnaty...* 'Come in! It's always open! Proletarians do not accept any locks. The door creaked open and on the threshold of the small room...'. This issue is also one of the sources of difficulty in disambiguating verbal homographs. One example is the homograph pair *razrézat'* – *razrezát'* that has been mentioned above: *Ded Isaak ochen' mnogo el. Batony* ***razrezal*** *ne poperek, a vdol'. V gostyah babka Raya postoyanno za nego krasnela* 'Grandpa Isaac ate a lot. He cut the loaves lengthwise instead of crosswise. Grandma Raya always blushed for him when they were on a visit'. The sentence with the target homograph (*Batony* ***razrezal*** *ne poperek, a vdol'*) might be interpreted in two ways: it could refer to the result of Isaac's action (perfective verb) or to Isaac's habit (imperfective verb). We could resolve the ambiguity by taking into account the neighboring sentences: the imperfective verbs *el* and *krasnela* explicitly confirm the second interpretation; therefore, the option *razrezála* has to be chosen. These examples demonstrate that limiting the context to one sentence is not always the appropriate solution.

9 Conclusion and Future Work

In this study we used contextualized word embeddings produced by BERT models in the disambiguation of Russian homographs. We showed that the proposed approach reaches the level of SOTA models (up to 97.6% accuracy) and has a wide range of advantages. Yet the approach also has a number of limitations. It is anticipated that the developed approach could improve the quality of speech synthesis.

The study puts forth the following avenues for future research:

- developing disambiguation approaches for other groups and subgroups of Russian homographs;
- improving the obtained results by a more careful selection of contexts and/or increasing the dataset;
- analyzing challenging cases of disambiguation;
- analyzing how the phrase boundaries and context window size affect disambiguation results;
- implementation of the developed algorithm in a speech synthesis system.

Acknowledgements The study was made possible owing to the support of SPbSU Scientific Project № 75254082 'Modeling the communicative behavior of residents of a Russian metropolis in the social, speech and pragmatic aspects with the use of artificial intelligence methods'.

References

1. Kozhina, M.N.: Stylistic Encyclopedic Dictionary of the Russian Language. Moscow (2003)
2. Lyashevskaya, O., Afanasev, I., Rebrikov, S., Shishkina, Y., Suleimanova, E., Trofimov, I., Vlasova, N.: Disambiguation in context in the Russian National Corpus: 20 years later. In: Computational Linguistics and Intellectual Technologies. Proceedings of the International Conference «Dialogue 2023». RSUH, Moscow, pp. 307–318 (2023)
3. Alexeyevsky, D., Temchenko, A.V.: WSD in monolingual dictionaries for Russian Word Net. In: Proceedings of the Eighth Global Word Net Conference. Bucharest, Romania, pp. 9–14 (2016)
4. Bolshina, A., Loukachevitch, N.: All-words word sense disambiguation for Russian using automatically generated text collection. Cybern. Inf. Technol. **20**(4), 90–107 (2020)
5. Lopukhin, K.A., Lopukhina, A.A.: Word sense disambiguation for Russian verbs using semantic vectors and dictionary entries. In: Computational Linguistics and Intellectual Technologies. Proceedings of the International Conference «Dialogue 2016». RSUH, Moscow, pp. 393–404 (2016)
6. Panicheva, P.V., Protopopova, E.V., Mirzagitova, A.R., Mitrofanova, O.A.: Development of an NLP toolkit for morphological analysis of Russian text corpora based on PyMorphy and NLTK. In: Proceedings of the International Conference «Corpus Linguistics – 2015». Saint-Petersburg, pp. 361–373 (2015)
7. Inshakova, Ye.S., Iomdin, L.L., Mityushin, L.G., Sizov, V.G., Frolova, T.I., Tsinman, L.L.: The syntagrus today. In: Proceedings of Vinogradov Russian Language Institute of the Russian Academy of Sciences, vol. 21, pp. 14–40 (2019)

8. Kolesnikov, N.P.: The system of word homonyms in Russian. In: 12th Session of the Faculty of Philology. Work plan and abstracts. Tbilisi University Press, Tbilisi, pp. 27–29 (1968)
9. Melnikova, A.I.: On the subject of Russian homographs. In: Russian Language at School, vol. 4, pp. 80–84 (1974)
10. Tsirulnik, L.I., Barbuk, S.G., Lobanov, B.M.: Statistical analysis and contextual rules of disambiguation of graphic homonymy in TTS. In: Computational Linguistics and Intellectual Technologies: Paper from the Annual International Conference «Dialogue 2009». RSUH, Moscow, pp. 530–536 (2009)
11. Khomitsevich, O.G., Rybin, S.V., Anichkin, I.M.: Using linguistic analysis to normalize text and disambiguate homonyms in the Russian speech synthesis system. In: Proceedings of Higher Education Institutions. Instrumentation Engineering, vol. LVI. Issue 2, pp. 42–46 (2013)
12. Gorman, K., Mazovetskiy, G., Nikolaev, V.: Improving homograph disambiguation with supervised machine learning. In: Proceedings of the 11th International Conference on Language Resources and Evaluation (LREC 2018). Miyazaki, Japan. European Language Resources Association (ELRA), pp. 1349–1352 (2018)
13. Nicolis, M., Klimkov, V.: Homograph disambiguation with contextual word embeddings for TTS systems. In: Proceedings of the 11th ISCA Speech Synthesis Workshop (SSW 11), pp. 222–226 (2021)
14. https://www.dialog-21.ru/evaluation/2018/disambiguation/
15. https://ruscorpora.ru/
16. Kaliszan, J.: Grammatical substantive homography in Russian. In: Studia Rossica Posnaniensia, vol. 38, pp. 119–123 (2013)
17. https://ruwordnet.ru/en
18. https://github.com/avidale/python-ruwordnet
19. https://github.com/IlyaGusev/rnnmorph
20. https://spacy.io/models/ru
21. https://huggingface.co/DeepPavlov/rubert-base-cased
22. https://huggingface.co/ai-forever/ruBert-base
23. https://huggingface.co/ai-forever/ruBert-large

Idioms Database: Evidence from Nineteenth-Century Russian Texts

A. N. Baranov, D. O. Dobrovol'skij, K. L. Kiseleva, A. D. Kozerenko, E. V. Sharapova, and M. M. Voznesenskaja

Abstract The article presents the main areas of research within the framework of the project for the study of Russian idioms of the nineteenth century and their development trend. We discuss the lexicographic sources relevant for the project: both general explanatory dictionaries of the eighteenth-nineteenth centuries and special ones focusing on the various aspects of phraseology. We briefly describe and characterize the specific features of representing information about idioms in every dictionary under discussion. The source of corpus data for the project is the Russian National Corpus (RNC). Special attention is paid to difficulties that accompany the study of Russian idioms of the nineteenth century. These difficulties are associated, firstly, with the limitations of corpus data. The RNC-data mostly consist of written texts. As for the nineteenth century, the oral data do not exist in principle. Secondly, the linguistic intuition of modern Russian speakers differs from the speech practices of the nineteenth century. The study aims at determining various changes in the inventory of Russian idioms from the nineteenth to the twenty-first century, their dynamics in form and meaning. In this paper, we also analyze several idioms that demonstrate the development of the Russian phraseology system.

Keywords Russian language · Phraseology · Idioms · Diachronic dynamics

1 Target Setting

The Russian language of the nineteenth century is not sufficiently studied in modern Russian linguistics, both in terms of syntax and lexical units—even at the level of lexicographic description. The St. Petersburg project aimed at compiling a dictionary of the Russian language of the nineteenth century is in the preparation stage judging by the available publications [1]. Similar is the case with the study of the nineteenth-century phraseology. Existing precedents pertain to the works of individual writers

A. N. Baranov · D. O. Dobrovol'skij (✉) · K. L. Kiseleva · A. D. Kozerenko · E. V. Sharapova · M. M. Voznesenskaja
Vinogradov Russian Language Institute of the Russian Academy of Sciences, Moscow, Russia
e-mail: dm-dbrv@yandex.ru

P. Eismont et al. (eds.), *Literature, Language and Computing*,
https://doi.org/10.1007/978-981-96-0990-1_8

and poets. The phraseological component is present in author dictionaries: e. g., in "Pushkin's Language Dictionary" [2], in "Dostoevsky's Language Dictionary" [3, 4], as well as in "Griboedov's Language Dictionary" [5]. There are also phraseological dictionaries of individual authors of the nineteenth century. For example, the phraseology of Alexander Ostrovsky is represented in [6], aphorisms of Alexander Pushkin in [7], the phraseology of Leo Tolstoy in [8], elements of Ivan Turgenev's phraseology are described in [9]. Thus, a consistent, systematic study of the inventory, structure and functioning of the idiom system in the given period of time is absent in modern Russian linguistics.

When compiling a database of nineteenth-century idioms, which can be used as a source of comprehensive dictionary, a researcher faces a number of problems. Firstly, well-known dictionaries by Maksimov, Snegirev or Dal [10–12] where idiomatic expressions are fragmentarily recorded do not meet the modern understanding of the essence of idioms and include diverse and unverified information about figurative expressions of various structures, semantics, and pragmatics. Although Morits Mikhelson's dictionary [13] is titled as a phraseological lexicon, it includes various speech phenomena—just what the author finds interesting.

Secondly, the Russian language of the nineteenth century is only available in written form, in other words, it is impossible to analyze the spoken language of the nineteenth century. Thirdly, the Russian language of the nineteenth century differs lexically and often grammatically from modern Russian. Therefore, the intuition of native speakers of modern Russian does not allow them to qualify some expressions and to judge about their meaning. Nevertheless, the task of describing the idiomatic expressions of the nineteenth century remains relevant and requires its solution.

The project carried out at the V. V. Vinogradov Russian Language Institute (project participants: A. N. Baranov, D. O. Dobrovol'skij, K. L. Kiseleva, A. D. Kozerenko, E. A. Osokina, E. V. Sharapova and M. M. Voznesenskaja) aims to create a dictionary of idioms, representative of written Russian texts of the nineteenth century. This requires identifying the contexts of idiom usage and describing their meanings as accurately as possible within the competence of the research team. Another important task within the project is to trace the dynamics of Russian idioms from the nineteenth to the twenty-first century.

Achieving these goals involves the use of modern computer technologies, primarily corpus methods. One of the crucial stages of the project is the creation of a database containing information about the dictionary form of idiomatic expressions, their usage, presence in dictionary sources, and specific characteristics of their semantics. Currently 8,000 idioms are included in the database.

2 Lexicographic Resources

The general inventory of the idioms under study was composed on the base of the dictionaries that present the Russian phraseology through the nineteenth century. The earliest one was *Slovar' Akademii Rossijskoj* (the Dictionary of the Russian

Academy [14]) published at the end of the eighteenth century, the last one was Morits Mikhelson's dictionary [13] published in the beginning of the twentieth century. The dictionary [13] was the first to present the Russian phraseology as both an independent scientific discipline and as a separate subsystem within the Russian lexis. During the nineteenth century, there were no Russian phraseological dictionaries in its present form, since there was no modern conception of idiom. Idioms were included in dictionaries as illustrative examples together with various free word combinations. Some idioms were included in various collections of set and figurative expressions. Hence, the sources of this study include the general explanatory dictionaries—[14, 15], as well as [10, 12, 13].

The dictionary [14] was the first academic explanatory dictionary published from 1789 to 1794. This dictionary was arranged by the principle of word families and included numerous set expressions (idioms or collocations) as illustrative examples (e. g. *horonit' koncy* (lit. to bury the ends)—"to hide the traces, destroy the evidence of some reprehensible or criminal action" [16: 301], *hlebnoe mesto* (lit. a bread place)—"a profitable, rewarding job" [16: 365], *pravaja ruka* (lit. one's right hand)—"a person of great value and usefulness to sb., sb.'s most trusted assistant" [16: 559]). The dictionary [14] describes the "Slavonic-Russian language", i. e. it presents the diglossia (additional distribution of Church Slavonic and Russian languages in different spheres of society) that was typical for Russia of that era, therefore it contains a large number of Church Slavonic expressions, which later would become idiomatic, e. g. *mir domu semu* (lit. peace to this house)—lat. *pax huic domui*, Christians' greetings; *vlit' vino novoe v mehi novye* (lit. to pour new wine into new wineskins)—"new substance needs new form", etc.

The dictionary [15] compiled by Vladimir Dal since 1819, was first published in 1863–1866. The main source of this dictionary was oral folk speech collected by the author and his contemporaries. The 2nd edition came out in 1880–1882. We used the 3rd edition, revised and enlarged by Jan Baudouin de Courtenay and published in 1903–1909. Baudouin de Courtenay corrected the composition of some word families in compliance with their meaning and eliminated unfounded etymological convergences. He also expanded the dictionary using some words and expressions from his own notes.

The dictionary [12] by Vladimir Dal (first published in 1862) is a collection of oral folk expressions and folklore. The dictionary [10] by Sergey Maksimov is a belletristic view on the aphorisms, rather than a scientific description of these expressions. Although the term *krylatye slova* (lit. winged words, or aphorisms) is in the title of Maksimov's book, the author was interested in words and expressions with obscure inner form, rather than in aphorisms themselves. For these reasons, Maksimov's collection includes numerous idioms: *v dugu gnut'* (lit. to bend in a bow)—"to keep under control", *vprosak popast'* (lit. to get into rope spinning frame)—"to get into trouble", *ljasy tochit'* (lit. to make small decorative columns at banisters)—"to be occupied with idle chatter (often to the detriment of the matter in hand)" [16: 347], etc.

The study uses the 2nd edition of Morits Mikhelson's dictionary (1912). The 1st edition was published in 1903–1904. The dictionary includes various words and expressions that the author considers to be phraseological units, among them idioms, proverbs, aphorisms (quotes), terminological collocations, as well as some single words with figurative meaning.

Our project is based not only on lexicographic sources, but also on corpus data from the Russian National Corpus (RNC) [17]. The idioms presented in the dictionaries we used were included in the general inventory of our study only in case if some illustrative examples could be found in the nineteenth-century texts from the RNC.

3 Structure of the Database

The records of the database are correlated with idioms, which are multiword expressions characterized by a high degree of idiomaticity and stability [18]. Technically, the dictionary of the nineteenth-century idioms is presented as a relational database in the form of tables, created on the Google Docs platform. Each record of the database includes nine fields:

1. the original form in the source dictionary;
2. meaning;
3. reference to the source dictionary;
4. proposed lemma (with the number of the meaning);
5. idiom component used for alphabetization;
6. examples from the source dictionaries and the RNC texts of the nineteenth century;
7. examples from the RNC texts of the twentieth and twenty-first centuries;
8. indicator of dynamics (disappearance of the unit, its preservation and changes);
9. notes.

Let's briefly characterize each of these fields. One of the well-known characteristics of idioms is that they allow for significant variation in form. This variation is recorded differently in different dictionary sources. Since it is not a priori clear which form was primary for the nineteenth-century Russian, all formal variants presented in the researched dictionaries were recorded during the data collection process. This information was placed in field 1 "original form in the source dictionary".

The description of the idiom's meaning is a complex research task, and the analyzed dictionaries addressed it differently. In some cases, it was not provided at all, for example, in [12] (with a brief comment from the author—especially in cases when the expression was extremely dialectal or little-known). In other cases (for instance, in Mikhelson's dictionary), explanations were present. Information of this type is presented in field 2 "meaning". In field 3 "reference to the source dictionary", an abbreviation was given to denote the corresponding dictionary—one or several.

The recorded variants of the idiom (field 1) were then reduced to a basic form. In this process, information from the RNC about the functioning of the given idiom was taken into account, as well as the researcher's intuition, and the "Thesaurus of Modern Russian Idioms" [19] was also considered, which contains over 8000 Russian idioms in lemmatized form, many of which were also present in the nineteenth-century Russian. The standardized dictionary form of idioms is recorded in field 4 "proposed lemma (with the number of the meaning)".

The principles for selecting the base component for the alphabetization of idioms are described in [18: 265–266]. We followed these rules during the lemmatization of the general inventory of idioms. Field 5 "idiom component used for alphabetization" allows us to group idioms by formal characteristics and avoid duplication.

An important part of the implemented project is illustrative examples, sourced from the RNC and the analyzed dictionaries. The selected examples are presented in fields 6 "examples from the source dictionaries and the RNC texts of the nineteenth century" and 7 "examples from the RNC texts of the twentieth and twenty-first centuries". Comparing usages from different time periods allows for the investigation of dynamics in changes within the Russian phraseological system. The results of this comparison are reflected in field 8 "indicator of dynamics", which records the disappearance of a unit, its preservation, and changes. Finally, field 9 "notes" serves an auxiliary purpose and is filled out only in cases where it is necessary to provide a comment regarding the form and semantics of the idiom and other features of its usage in discourse.

4 Dynamics of the Development of Russian Idioms

4.1 Dynamics of the Inventory

Dynamics of the idioms' inventory includes the emergence of the new idioms in the twentieth and twenty-first centuries and the disappearance of the idioms used in the texts of the nineteenth century. For this reason, we distinguish three main groups of idioms (see also [20]):

- new idioms that emerged in the twentieth–twenty-first centuries,
- old idioms found in nineteenth-century texts that disappeared in the twentieth century,
- invariable part—idioms found in texts of the nineteenth century that are used in the twentieth and the twenty-first centuries as well.

At the same time, we drew data on the idioms of the nineteenth century from the sources that include materials of the eighteenth century (see [14]). The Russian language, however, began to change greatly not at the turn of the twentieth century, but rather after the First World War and the Revolution in Russia. Thus, two large periods are compared: from the nineteenth century to the beginning of the First World War and from 1914 to the present.

Emergence of New Idioms. According to our observations, the idiomatization of a number of Russian colloquial expressions took place in the nineteenth century. While a variety of biblical expressions and quotations from precedent texts are found earlier (e. g., *agnec neporochnyj* (lit. the immaculate lamb)—"a timid, harmless person"; *prinjat' svoj krest* (lit. accept one's cross)—"patiently endure suffering"; *otec lzhi* (lit. the father of lie)—a euphemism for Satan), many common modern colloquial expressions are formed precisely in the texts of the nineteenth century that we have analyzed. The evidence to this is, in particular, the instability of the form and set of meanings of a number of idioms: see the description of idioms with *glaz* (eye) component, as well as the change in the set of meanings of the idiom *imet' v vidu* (lit. to have in view)—"to keep in mind" from the nineteenth to the twentieth century in [21, Sects. 3.2 and 3.3].

However, it is not the emergence of new idioms in the nineteenth century that we are focusing on, especially since we do not have sufficient information about the inventory of idioms used in the texts of the eighteenth century. What we are focusing on is the subsequent dynamics of the inventory of idioms from the nineteenth to the twenty-first centuries. We will draw our conclusions based on the inventory of idioms of the nineteenth century, which we collected from the available dictionaries (see Sect. 2).

Note that the absence of an idiom in dictionary sources and corpora of the nineteenth century does not automatically mean that it was not used. Such a lack may as well indicate the insufficiency of the corpora or the incompleteness of the dictionaries used.

We can only state with certainty that some idioms could not be used in the nineteenth century. It concerns the following types of idioms:

- idioms with new lexical components,
- idioms that denote new realities,
- idioms that arose on the basis of precedent texts of the twentieth and twenty-first centuries,
- idioms that arose on the basis of official or public discourse of the twentieth and twenty-first centuries.

Let us take a closer look at what these idioms are. Idioms with new lexical components contain words that did not exist in the nineteenth century, e. g., *na avtopilote* (lit. on autopilot)—"without thinking"; *pod dulom avtomata* (lit. at gunpoint)—"under duress"; *avos'koj stebanutyj* (lit. hit with a string bag)—"strange, inhibited"; *interesnoe kino* (lit. an interesting movie)—"sth. unexpected and strange"; *strashnee atomnoj vojny* (lit. uglier than nuclear war)—"terribly ugly".

New idioms denote new artifacts and realities, e. g., *bol'shoj brat* (lit. big brother)—in the meaning of "video camera"; *goluboj ekran* (lit. blue screen)—"TV"; *odnorukij bandit* (lit. one-armed bandit)—"slot machine", or name phenomena discovered only in the twentieth-twenty-first centuries, e. g., *chernaja dyra* (lit. black hole)—"space object formed by gravitational compression of space bodies"; *brounovskoe dvizhenie* (lit. Brownian motion)—"random movement of small particles"; *belyj karlik* (lit. white dwarf)—"a star type". This group also includes idioms with proper names of people, literary characters or phenomena of the twentieth-twenty-first centuries, e. g., *bogaten'kij Buratino* (lit. rich Pinocchio)—"someone rich"; *rabotat' kak papa Karlo* (lit. work like Papa Carlo)—"work hard"; *starik Baturin* (lit. old man Baturin)—"Luzhkov", the mayor of Moscow described by the name of his wife; *zheleznyj Feliks* (lit. iron Felix) – "Dzerzhinsky"; *Papa Zyu* (lit. father Zyu)—"Zyuganov"; *Stepanida Vlas'evna*—a euphemism for the Soviet government made of a typical Russian female name.

Idioms that arose on the basis of precedent texts of the twentieth and twenty-first centuries are based on quotes from popular novels, e. g., by Ilf and Petrov: *led tronulsja, gospoda prisjazhnye zasedateli!* (lit. the ice has broken, gentlemen of the jury!)—"sth. important has begun!", as well as on quotes from famous films of the Soviet and post-Soviet periods: *Mulja, ne nerviruj menja!* (lit. Mulya, don't irritate me!)—"do what I say"; *elementarno, Vatson!* (lit. It's elementary, Watson!)—"sth. is very easy"; *rezat', ne dozhidajas' peritonita* (lit. operate without waiting for peritonitis)—"do sth. decisively".

Idioms that arose on the basis of official or public discourse of the twentieth and twenty-first centuries, primarily, came from the official Soviet discourse: *luchshij drug pozharnikov* (lit. best friend of firefighters); *velikij kormchij* (lit. great helmsman); *otec narodov* (lit. father of nations) are propaganda names for Stalin; *um, chest' i sovest' nashej epohi* (lit. the mind, honor and conscience of our era)—'the communist party of the Soviet Union'.

This group also includes the newest idioms that have to be attributed to the statements of newsmakers: *deneg net, no vy derzhites'* (lit. there is no money, but you hold on)—"you will get nothing from the state, save yourself"; *hajli lajkli*—Russian transcription for *highly likely*. Some idioms come from gaming and other jargons: *izi katka* (lit. easy game)—"sth. easy"; *van lav* (lit. one love)—"sth. special"; *zaskamit' mamonta* (lit. to scam a mammoth)—"to fool an old man". Blogs and social networks are another source of the new phraseology: *beloe pal'to* (lit. white coat)—"sb. thinking himself/herself to be perfect among others"; *bombit' Voronezh* (lit. to bomb Voronezh)—"to punish one's citizens instead of one's enemies", for more details see [22].

Disappearance of the Old Idioms. Some idioms present in the dictionaries and in the texts of the nineteenth century are no more used in the texts of the twentieth and twenty-first centuries. These are, for example, *vyzhit' iz pamjati* (lit. outlive one's memory)—"go crazy"; *vozdat' osmericeju* (lit. repay eight times)—"thank sb. several times"; *smotret'/gljadet' von* (lit. to look out)—"to want to leave some place", and many others. These idioms are present in the sources on which we relied; according to the RNC, they are found in the texts of the nineteenth century, but not in the texts of the twentieth and twenty-first centuries.

Just as in the case of the appearance of new idioms for denoting new realities, the disappearance of old realities often entails the disappearance of the corresponding idiom, e. g., *krasnaja podkladka* (lit. a red lining) meaning "a general" (and referring to the general's uniform in a certain historical period); *znachkovyj tovarisch* (lit. badge comrade) meaning "military official in Malorussia".

However, there are also idioms that disappeared from use in the twentieth century despite the fact that the entities or phenomena they denote still exist: *brat' devicu* (lit. to take a girl) meaning "to marry"; *znat' sebja* (lit. know oneself) meaning "not to interfere in other people's affairs".

Idioms with lexically or morphologically obsolete components can either still be used, e. g., *peret' na rozhon* (lit. go on a stake pointed at sb.)—"to seek for troubles"; *denno i noschno* (lit. day and night)—"constantly"; *odin kak perst* (lit. one like a finger)—"alone", or disappear from use in the twentieth century, e. g. *nesti/molot' gil'* (lit. to carry/grind rubbish)—"talk nonsense"; *vozdat' osmericeju* (lit. repay eight times)—"thank sb. several times".

There are several authors of the twentieth century, however, who deliberately use obsolete idioms in their works as if re-introducing them into everyday life. Corpus data shows that these idioms are not found in any other authors' texts, though. These authors include, first of all, E. Lukin and Aleksandr Solzhenitsyn. Cf. the following obsolete expressions from the Dal's dictionary [15] which are present in their works: *pal'cy torchat—rabotat' meshajut* (lit. fingers stick out and interfere with work)—"bad work"; *rabotat' po konec pal'cev* (lit. work at the end of the fingers)—"work badly", *oboe rjaboe* (lit. both are pockmarked)—"the same".

Unchanging Part of Inventory. A significant part of the inventory of the idioms has remained unchanged from the nineteenth to the twentieth and twenty-first centuries. Some of these units are now regarded as obsolete, e. g., *pitat'sja akridami i dikim medom* (lit. eat locusts and wild honey)—"to starve"; *myshinyj zherebchik* (lit. a mouse stallion)—"an old man pretending to act like a young one"; *pochit' v boze* (lit. to rest in god)—"to die". Many idioms have survived unchanged and are not perceived as obsolete either, e. g., *guba ne dura* (lit. one's lip is not a fool)—"one has good taste"; *sled prostyl* (lit. sb's trace is cold)—"sb. is long gone"; *syt po gorlo* (lit. well-fed up to the throat)—"too much"; *zadet' za zhivoe* (lit. touch the tender spot)—"to offend"; *rodit'sja pod schastlivoj zvezdoj* (lit. to be born under a lucky star)—"to be lucky", and many others.

The percentage of new idioms, old idioms and unchangeable part in the general corpus of Russian idioms of the nineteenth-twenty-first centuries can only be obtained when the project is finished and its results are analyzed.

4.2 Dynamics of the Form

Under form dynamics we understand changes in the lexical structure of an idiom (its expansion or contraction as well as the substitution of components, or changes in their morphological structure). For any given idiom, such variation is difficult to predict, but a posteriori we can identify several common types of such changes.

Grammatical Deviations. The form of an idiom is rather stable, so that in some cases the morphology of its components remains frozen, even when such grammatical forms are no longer found elsewhere. These cases include exotic archaisms such as the biblical expressions *temna voda vo oblaceh* (lit. the water is dark in the clouds)—"it's unclear", or *blagorastvorenie vozduhov* (lit. mildness of the air (pl.))—"healthy climate", where we have obsolete grammatical forms of the words *oblako* ("cloud") and *vozduh* ("air") as well as a lexical archaism *blagorastvorenie* ("mildness").

This phenomenon also concerns much more common idioms. For example, in the idiom *polozha ruku na serdce* (lit. having put one's hand on one's heart)—"to be honest" we see the form *polozha* instead of *polozhiv* (both meaning "having put"). Short adjectives, that are no longer used before a noun, are often retained in this position even in the twenty-first century when they are part of an idiom: *krasna devica* (lit. red maiden)—"a beauty", *na skoru ruku* (lit. on a quick hand)—"in haste", *liha beda nachalo* (lit. [a] terrible trouble [is the] beginning)—"the first step is the hardest". This may not be a general rule: for the idiom *vyjti suhim iz vody* (lit. come out dry out of the water)—"to get away with it", the variant with the short form *suh* of the adjective *suhim* ("dry"), common in the nineteenth century, is not found in the RNC after 1930.

In other cases, a rare grammatical form may be invented by the author. For example, Dostoevsky used the plural form *porjadki veschej* (lit. orders of things) while the standard form is *porjadok veschej* (lit. order of things)—"the way things are, the course of nature". For other authors, no occurrences of this idiom in the plural form were found in the RNC.

Finally, in a number of idioms we observe the actual dynamics of the grammatical form. For example, the analysis shows that the idiom *ni zgi ne vidno/ne videt'* (lit. not a thing can be seen/can see)—"it's totally dark" does not occur without the negative particle *ni* since the twentieth century. This particle has now become obligatory, which was not the case in the language of the nineteenth century.

Reduction or Expansion of the Lexical Structure. Let us start with the change in the number of components. In the nineteenth century, the idiom *temna voda vo oblaceh* (lit. the water is dark in the clouds)—"it's as clear as mud" had one extra component—the attribute *vozdushnyh/nebesnyh* ("airy"/ "celestial"), which does not appear in the twentieth century.

A common case of reduction in the number of components is the clipping of proverbs and sayings. Such examples are regularly found in our material and lie at the intersection of the dynamics of the inventory and the dynamics of the form. On the one hand, such development of proverbs and sayings produces new expressions that replenish the inventory of idioms. On the other hand, it is precisely this clipping that leads to a change in the form of the expression, reducing the number of its components.

Clipping also occurs in idioms themselves. Most speakers of modern Russian do not suspect that originally many widespread idioms were extended maxims with a different meaning. This is what happened, for example, with the phrase *bogat kak Krez, a zhivet kak pes* (lit. rich as Croesus, but living like a dog)—"sb. extremely rich who lives in very bad conditions" which is now used in its clipped form *bogat kak Krez* (which simply means "extremely rich"). The disappearance of some components of an idiom can be considered the most common case of form change.

Variation of One of the Components. The simplest case is when one of the components slightly changes its form. For example, the idiom *kak ob stenu/ob stenku goroh* (lit. like peas against the wall)—"like talking to a brick wall" appears in the nineteenth century only with the component *ob stenu.* The *ob stenku* variant does not appear in the RNC until 1921. In this case, we have the simultaneous disappearance of one variant of an idiom and the appearance of another. There are a number of idioms with the identical morphological dynamics, e. g. *kak na iglah/na igolkah [sidet']* (lit. to sit as if on thorns)—"to be very impatient, anxious". The first variant *na iglah* was common in the nineteenth century, and was then replaced by the variant *na igolkah.*

Here are some other examples of variation reduction. In the idiom *vody ne zamutit* (lit. won't muddy the water)—"innocuous, quiet, gentle" the nominative part *vody/vodoj* varied. The *vodoj* variant was lost, and with it the variability of the noun.

The verb components of idioms often have several variants, and their set may change over time. For example, the idiom *vskruzhit' golovu* (lit. make sb.'s head spin)—"impair one's judgment, enthrall sb." used to have the variant *svertet' golovu* (lit. twist sb.'s head). In the idiom *[i] pal'cem ne poshevelit'* (lit. not to stir a finger)—"not to make the slightest effort" the verbs *sognut'* and *razognut'* ("to bend"/ "to unbend") instead of *poshevelit'* ("to stir") were possible: *palec ne sognut'/ ne razognut'* (lit. not to bend/to unbend a finger).

Noun components also allow for lexical variation. For example, in the idiom *babushka nadvoe skazala* (lit. grandmother said in two)—"it remains to be seen" the noun component in the nineteenth century could be either *babushka* "grandmother" or *staruha* "old woman". The latter variant is not found in the RNC later on. Similarly, in the nineteenth century, the idiom *krugovaja poruka* (lit. circular commitment)—"mutual cover-up" had a variant with the adjective *kruglyj* ("round").

The appearance of new variants for one of the idiom components is also possible, but, according to our estimates, these cases are rather rare. An interesting case is represented by the idiom *ni v zub [tolknut']* (lit. not to the tooth [push])—"to have no idea, to be ignorant". In the nineteenth century it was used in two variants, with and without the verb *tolknut'* ("to push"). The variant with the component *nogoj* (with one's leg) appears for the first time in the early twentieth century: *ni v zub nogoj.* The variant with the verb appears for the last time in the RNC in the 1930s. Thus, the idiom retained the short variant *ni v zub* (which is now rarely used), while the old variant with the verb *tolknut'* disappeared and a variant with the new component *nogoj* appeared and quickly became dominant.

Changes in Transparency of the Inner Form. By the inner form we understand the image on which the idiom is based as well as its semantic motivation [18]. In the nineteenth century, however, the image underlying the semantics of many idioms was much clearer than today. This applies not only to expressions such as *bit' baklushi* (lit. beat the woodblocks) — "to fool around" and *igrat' v birjul'ki* (lit. play at spillikins)—"to waste one's time on trifles", which are associated with past realities, but also, for example, a number of expressions associated with religious texts, such as *angel vo ploti* (lit. an angel in the flesh)—"an angel on earth" or *angel-hranitel'* (lit.

a guardian angel). Thus, for many idioms the opacity of the inner form has increased today compared to the nineteenth century.

4.3 Dynamics of the Meaning

The trends in the development of Russian idiomatics discussed above (the dynamics of its inventory and form) are closely related to the dynamics of the meaning of idioms. A change in the phraseological inventory, the appearance and disappearance of one or another idiom naturally implies the appearance or disappearance of its meaning. When the lexical structure of an idiom changes, its semantics can either be preserved or changed. Below we will consider the main directions in the dynamics of the meaning of idioms, including the preservation, change, or disappearance of existing meanings, as well as the emergence of new ones.

Dynamics of the Meaning of Monosemantic Idioms. As mentioned in Sect. 4.1, a significant part of Russian idioms has remained unchanged, preserving its semantics from the eighteenth to the twenty-first century. However, there are many cases of change in the meaning of idioms.

Firstly, the change in the meaning of an idiom can be due to the highlighting of different features in its image. An example of this type of change in semantics is the expression *kisejnaja baryshnja* (lit. muslin lady), first used in Nikolai Pomyalovsky's work *Meshchanskoe schast'e* ("Bourgeois Happiness"). In the nineteenth century, this idiom was used to denote a whole range of characteristics of a young girl—'frivolous', 'simple', 'modest', 'not emancipated', 'poorly educated', 'with petty interests', 'prudish', 'spoiled'. As a result of the semantic development of the idiom, many of these features disappeared, the meaning of the idiom was generalized, and in modern Russian, *kisejnaja baryshnja* is used to describe a 'coddled person who is unable to adapt to real life' [23: 32]. (For more details on the semantic development of the idiom *kisejnaja baryshnja*, see [24, 25]).

Secondly, the semantic change of the idiom may lie in the fact that the idiom, while preserving the meaning that existed in the nineteenth century, gets a new one in the twentieth century and becomes polysemous. In the nineteenth century, the expression *volchij bilet* (lit. wolf's ticket) was used to refer to 'a document containing notes on its holder's unreliability and the restriction of his civil rights'. In modern Russian, the idiom has a second meaning: 'an extremely negative written evaluation (often a notation in a person's work record) of a person's work, political views, etc., which does not allow this person to get a job, occupy a certain position, etc'.

Dynamics of the Meanings of Polysemous Idioms. The processes characterizing the development of polysemous idioms are very diverse and concern both quantitative and qualitative (semantic) characteristics of the set of meanings of an idiom.

Polysemous idioms can retain the structure of their polysemy by having the same set of meanings throughout the eighteenth-twenty-first centuries. For example, the expression *Bog s toboj* (lit. God with you) [26: 38] has three meanings ('wishing goodbye'; 'expressing disagreement with the interlocutor' and 'reluctant agreement with the interlocutor'), the same meanings are recorded in [14].

The number of meanings of polysemous idioms can vary—increase or decrease. For example, the expression *prikazat' dolgo zhit'* (lit. to order to live a long time) was used in nineteenth-century texts in two meanings 'to die' and 'to cease to exist'. In modern Russian, while retaining these two meanings, the idiom has a third meaning 'to break, to get out of order', which is used to characterize various technical devices [26: 186–187].

The idiom *pod rukoj/rukoju* (lit. under the hand) had several meanings in the eighteenth and nineteenth centuries: to be 'under the authority of sb.', to do sth., usually to report, to transmit any information 'secretly, covertly, implicitly' and to be 'near, in close proximity'. Nowadays, only the third meaning remains in active usage.

A change in the structure of a polysemous idiom can involve both a reduction and an increase in the number of meanings. For example, the expression *postavit' na nogi* (lit. to put on feet) was used in nineteenth-century texts in four meanings: 'to cure sb.', 'to bring up sb.', 'to awaken sb.', 'to make sb. act energetically'. In the twenitieth century, the meaning 'to awaken' was lost, the compatibility of the idiom extended, and it became possible to use inanimate nouns as direct objects, as a result of which two new meanings appeared: 'to restore, to revive sth.' and 'to strengthen, develop sth.'.

The simultaneous increase and decrease in the number of meanings can be accompanied by semantic modifications of the meanings themselves. Thus, the use of the idiom *imet' v vidu* (lit. to have in view) in nineteenth-century texts allows us to distinguish the following meanings: 'to imply', 'to take sth. into account', 'to take sb. into account', 'to plan to do sth.', 'to count on sth. positive in the future' and 'to seek to achieve some goals in the future'. In the twentieth century, the number of meanings of the idiom changed—the last two meanings disappeared, a new meaning 'to ignore sb./sth.' appeared, and the second and third merged into one 'to take sb./ sth. into account ' [26: 77]. (For more details on the idiom *imet' v vidu*, see [21: 72–86]).

5 Main Trends in the Development of Russian Idioms

At the current stage of the project, any generalized conclusions inevitably have a preliminary nature. Moreover, the nature of the research and the state of existing sources do not allow one to expect unequivocal and strictly proven statements regarding the phraseology of the nineteenth century. Nevertheless, even taking into account the existing limitations, the setting of the task itself is significant for understanding the development of the Russian lexical system. It should also be borne in mind that the higher the level at which generalization is made, the less informative and more trivial it is. The thesis about the change in the lexical and phraseological system is obviously indisputable. However, the specific ways of change and especially the prevalence of certain methods are already questions that require representative data, which is not always achievable.

A significant portion of changes in the Russian idiom system can be described in terms of dynamics, as has been mentioned earlier. Let us note the main points. The inventory of idiomatic expressions has changed: some idioms disappeared from actual usage, while new idioms have emerged (for examples see Sect. 4.1). Meanwhile, the basic part of the inventory of Russian idioms has been preserved, especially for idioms that lack stylistically neutral one-word-synonyms, e.g., *guba ne dura* (lit. one's lip is not a fool)—"one has a good taste". Often (but not always) the disappearance of an idiom can be explained by the disappearance of the corresponding reality fragment. Similarly, a new phenomenon can give rise to a new idiom; compare the idiom *byt' na odnoj volne* (lit. to be on the same wavelength)—"to understand each other well", which could only emerge with the advent of radio communication.

Semantic change has been divergent: the meaning of an idiom could both simplify (e. g., *na otlete* (lit. on the sidelines), which had two meanings—"at an advanced age" and "on the eve of departure"—in the nineteenth century) and become more complex.

Another fairly obvious trend is the stabilization of the variability of the idiom's structure (for examples see Sect. 4.2). Some word combinations that were perceived as almost free in the nineteenth century, were later fixed in a limited set of variants and became part of phraseology.

Preliminary analysis shows that compared to the nineteenth-century language the range of constructional phrasemes is expanding, which have come into the scope of our research due to the fact that many of them give rise to idioms. For instance, according to data from the RNC, the expression *X—eto Y dlja bednyh* (lit. X is Y for the poor)—"X is a substandard version of Y" only emerged in the mid-twentieth century (e. g., *kitajskoe radio—eto BBC dlja bednyh*—lit. broadcast from China is BBC for the poor, *etot novyj spektakl'—eto Ibsen dlja bednyh*—lit. this new performance is Ibsen for the poor, etc.), and the construction *X on i v Afrike X* (lit. X is even in Africa X)—"X is [still] X" appeared in the 1970s, e. g., *tank on i v Afrike tank* (lit. a tank is even in Africa, a tank). In this sense, the sphere of phraseology is expanding and becoming more complex, which is a reflection of the general trend toward an increase in the complexity of discourse in Russian.

References

1. Materials for the Dictionary of the 19th Century Russian: trial entries [Materialy k "Slovarju russkogo jazyka XIX veka": probnye stat'i]. 19th Century Russian: Language Dynamics [Russkij jazyk XIX veka: dinamika jazykovyh processov]. Edited by V. N. Kalinovskaja. (Acta Linguistica Petropolitana: Proceedings of the Institute for Linguistic Studies. Edited by N. N. Kazansky. Vol. IV, part 3). Nauka Publ., St. Petersburg (2008). pp. 311–364. (In Russ.)
2. Pushkin's Language Dictionary [Slovar' jazyka Pushkina]: in 4 v./Ed. V. V. Vinogradov.—2nd ed. suppl./Russian Academy of Sciences, Vinogradov Russian Language Institute. Azbukovnik, Moscow (2000). (In Russ.)

3. Dostoevsky's Language Dictionary. The lexical structure of the idiolect [Slovar' jazyka Dostoevskogo. Leksicheskij stroj idiolekta]./Russian Academy of Sciences, Vinogradov Russian Language Institute; Ed. Ju. N. Karaulov. Azbukovnik, Moscow (2001). (In Russ.)
4. Dostoevsky's Language Dictionary. Idioglossary [Slovar' jazyka Dostoevskogo. Idioglossarij] (A–S)/Ed.-in-Chief Ju. N. Karaulov. Azbukovnik, Moscow (2008–2021). (In Russ.)
5. Poljakov, A.E.: Griboedov's Language Dictionary [Slovar' jazyka A. S. Griboedova]. Jazyki russkoj kul'tury Publ., Moscow (2008). (In Russ.)
6. Lomov, A.G., Phraseological Dictionary of A. N. Ostrovsky's Dramaturgy [Frazeo-logicheskij slovar' dramaturgii A. N. Ostrovskogo]. Issue 1. Uzhiruvchi Publ., Tashkent (1988). (In Russ.)
7. Mokienko, V.M., Sidorenko, K.P.: Dictionary of Pushkin's Aphorisms [Slovar' krylatyh vyrazhenij Pushkina]. St. Petersburg State University; Folio-Press, St. Petersburg (1999). (In Russ.)
8. Lomakina, O.V.: Phraseology in the Text: Functioning and Idiostyle [Frazeologija v tekste: funkcionirovanie i idiostil']. Edited by V. M. Mokienko. RUDN, Moscow (2018). 344 p. (In Russ.)
9. Markanova, F.A.: Dictionary of Colloquial Lexicon and Phraseology, compiled from the collected works of I. S. Turgenev [Slovar' narodno-razgovornoj leksiki i frazeologii, sostavlennyj po sobraniju sochinenij I. S. Turgeneva]. Fan Publ., Tashkent (1968). (In Russ.)
10. Aphorisms according to S. Maksimov's Interpretation [Krylatyje slova po tolkovaniju S. Maksimova]/Preface and notes by N. S. Ashukin. Goslitizdat, Moscow (1955). 447 p. (In Russ.)
11. Snegirev, I.M.: Russian People's Proverbs and Parables [Russkie narodnye poslovicy i pritchi]. Indrik, Moscow (1999). 621 p. (In Russ.)
12. Proverbs of the Russian People [Poslovicy russkogo naroda]. Collected by Vladimir Dal. In 2 volumes. Hudozhestvennaja literatura Publ., Moscow (1989). (In Russ.)
13. Mihel'son, M.I.: Russian Thought and Speech. Our own and foreign. Study of Russian phraseology. Collection of figurative words and allegories. [Russkaja mysl' i rech'. Svojo i chuzhoje. Opyt russkoj frazeologii. Sbornik obraznyh slov i inoskazanij]. Akademija Nauk, St. Petersburg (1912). 103 p. (In Russ.)
14. Dictionary of the Russian Academy [Slovar' Akademii Rossijskoj]. Parts I-VI. Pri Imperatorskoj Akademii Nauk, St. Petersburg (1789–1794). (In Russ.)
15. Explanatory Dictionary of the Living Great Russian Language by Vladimir Dal [Tolkovyj slovar' zhivogo velikorusskogo jazyka Vladimira Dalja], Third, corrected and greatly enlarged edition edited by prof. I. A. Baudouin de Courtenay. V. 1–4. Izdanie Tovarishchestva M. O. Volf, St. Petersburg (1903–1909). (In Russ.)
16. Lubenskaja, S.I.: Russian-English Dictionary of Idioms [Russko-anglijskij frazeologicheskij slovar'], p. 1056. Jazyki russkoj kul'tury Publ, Moscow (1997)
17. The Russian National Corpus (RNC) [Nacionalnyj korpus russkogo jazyka]: ruscorpora.ru
18. Baranov, A.N., Dobrovol'skij, D.O.: Fundamentals of Phraseology [Osnovy frazeologii]. Nauka Publ., Moscow, Flinta (2013). (In Russ.)
19. Dictionary-Thesaurus of the Modern Russian Idioms [Slovar'-tezaurus sovremennoj russkoj idiomatiki]. Baranov, A.N., Dobrovol'skij, D.O. (eds.). Mir enciklopedij Avanta+, Moscow (2007). 1135 p. (In Russ.)
20. Baranov, A.N., Dobrovol'skij, D.O. Evolution trends in Russian idiomatics from 19th to 21st century (the statement of the problem) [Tendencii razvitija russkoj idiomatiki s XIX po XXI vv. (k postanovke problemy)]. The report read at the Academic Council in Vinogradov Russian Language Institute on November 21, 2021
21. Balashov, E.A., Baranov, A.N., Dobrovol'skij, D.O., Kiseleva, K.L., Kozerenko, A.D., Korobova, M.M. et al.: Corpus Model of Dostoevsky's Idiostyle [Korpusnaja model' idiostilja Dostoevskogo]/eds. A.N. Baranov, D.O. Dobrovol'skij, LEKSRUS Publ., Moscow (2021). (In Russ.)
22. Kiseleva, K.L., Kozerenko, A.D. *Izi katka, van lav, Dobbi svoboden* and other frequent colloquial neologisms: sources and mechanisms of idiomatization [*Izi katka, van lav, Dobbi*

svoboden i drugie chastotnye razgovornye neologizmy: istochniki i mehanizmy idiomatizacii] (2023). (In Russ.) https://ruslang.ru/sites/default/files/2023-02/tezisy_ Shmelev14_ v16022023.pdf
23. Molotkov, A.I. Phraseological Dictionary of the Russian Language [Frazeologicheskij slovar' russkogo jazyka]. AST, Astrel Publ. Moscow (2006). 524 p. (In Russ.)
24. Babkin, A.M.: Russian Phraseology, its Evolution and its Origins [Russkaja frazeologija, ejo razvitie i istochniki]. Nauka Publ., Leningrad (1979). 264 p. (In Russ.)
25. Kiseleva, K.L., Kozerenko, A.D.: *Turgenev's girl, a superfluous man* and other cultural allusions as a component of the meaning of an idiom [*Turgenevskaja devushka, lishnij chelovek* i drugie: kul'turnye alljuzii kak komponent znachenija frazeologizma]. Word. Dictionary. Literature. Problems of Functional Lexicology. Collected works in the honour of Professor Vera Stepanova's 100th anniversary [Slovo. Slovar'. Slovesnost'. Problemy funkcional'noj leksikologii. Sbornik nauchnyh statej k 100-letiju professora Very Vasil'evny Stepanovoj]. (2023). (In print) (In Russ.)
26. Academic Dictionary of Russian Phraseology [Akademicheskij slovar' russkoj frazeologii]. Baranov, A.N., Dobrovol'skij, D.O. (eds.), 3rd edn. LEKSRUS Publ., Moscow (2020). 896 p. (In Russ.)

Possessor Doubling Strategies in Modern Vernacular Russian as Represented in the "One Speech Day" Oral Corpus

Evgenii Sokolov and Mariia Korolkova

Abstract In this article we try to describe and explain the nature of possessor doubling constructions, as we call structures containing both external and internal possessors, in Russian spontaneous oral speech. Drawing from the data extracted from the "One Speech Day" corpus of oral vernacular Russian we try to single out the reasons for using such constructions which are generally believed to be semantically redundant. We demonstrate that this redundancy is in many respects imaginary and claim that the two separate parts of this construction do not convey the same possessive meaning and their pragmatic orientation is quite different. The external possessor may in fact lack possessive semantics at all, being just the way of encoding the discursively central entity or the bearer of the local point of view, while the internal possessor may be overt or covert depending on its saliency and secondary meanings. This difference allows these constructions to appear in the same utterance simultaneously.

Keywords Corpus · Oral speech · Possessum · External possessor · Internal possessor · Free affectee · Discourse · Semantics · Redundancy

1 Introduction

Practical handbooks of Russian style claim that unwary use of pronouns may produce semantic redundancy [5: 288]. In this respect possessives are believed to be one of the most treacherous classes of pronouns [18: 187]. At the same time the excessive use of possessive pronouns has a long history [16: 77–78] and as such is undoubtedly predefined by some basic features of Russian language. In this article we are going

E. Sokolov (✉)
Institute for Linguistic Studies, Russian Academy of Sciences, Tuchkov per. 9, 199004, Saint-Petersburg, Russia
e-mail: pan_liwcrij@mail.ru

M. Korolkova
St. Petersburg State University, University emb, 199034 Saint-Petersburg, Russia
e-mail: skifane@gmail.ru

P. Eismont et al. (eds.), *Literature, Language and Computing*,
https://doi.org/10.1007/978-981-96-0990-1_9

to examine a certain syntactic construction which is not infrequent in Russian oral speech and is generally identified as formally pleonastic—namely, the possessor doubling construction exemplified below:

(1a) U menja moj otec na fronte byl [4: 162]
At I.GEN my.NOM father.NOM on frontline.LOC be.PST.MASC
'As for me, my father was on the frontline'
(1b) U nas naš narodnyj dux... [13: 187]
At we.GEN our.NOM national.NOM spirit.NOM
'As for us, our national spirit...'

Our goal is to determine whether this construction really appears in Russian vernacular speech completely by chance, or there are some underlying factors which predetermine its usage in certain contexts. If discovered, these factors could question the very idea of its erroneous or at least redundant character.

2 Data and Examples

For our current research we examined the data of the Russian sound corpus "One speech day" (further OSDC) [3: 101]. This corpus was designed as a complex structure aimed at documenting modern vernacular Russian oral speech, describing the language in its most natural form, and solving a bunch of applied didactic and linguistic tasks [19: 17]. Spontaneous speech is often generated hastily and abounds in hesitations, bloopers, repetitions, self-correction, etc. [20: 4]. Thus, the natural character of examples in OSDC is of great moment to us, for we believe that by scrutinizing the structure of spontaneous utterances researchers can elicit much more information on the actual machinery of the human language than by observing refined standard examples.

Our work being to a great extent preliminary, we are still collecting and processing the data and thus we reserve their statistical analysis to our future publications. In the current article we are going to focus on the structure of the constructions in question as represented in OSDC.

Our examples are of a threefold manner. Their larger part consists of utterances taken from OSDC. They are preceded by the corresponding abbreviation, as in (2a). Artificial examples are marked with the abbreviation FICT, as in (2b), and those borrowed from other works are provided with a link, as in (1a, b) above.

(2a) OSDC: u nas teper' *P naša federacija ...
at we.GEN now our.NOM federation.NOM
'Now we have got our own federation...'
(2b) FICT: U derevjev net svoego mnenija.
At trees.GEN no self.POSS.GEN opinion.GEN
'Trees lack their own opinion'.

3 The Problem

Below we are going to thoroughly examine the possessor doubling constructions. In order to present the data more clearly, we shall first introduce the notions of possession, possessor and possessum, as well as show the structural differences between the external and internal possessor encoding strategies. Then we shall analyze the conditions and circumstances under which these strategies tend to cooperate, resulting in possible semantic redundancy.

3.1 Possession, Possessor and Possessum

Proper possession, or *possessive relation* sensu stricto, is, in fact, an ownership relation which holds between an owner, called possessor, and this owner's property, called possessum [10: 122].

Possession in general, or *possessive relation* sensu lato, is a set of at least 27 semantically diverse relations [8: 25, 26] which, in particular languages, can be encoded by the expedient of the same grammatical means as proper possession [10: 122]. The only common semantic feature of all these relations is their abstract ability to link two arbitrary entities [2: 239–242] by any connection closer than spacial vicinity [4: 11]. Two entities engaged in general possessive relation retain the names of possessor and possessum.

Usually possessor is perceived as a communicatively salient, animate entity; as a language expression it has autonomous reference and tends toward the position of empathy focus, i.e. that of the participant whose point of view is prioritized by the speaker [2: 242, 9:442]. Posessum generally lacks at least some part of these features.

3.2 Internal Versus External Possessors

The two central elements of a possessive construction can be arranged in a twofold manner. The first case, called *Internal Possessor Construction* (henceforth *IPC*), consists in that the possessor PSR and the possessum PSM are located inside the same constituent, namely a NP, whereas the possessum acts as its nominal head and the possessor occupies the position of a possessive adjective (3a) or a pronoun (3b), a reflexive pronoun (3c) or the genitive complement of the head noun (3d) [8: 17]:

(3a) FICT: *Ivan* *poterjal* *[NP papin PSR* *[N pasport PSM]]*
Ivan.NOM lose.PST.MASC father.POSS.ACC passport.ACC
'Ivan lost his father's passport'
(3b) FICT: *Ivan* *poterjal* *[NP moj PSR* *[N pasport PSM]]*
Ivan.NOM lose.PST.MASC my.ACC passport.ACC
'Ivan lost my passport'
(3c) FICT: *Ivan* *poterjal* *[NP svoj PSR* *[N pasport PSM]]*
Ivan.NOM lose.PST.MASC own.ACC passport.ACC
'Ivan lost his own passport'
(3d) FICT: *Ivan* *poterjal* *[NP [N pasport PSM] otca PSR]*
Ivan.NOM lose.PST.MASC passport.ACC father.GEN
'Ivan lost the passport of his father'

In the second case, called *External Possessor Construction* or *EPC*, the possessor is located outside the NP which hosts the possessum [7: 1]. Compared to the corresponding IPCs (4a,b), EPCs feature two structural variants [Ibid.]:

1. *possessor extraposition* [8: 17; 12: 136; 4: 21]: the possessum is in the same position as in the respective IPC, while the possessor is raised into a separate constituent (4c,d);
2. *possessum extraposition* [8: 17; 4: 22]: the possessor retains the position in which an IPC could have been placed, and the possessum receives a new one (4e).

(4a) FICT: *[**Moja** PSR **duša** PSM]* *stradaet.*
My.NOM soul.NOM suffer.PRES.3SG
'My soul is suffering'
(4b) FICT: *Etot* *tip* *slomal* *[**moju** PSR **ruku** PSM].*
This.NOM subject.NOM break.PST.MASC my.ACC arm.ACC
'This subject has broken my arm'
(4c) FICT: *[U menja PSR]* *[**duša** PSM]* *stradaet.*
At I.GEN soul.NOM suffer.PRES.3SG
'My soul is suffering'
(4d) FICT: *Etot* *tip* *slomal* *[mne PSR]* *[**ruku** PSM].*
This.NOM subject.NOM break.PST.MASC I.DAT arm.ACC
'This guy has broken my arm'
(4e) FICT: *[**Ja** PSR]* *stradaju* *[dušoj PSM].*
I.NOM suffer.PRES.1SG soul.INS
'My soul is suffering'.

3.3 Possessor Doubling as a Simultaneous Use of Both External and Internal Possessors

OSDC contains multiple entries of both internal (5a–c) and external (5d–f) possessor constructions:

(5a) OSDC: *tak* [$_{NP}$ *mamina*$_{PSR}$ [$_{N}$ *sumka*$_{PSM}$]]
well mother.POSS.NOM bag.NOM
'Well, mother's bag…'

(5b) OSDC: *Vitja%* *popalsja* *s* [$_{NP}$ *moej*$_{PSR}$ [$_{N}$ *kartočkoj*$_{PSM}$]] *prosto*
Vitja get-captured.PST.MASC with my.INS card.INS just
'Well, Vitja has just been nailed with my card'

(5c) OSDC: *est'* [$_{NP}$ *direktora*$_{PSR}$ [$_{N}$ *telefon*$_{PSM}$]] *kstati ?*
be.PRES.3SG. director.GEN phone.NOM by-the-way
'By the way, have we got the director's phone number?'

(5d) OSDC: *čto-to* *tam* [$_{PP}$ *u mamy*$_{PSR}$] *perebrodilo* *v* [$_{NP}$ *nosu*$_{PSM}$]
Something.NOM there at mother.GEN ferment.PST.NEUT in nose.LOC
'Something has fermented in mother's nose'

(5e) OSDC: *vot* [$_{PP}$ *u tebja*$_{PSR}$] *počemu* [$_{NP}$ *nosik*$_{PSM}$] *to* *ne* *dyšit*
here at you.GEN why nose.NOM DET not breath.PRES.3SG
'That is why your nose is stuffy'

(5f) OSDC: *kak* [$_{NP}$ *mne*$_{PSR}$] *v* [$_{NP}$ *golovu*$_{PSM}$] *udarilo*
how I.DAT in head.ACC strike.PST.NEUT
'And then, out of the blue, I realised'

But topicalized external possessor PPs projected by the preposition *u* do not disallow a simultaneous use of internal possessor constructions pertaining to the same possessum [4: 64], which results in their simultaneous use and tentative semantic redundancy:

(6a) OSDC: [*u nas*$_{PSR}$] *v* [$_{NP}$ *našix*$_{PSR}$ *nasosnyx*$_{PSM}$] *byvaet /* *vonjaet* *užas*
At we.GEN in our.LOC pumping-rooms.LOC sometimes stink.PRES.3SG terribly
'Sometimes it stinks terribly in our pumping-rooms'

(6b) OSDC: *vot* [*u vas*$_{PSR}$] [$_{NP}$ *svoi*$_{PSR}$ *natural'nye* *nogotočki*$_{PSM}$]
here at you.GEN own.NOM natural.NOM nails.NOM
'Well, you've got natural nails'

Let Us Call Such Cases of Co-Occurrence of External and Internal Possessors *Possessor Doubling Constructions*, or *PDC*s.

3.3.1 Normal Possessor Doubling Constructions: *Svoj*

In the most common case, the internal possessor in PDCs is encoded by the reflexive possessive pronoun *svoj*. E. Paducheva notes that in the example (7) the external possessor topic *u kolxoznikov* controls the reference of the PP *na učastkax* so that it necessarily means 'in the gardens of these cottagers':

(7) *U kolxoznikov na svoix učastkax čudesa agrotexniki* [14: 12]
At cottagers on own.LOC gardens.LOC miracles.NOM agricul-ture.GEN
'In their gardens cottagers show miracles of agriculture'

According to Paducheva, this fact implies that the pronoun *svoj* in such contexts can, in addition to its proper function of encoding the possessor, convey some secondary meaning, for example, that of private property [Ibid.]. In general, E. Paducheva distinguishes six separate (but connected) meanings of the pronoun *svoj*: $svoj_1$ = reflexivity & possession; $svoj_2$ = 'svoj_1' & the opposition of 'one's own' and 'someone else's'; $svoj_3$ = 'svoj_1' & distributive interpretation; $svoj_4$ = 'svoj_1' + 'special'; $svoj_5$ = 'svoj_1' + 'proper, right, suitable', and $svoj_6$ = 'being one's kinsman or friend' [Ibid.: 4–6].

Most PDCs with *svoj,* or even all of them in OSDC, feature semantically complex meanings of this pronoun:

(8a) OSDC: *tak a čto u nego / svoj restoran doma* — svoj_2
well and what at he.GEN own.NOM restaurant at-home
'Well, and what? He's got a private restaurant at home'
(8b) OSDC: *i voobšče kak-to u nego svoi dela u menja svoi* — svoj_3
And generally somehow at he.GEN own.NOM problems.NOM at I.GEN own.NOM
'And generally, I do not know how, he does his own business, I do mine'
(8c) OSDC: *u menja est' kakoe-to svoje videnie ustanovki unitaza* — svoj_4
at I.GEN be.PRES.3SG some.NOM own.NOM idea.NOM set-ting.GEN toilet GEN
'As for me, I've got my own idea about how the toilet has to be set up'
(8d) OSDC: *nu u nix svoi soobraženija značit na eto* — svoj_5
well at they.GEN own.NOM ideas.NOM well about that.ACC
'Well, they have their own ideas about that'

We may assume that possessor doubling in such cases is largely standard or normal, because aside from marking the possessor the reflexive pronoun *svoj* plays here some additional roles which are probably justified by the situation. In somewhat more complicated cases additional semantic components of the pronoun *svoj* can be detected only in wider contexts. For instance, example (9) contains a fragment of a conversation in which two women discuss the habits of the daughter of one of them:

(9) A dialogue about a girl and a cat, OSDC:
Speaker 1. *ja vot smotrju / sryvov v obščem to takix *N //*
I here look.PRES.1SG / outbreaks.GEN in general DET such *N
'Well, as far as I am concerned, there are no problematic outbreaks'
nu v vyxodnye skol'ko spit
well on weekend.ACC how-much sleep.PRES.3SG
'Well, on weekends, she sleeps as long as she wants…'
/ stol'ko ne trogajut / vse //
that-much NEG touch.PRES.3PL. all.NOM
'…and nobody disturbs her.'
Speaker 1@Speaker 2. *skol'ko ležit // @ ugu //*
how-much lie.PRES.3SG. @ yeah
'as long as she lies. — Yes.'
Speaker 2. *da da da //*
yes yes yes
'Oh, surely'
Speaker 1. *vse // u nee tam koška svoja*
Well at she.GEN there ca
'Well, she's got her own cat there…'
/ oni tam určat vdvoem //
They there purr.PRES.3PL together
'They purr there together'

Here one can deduce that the pronoun *svoj* inside the NP *koška svoja* belongs to the type of $svoj_4$ = 'svoj_1' & 'special' only having taken into consideration the context of the situation, which tells us that the girl, after returning from school, uses to retire to her own room where she pets her cat, whereas the cat prefers her to the rest of the inhabitants.

3.4 *Abnormal Doubling:* Moj, Tvoj, Ego

A. Kibrik believes the reflexive pronoun *svoj* to be a trace[1] left by the external possessor in process of its extraction outside of the initial NP-internal position [9: 441]. Admitting the necessity or at least permissibility of traces in several contexts, Kibrik nevertheless points out the ungrammaticality of their emergence in some examples like those given below:

(10a) **U nego net svojej ženy* [Ibid.]
At he.GEN be.NEG own.GEN wife.GEN
'He's got no wife'
(10b) **U nego svoj život bolit* [Ibid.]
At he.GEN own.NOM stomach.NOM ache.PRES.3SG
'He's got a stomach ache'

---

[1] Undoubtedly, A. Kibrik uses the notion of *trace* independently from the generative, Chomskyan tradition, where *traces* are believed to be phonologically empty copies of displaced elements.

Contrary to Kibrik's claims, in OSDC there are multiple utterances similar to (10a) and (10b), and the internal possessor position in these utterances is occupied by a full-scale duplicate of the raised possessor, namely, a personal possessive pronoun, as exemplified in (11a–e):

(11a) OSDC: *[u nego$_{PSR}$] umerla [$_{NP}$ žena$_{PSM}$ ego$_{PSR}$]*
At he.GEN die.PAST.3SG wife.NOM he.POSS
'(As to him), his wife died'

(11b) OSDC: *[u menja$_{PSR}$] [$_{NP}$ ves$_{PSM}$ obyčnyj moj$_{PSR}$] devjanosta četyre kilogramma*
At I.GEN weight.NOM usual.NOM my.NOM ninety-four.NOM kilograms.NOM
'(As for me,) my average weight is ninety-four kilograms'

(11c) OSDC: *[u menja$_{PSR}$] [$_{NP}$ ni odin moj$_{PSR}$ odnogruppnik$_{PSM}$] /*
At I.GEN no one.NOM my.NOM group-mateNOM.
'(As for me,) none of my group mates…'
[$_{NP}$ ni odin moj$_{PSR}$ sokursnik$_{PSM}$] ne znajet!
no one.NOM my.NOM fellow student.NOM NEG know.PRES.3SG
'…none of my fellow students knows'

(11d) OSDC: *vot [u menja$_{PSR}$] v naprimer daže v [$_{NP}$ moem$_{PSR}$ sadovodstve$_{PSM}$]…*
well at I.GEN in say even in my.LOC gardening-community.LOC
'Well, (as for me,) even in, say, my gardening community…'

(11e) OSDC: *navigator [u nas$_{PSR}$] ne vidit [$_{NP}$ naših$_{PSR}$ dorog$_{PSM}$]*
GPS-navigator.NOM at I.GEN NEG see.PRES.3SG our.NOM roads.NOM
'Our navigator does not recognize our roads'

Moreover, sometimes discourse-configurational requirements demand that internal possessor constituent be placed to the left of the EPC, which makes the appearance[2] of the latter even more enigmatic:

(12) OSDC: *vot [$_{NP}$ moja$_{PSR}$ pervaja palatka$_{PSM}$] … [u menja$_{PSR}$] byla bez tenta //*
well my.NOM 1st.NOM tent.NOM … at I.GEN be.PST without canopy.NOM
'Well, my first tent had no canopy'

As to the examples (10a,b), we believe that the only thing which interdicts the use of the pronoun *svoj* in these contexts is the fact that *svoj* as a reflexive pronoun has to be properly governed by a coreferent element in subject or subject-like position, and these sentences lack such an element.

---

[2] The alternative choice is to assume the generative interpretation, according to which the IPC is topicalised to its visible position from the initial location c-commanded by the EPC.

3.5 Possible Explanations

Possessor doubling, especially its abnormal cases as more important for us, can be explained in several ways. The first possible explanation rests on the fact that in the case of pure, non-doubled EPC the possessum NP necessarily contains an empty variable bound by the external possessor [15: 333; 6: 9[3]]:

(13a) OSDC: *[u nee$_{PSR}$] kak by gematoma na [$_{NP}$ Ø$_{PSR}$ golove$_{PSM}$]*
at she.GEN like bruise.NOM on head.LOC
'She has something like a bruise on her head'

(13b) OSDC: *[u nego$_{PSR}$] [$_{NP}$ Ø$_{PSR}$ skorost'$_{PSM}$] sejčas (...) desjat' metrov v sekundu*
at he.GEN speed.NOM now ten meters.NOM in second.ACC
'Now his speed is 10 meters per second'

In the languages which feature both EPC and an overt article system such an empty variable is often replaced by a definite article [15: 334]:

(14) *Der Gedank, Mathurine zu verlassen... brach [mir$_{PSR}$] fast [$_{NP}$ das$_{PSR}$ Herz$_{PSM}$].*
The.NOM thought.NOM Mathurine to lose.INF… break.PAST I.DAT nearly the.ACC heart.ACC
'The idea of losing Mathurine … nearly broke my heart'

As we have already seen, in Russian this function (though complicated with a bunch of additional meanings) can be served by the reflexive possessive pronoun *svoj*. One may conjecture that in some cases where the use of the form *svoj* is undesirable the search for the elements able to fill the aforementioned position urges the speaker to resort to the seemingly superfluous pronouns *moj, tvoj, ego, ee.* Let us note here that such an "excessive" pronoun usage (even in contexts with no EPCs) has a long history, for possessive pronouns "contributing nothing to the meaning of an utterance" were already widespread in the Russian fiction of the first half of the nineteenth century [16: 77]. Moreover, even though the hypothesis that it could result from the French influence on this fragment of Russian syntax is to some extent justified, one has to admit that the competition between personal possessive and reflexive possessive pronouns dates back as far as the Old and Middle Russian periods, that is, it emerges much earlier than one may believe the everyday language usage of the educated part of the Russian society to be massively contaminated with any modern European language [Ibid.: 82–83]. Finally, notwithstanding that personal possessive pronouns were hugely widespread in the nineteenth century, they nevertheless were not the basic way of possessor encoding [Ibid.: 89].[4]

---

[3] The accessible text of [6] lacks page numeration. The page numbers are given according to their count.

[4] One must consider though that the Old Russian examples chosen by O. Pekelis come from "The Jewish War" by Joseph Flavius and "Alexandria", both translated into Old Russian from Greek.

The second explanation of PDC is based on a more radical hypothesis which implies that, in fact, the so-called external possessor constructions do not encode possessive relations at all [20: 132] or that constructions labeled as possessive can express a non-possessive meaning as well [22: 51]. For instance, I. Seržant gives an in-depth analysis of the European constructions which place the possessor and the possessum in separate constituents and demonstrates that the connection between the so-called external possessor and its possessum results from the application of various pragmatic rules aimed at finding the potential possessors for NP and consequently has nothing to do with the proper semantics of the construction in question [Seržant 2016: 138]. It is quite convincing especially in the light of the fact that EPCs tend to yield to various pragmatic limitations [13: 180]. Seržant also argues that there are multiple instances of "cancelling" the possessive relation between the potential external possessor and its possessum. Our data also provide us with such examples, cf. pair (15a) and (15b):

(15a) FICT: *gde? a / [u nee$_i$] da / mnogo [Ø$_i$ platjev]*
where? well at she.GET yes lot-of dresses.GEN
'Where? Well, she has got plenty of dresses.'
(15b) OSDC: *gde? a / [u nee$_i$] da / mnogo [našix$_j$ platjev]*
where? well at she.GET yes lot-of our.GEN dress-es.GEN
'Where? Well, she has got plenty of our dresses.'

The artificially constructed example (15a) features the null internal possessor $Ø_i$, which, by default, binds[5] the personal possessive pronoun *nee$_i$* contained in the *u-PP*.[6] Meanwhile, in the real example (15b) taken from OSDC the same pronoun has the referent *i* which obviously differs from the referent *j* of the internal possessor, and this mismatch of referents cancels the possible binding of the second element by the first one. Seržant proposes that the EPCs be better called *free affectee constructions* (or *FAC*), which he defines to be constructions which license the encoding of an extrathematic participant which (a) is to a certain degree affected by the situation and (b) does not change the syntactic positions of the core argument of the verb or become one of the core arguments [Ibid.: 153]. In addition, A. Zimmerling also states that no direct mapping holds between Russian *u*-PPs and the semantic domain of possession, calling the examples of non-possessive *u*-PPs pseudo-possessives [22: 51].

This idea means that PDC has got, in fact, only a single possessor, namely the internal one, whereas the external element has a different, non-possessive interpretation. This element denotes the entity, such that the actual situation takes place in its semantic domain and affects it in some manner. E. Paducheva, though not denying

---

[5] Informally: becomes the antecedent; for formal definition of binding and its conditions applicable in Standard Modern Russian see [17].

[6] Russian personal possessive pronouns are bound inside their finite clause by any nominal element except subject, and therefore they are said to feature anti-subject orientation [1: 709–10; 713–16].

the possessive character of *u*-PPs, nevertheless proposes a somewhat similar explanation, showing that the *u-PP* construction delimits a special world for the utterance, in which all relational terms are referentially dependent on it [Padučeva: 353]. In other words, this construction encodes the discursively salient participant which is at the same time not necessarily the possessor. The privileged status of this participant consists in the fact that it features autonomous reference and thus tends to appear in the utterance earlier than the elements which referentially depend on it [Ibid: 355]. The idea of privileged status and discursive saliency of the *u-PP* is considerably well fitted for the utterances (16a–c), especially considering the fact that even the works like [15], which generally do not doubt the possessive character of the u-PPs, nevertheless ascribe to them the semantic role of PLACE, as if they were designed to outline the stage for *un petit drame* of the utterance [21: 102]:

(16a) OSDC: *u nas v Sankt-Peterburge / iz vsej našej semji…*
at we.GEN in St. Petersburg from all.GEN our.GEN family.GEN
'Here in St. Peterburg from all our family…'

(16b) OSDC: *u nas / v naših komnatax net //*
at we.GEN in our.GEN rooms.GEN no
'There are none of them in our rooms'

(16c) OSDC: *čtoby u nas opjat' ne zatopilo naši mestnyje pul'ty upravlenija*
to at we.GEN again not flood.CONJ our.ACC local.ACC panels.ACC control.GEN
'In order to prevent another flooding of our local control panels'

It is also of some interest that when the scope of a *u*-PP contains several NPs, the choice of the NP for the overt possessum to appear may be also pragmatically motivated, as in (17):

(17) OSDC: *budut [$_{PP}$ u tebja$_i$] / v [$_{NP}$ tvoem$_i$ politexe] prosto [$_{NP}$ Ø$_i$ mozgi] () sušitsja*
be.FUT at you.GEN in your.LOC polytechnical.LOC just brains.NOM dry.INF
'In this boasted Polytechnical Institute you'll just boil your brains'

Here two NPs, namely *tvoem politexe* and *mozgi* are referentially dependent on the same nominal element *tebja* inside the *u-PP*, but only the first of them has a manifest internal possessor. The use of the personal pronoun *tvoj* in this case is obviously triggered by the fact that the Polytechnical Institute is presumably associated with the addressee as his or her possible future place of study, whereas the NP with the relational head *mozgi* features no overt possessive elements. A similar case of choosing between two possible hosts for an overt IPC is presented below:

(18) OSDC: *a [PP u menja$_i$] tam [NP Ø$_i$ ball xorošij] na [NP mojem$_i$ vtorom profile]*
and at me there score.NOM good.NOM on my.LOC second.LOC profile.LOC
'And I've got a good score on the second programme I've applied for'

Note that such additional semantic component is also characteristic of *svoj* in utterances with no PDCs, as in (19a,b):

(19a) OSDC: *ne nu počemu ty lezeš so svoim russkim eto Latvija //*
but well why you.NOM interfere.PRES.2SG. with your.INS Russian.INS it Latvia.NOM
'Well, why do you interfere with your Russian? It is Latvia, after all!'

(19b) OSDC: *on uže priexal so svoego Dalnego Vostoka % /*
he.NOM already come.PAST.MASC from own.GEN Far.GEN East.GEN
'He has already returned from the Far East'

Also noteworthy is the fact that in Russian child speech *u*-PPs appear on a very early development stage. For instance, in the speech of 2-year-old children *u*-PPs definitely prevail over possessive pronouns [11: 654]. S. Krasnoščekova claims [Ibid.] that at that stage they are the default way of encoding possessive relations, but in our opinion, one may decide as well that they encode the most prominent entity in the discourse, whereas possessive meaning is just a concomitant effect thereof.

So, in some cases discourse and pragmatic factors may really have heavier influence on the possessor marking than the semantic subclass of a certain possessum; therefore, the possessive character of EPCs in general and inside PDCs has to be thoroughly examined.

To sum up, the second explanation implies that PDC construction contains no redundancy whatsoever, for both of its parts—that is the internal possessor and the free affectee construction—function differently and do not overlap.

Both explanations reveal grammatical or pragmatical causes which trigger the use of PDC, and thus the general idea of its redundant character does not seem trustworthy.

4 Conclusion

The preliminary analysis of vernacular possessor doubling construction undertaken in this article demonstrates that (a) the meaning and pragmatic behavior of the doubled external and internal pronominal elements do not coincide; (b) the construction in question cannot be regarded as truly tautological or pleonastic. Moreover, it seems that the occurrence of external possessor / free affectee and that of internal possessor may be caused by completely different grammatical and semantic mechanisms.

The independency or, vice versa, interdependency of the two parts of possessor doubling construction in vernacular Russian speech as well as the question of whether they rely on the same discourse factors or not must be tested against the statistical data collected from OSDC. This is going to be the topic of our further work in this domain.

Acknowledgements Financial support for Mariia Korolkova's participation in this study was provided by a grant from St. Petersburg University (project №75254082 "Modelling of Russian megapolis citizen's communicative behavior in social, speech and pragmatic aspects using artificial intelligence methods"). Evgenii Sokolov would like to thank the members of the project for granting him access to the data of the "One Speech Day" corpus.

References

1. Avrutin, S.: The Structural Position of Bound Variables in Russian. Linguistic Inquiry. **25**(1) (Autumn 1994). pp. 709–727
2. Baldi, P., Nuti, Possession, A., Baldi, P., Cuzzolin, P. (eds.): New Perspectives on Historical Latin Syntax. Vol. 3. Constituent Syntax: Quantification, Numerals, Possession, Anaphora. Berlin/New York: De Gruyter Mouton, pp. 239–387 (2010)
3. Bogdanova-Beglarian, N., Sherstinova, T., Blinova, O., Martynenko, G.: An Exploratory Study on Sociolinguistic Variation of Russian Everyday Speech. In: Ronzhin, A., Potapova, R., Németh, G. (eds.) Speech and Computer. SPECOM 2016. Lecture Notes in Computer Science, vol 9811. Springer, Cham. pp. 99–107 (2016)
4. Brykina, M.M.: Jazykovye sposoby kodirovanija posessivnosti [Natural language possession encoding]. PhD Thesis. Moscow, (2009)
5. Golub, I.B.: Stilistika russkogo jazyka [Russian stilistics]. Iris Press, Moscow (2010)
6. Grashchenkov P., Grashchenkova A.: Possessive Reflexives in Russian. In: Proceedings of FASL-15. Toronto: Ann Arbor, (2006) No pages.
7. Haspelmath, M.: External Possession in a European Areal Perspective. Barshi, I., Payne, D. (eds.) External Possession. Amsterdam: Benjamins, pp. 1–20 (1999)
8. Kibrik, A.E., Brykina, M.M., Leontjev, A.P., Xitrov, A.N.: Russkije posessivnyje konstrukcii v svete korpusno-statističeskogo issledovanija [A corpus and statistical approach to Russian possessive constructions]. In: Voprosy jazykoznanija [Issues in Linguistics], 1. pp. 16–45 (2006)
9. Kibrik, A.E.: Vnešnij possessor kak rezul'tat raščeplenija valentnostej [External possessor as the result of argument split]. In: Lomdin, L.L., Krysin, L.P., (eds.) Slovo v tekste i v slovare. Sbornik statej k semidesjatiletiju akademika Yu.D. Apresjana [Word in text and vocabulary. A Festschrift for Yu. D. Apresjan's 70th anniversary]. Moscow: "Jazyki russkoj kul'tury", pp. 434–446 (2000)
10. Kobozeva, I.M.: O posessivnosti v russkom jazyke: posessivnye predikaty vs. genitive [On Possession in Russian: Possessive Predicates vs. Genitive]. In: Acta Linguistica Petropolitana. Trudy Instituta linguvističeskix issledovanij. Vol. IX, part I. St. Petersburg: "Nauka", pp. 122–126 (2015)
11. Krasnoščekova, S.V.: Status pritjažatel'nyx mestoimenij 3 lica v reči rebenka [The Status of 3rd Person Possessive Pronouns in Child Speech]. In: Acta Linguistica Petropolitana. Vol. XI, Part II. pp. 647–658 (2015)
12. Mel'čuk, I.A. Iordanskaja L.N.: Glaza Mashi golubye versus Glaza u Mashi golubye: Choosing between two Russian constructions in the domain of body parts. In: I.A. Mel'čuk. Russkij jazyk v modelu "Smysl<=>Tekst" [Russian Language in the "Meaning<=>Text" Model]. Moscow: "Jazyki slavjanskoj kul'tury". pp. 135–165 (1995)
13. Nam Hye Hyun.: Study on the Russian external possessor constructions as a diathetic phenomenon and their semantic-discursive functions. In: Russian Linguistics **37**. pp. 175–191 (2013)

14. Paducheva, E.V.: Splitting of possessive NPs and external possessor in Russian, Kim, J.-Y., Partee, B. H., & Lander, Y. A. (Eds.), Possessives and beyond: semantics and syntax (University of Massachusetts Occasional Papers in Linguistics, 29. Boston, Massachusetts, pp. 351–363 (2004)
15. Paykin, K., Peteghem M.: van. External vs. Internal Possessor Structures and Inalienability in Russian. Russian Linguistics 2003, **27**(3). pp. 329–348 (2003)
16. Pekelis, O.: Moj ili svoj? Ob evolucii pritjažatel'nyx mestoimenij v russkom jazyke posle XVIII veka [Moj or svoj? On the Evolution of Possessive Pronouns in the Post-18th Century Russian]. In: Russian Linguistics, **45**. pp. 75–91
17. Rappaport, G.: On Anaphor Binding in Russian In: Natural Language and Linguistic Theory 4. D. Reidel Publishing Company. pp. 97–120 (1986)
18. Rosental, D.E.: Praktičeskaja stilistika russkogo jazyka [A Practical Handbook of Russian Stylistics]. 5th ed. Moscow: "Vysšaja škola", (1987)
19. Bogdanova-Beglarian, N.V., Sherstinova, T.Yu., Baeva, E.M., Blinova, O.V., Martynenko, G.Ya., Yermolova, O.B., Ryko, A.I. (ed.) Russkij jazyk povsednevnogo obščenija: osobennosti funkcionirovanija v raznyx social'nyx gruppax [Russian Vernacular Language and The Peculiarity of its Functioning in Various Social Groups]. St. Petersburg: LAIKA, pp. 244 (2016)
20. Seržant, I.: A. External possession and constructions that may have it. In: STUF—Language Typology and Universals, **69**(1), pp. 131–169 (2016)
21. Svetozarova, N.D. (ed.): Fonetika spontannoj reči [Phonetics of Spontaneous Speech]. L. (1988)
22. Tesnière, L.: Éléments de syntaxe structurale. Librairie C. Klinksieck, Paris (1959)
23. Zimmerling, A.: Possessor Raising and Slavic Clitics. In: Irina Kor Chahine (ed.) Current Studies in Slavic Linguistics. John Benjamins Publishing Company, (2013)

Spoken Corpora: Phonetics Studies

Formant Trajectories in Different Languages

Vera Evdokimova and Maria Maksimova

Abstract This paper compares formant transitions in English, French and German monophthongs after labial and lingual (tip, front and back) consonants. The monophthongs were extracted from words, sentences and texts read by female speakers. The formant values were measured at 9 points within each vowel. Formant transitions were plotted on line graphs. The derivatives of the resulting functions at 9 points were calculated to compare the slopes of different formant trajectories. The formant values were converted from Hertz to Bark in order to evaluate the variability of the formant structure. The results indicated that the formant transitions in English and German vowels were similar after tip and front consonants. In labial consonantal context, the dynamics of formant transitions did not show any clear trends. After back lingual consonants, the formant transitions were similar for all the three languages. The region in which the greatest slope occurred was the same for French and German monophthongs, but different for English vowels. The variability of formant structure was lower in the back monophthongs compared to the front vowels in English and German data. However, in French monophthongs, the transition from one critical bandwidth to another became more frequent with backness.

Keywords Acoustic phonetics · Formant transitions · Formant structure variability · Bark scale

1 Introduction

The quality of a speech sound is determined by the movement of articulators. Another important factor is the regions of the vocal tract that influence the sound spectrum. The spectrum is formed as a sound passes through the upper vocal tract (i.e. the oral cavity

V. Evdokimova · M. Maksimova (✉)
St. Petersburg State University, Saint-Petersburg, Russia
e-mail: st076821@student.spbu.ru

V. Evdokimova
e-mail: v.evdokimova@spbu.ru

P. Eismont et al. (eds.), *Literature, Language and Computing*,
https://doi.org/10.1007/978-981-96-0990-1_10

and the nasal cavity). The cavities of the upper vocal tract act as resonators increasing those sound frequencies that are equal or close to natural resonating frequencies of the resonators. The increased frequencies are referred to as formants. A natural resonating frequency of a cavity is determined by its shape, which can be changed by certain movements of articulators located in this cavity [3].

Since 1950s, a number of studies have reported a crucial role of the first two formants in vowel quality. The value of the first formant (F1) correlates with vowel height, while the second formant (F2) correlates with vowel backness. These parameters are essential for vowel discrimination and, consequently, for automatic speech recognition [3].

Besides formant values, formant trajectories (or formant transitions) are also important for vowel discrimination [4]. In connected speech, vowels rarely occur in isolation. Generally, they are preceded and/or followed by other speech sounds. Therefore, the acoustic features of vowels can change depending on the characteristics of the neighboring consonants or vowels. Vowel quality is primarily affected by the loci of the neighboring consonants and by secondary consonantal articulations (e.g. palatalization, labialization, etc.) that modify the shape of the vocal tract [8].

The dynamics of formant trajectories is studied in acoustic phonetics. Much of the previous research on this subject is based on two approaches. The first approach considers formant transitions as sets of discrete values. The second approach, on the contrary, assumes that there exists a quantitative relationship between formant values within a formant transition. The advantage of this latter approach might be that the dynamics of acoustic characteristics play a more significant role in speech perception than static features of sounds [4].

The second approach is adopted by Broad and Clermont [4]. Their hypothesis is that a set of formant trajectories produced by a speaker is characterized by similarity relations and therefore is connected by linear scaling. A linear scaling model is designed in order to define the relations between consonants and vowels in VC syllables. This model is based on the distance from the consonant locus to the vowel target and on the shape of the formant transition between the consonant and the vowel. The shapes of the formant trajectories are depicted as exponential relationships the asymptotes of which correspond to vowel targets. The model is evaluated on VC syllables containing vowels /ɪ, ɛ, æ, a, ɔ, u, ʌ, ɝ/ and consonants /b, d, g/ produced by a male American speaker.

The results indicate that loci and targets connect a speaker's range of formant transitions into a system characterized by scaling relationships between its elements. Another finding is that the relative positions of vowel formant trajectories on the frequency axis are not affected by phonetic context or position within the syllable. This suggests that phonetic context does not influence all acoustic features of a vowel. It can cause formant values within trajectories to increase or decrease. The context might also extend or narrow the range of formant values within transitions.

Sets of formant trajectories in a speaker formed the central focus of a study by Carre and Mrayati [5] who investigated formant transitions between French vowels. Carre and Mrayati found that, as a rule, trajectories between vowels are not straight. In addition, transitions between each pair of vowels often intersect formant spaces of other vowels. For example, a trajectory between the vowels /i/ and /œ/ is partly located in the formant spaces of /e/ and /ø/. Interestingly, some formant transitions could be produced by a speaker more frequently than others. As a result, trajectories from a vowel to several other vowels may intersect.

The dynamic acoustic characteristics of vowels were also studied by Stachurski and colleagues [14]. This research confirmed that formant trajectories are important for vowel perception. Therefore, incorrect formant transitions may increase the error probability in vowel recognition. However, vowel recognition can be improved due to a broader linguistic context (e.g. lexical cues).

While previously mentioned studies mainly focus on formant trajectories in monophthongs, Watson and Harrington [16] also address transitions in diphthongs. This research highlights the particular importance of formant trajectories for the recognition of diphthongs. Bladon (1985, cited in Watson and Harrington [16]) explains this by the fact that a transition between two vowel targets occurs in diphthongs. Moreover, Watson and Harrington draw on several works of Nearey [1, 10] which demonstrated that some monophthongs have a quasidiphthongal quality. Therefore, it is crucial to consider not only mean formant values at the target, but also formant movements within monophthongs. In particular, formant contours allow to distinguish pairs of tense and lax monophthongs.

Additionally, mean formant values are not sufficient for vowel recognition as a vowel with close F1 and F2 (or, F2 and F3) might be identified incorrectly. Moreover, the formants that are characterized by low amplitude may not be tracked [16].

Another significant feature for vowel recognition is duration. Using this parameter could enhance the discrimination of monophthongs as well as the distinction of monophthongs and diphthongs [16].

Vowels can also be characterized by the slope of their formant trajectories. This feature is determined by the distance between the consonantal locus and vowel target and, consequently, by the formant values of the consonant and the vowel. Slopes are of importance for distinguishing tense and lax monophthongs as well as for discriminating monophthongs from diphthongs that have similar formant values at the first target. However, similarly to mean formant values, slopes cannot possibly be used as a single parameter for vowel recognition as the slopes of most monophthongs are similar [16].

The aim of the present study is to compare formant transitions in English, German and French monophthongs in several consonantal contexts. The comparison is also based on the shape of formant slopes. The latter parameter has not been sufficiently examined in previous research.

2 Materials and Methods

The monophthongs in labial and lingual (tip, front and back) consonantal contexts were obtained from sentences, words and texts read by female speakers. Only the preceding consonantal context was considered. In total, voices from 5 English speakers, 4 French speakers and 5 German speakers were used for the study. The English speech samples were taken from the LUCID corpus (London UCL Clear Speech in Interaction Database) designed by Baker and Hazan [2], and from the audio recordings for the manual "MyGrammarLab: Advanced C1/C2" [6]. The French data were drawn from the audio application for the manual "EDITO C1 Méthode de français" [12]. The German recordings were collected from the audio course which was a part of the manual "Wir-3" [9].

In total, 12 English, 10 French and 16 German phonemes were examined. For each language, 20 examples of each vowel in each context were analyzed. The vowels selected were labeled phonetically using Praat. Diphthongs and nasal vowels were not included in this set for the reason that diphthongs are not presented in the phoneme inventory of French, while nasal vowels do not exist as phonemes in English and German.

To plot formant trajectories, F1 and F2 values were measured at 9 points within each vowel using a script from the SpeCT (The Speech Corpus Toolkit for Praat). After that, the derivatives of the resulting functions were calculated in order to compare the slopes of formant transitions in the three languages. To evaluate formant structure variability, the formant values were converted from Hz to Bark.

The formant trajectories in English, French and German monophthongs were compared on the basis of shape, slope and the variability of formant structure.

3 The Shapes of Formant Transitions

Some formant values that were obtained using a script corresponded neither to theoretically expected values, nor to those that were actually observed in a spectrogram. In such cases, formant values were manually corrected.

The formant trajectories for each vowel were constructed as scatter plots with smooth lines using Excel (see Fig. 1). To illustrate the formant transitions that are characteristic of each vowel in all the three languages in each of the contexts, averaged plots were designed (see Figs. 2, 3 and 4).

The results indicated that formant transitions differed most after nasal consonants. Interestingly, formant values were observed to decrease as well as to increase in nasal context, although formant values generally fall when surrounded by nasal consonants [8]. F2 values in German vowels in each context were higher than in the other languages. Relative to German and French monophthongs, F2 values in English vowels were the lowest. Nevertheless, F1 values were, as a rule, the greatest in English monophthongs (see Figs. 2, 3 and 4).

Regarding French vowels, a difference was observed between rounded and unrounded phonemes. French unrounded monophthongs were characterized by less significant formant movements in the first transition region compared to English and German unrounded vowels. However, French rounded vowels showed more steep contours of the first transition region in comparison with rounded monophthongs of the other languages. This means that formant changes were, on average, greater in

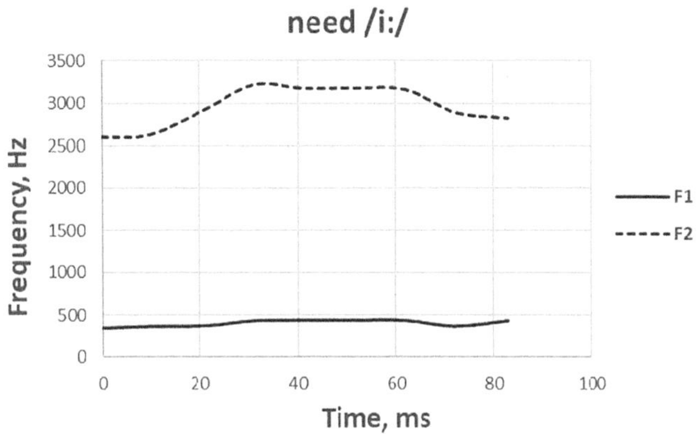

Fig. 1 A plot of F1 and F2 trajectories of the vowel /i:/ in the English word 'need'

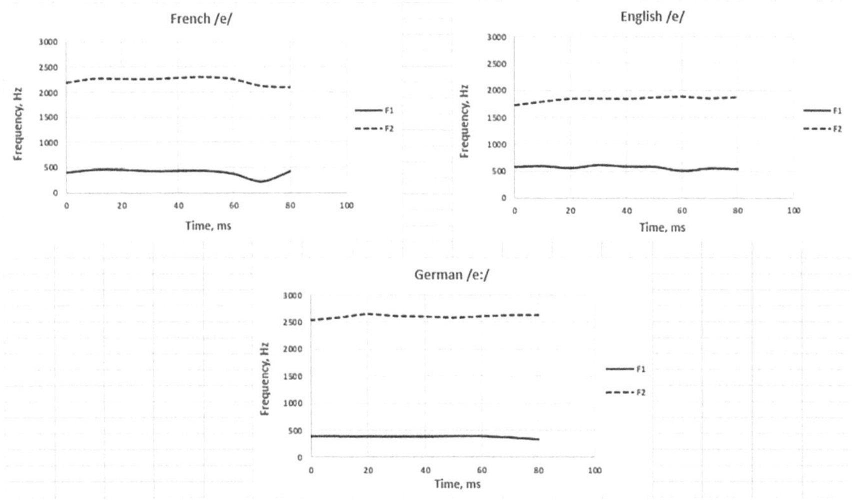

Fig. 2 Averaged plots of the formant trajectories of the vowel /e/ (/e:/) after labial consonants in English, French and German

the first transition region of French rounded vowels relative to English and German rounded monophthongs.

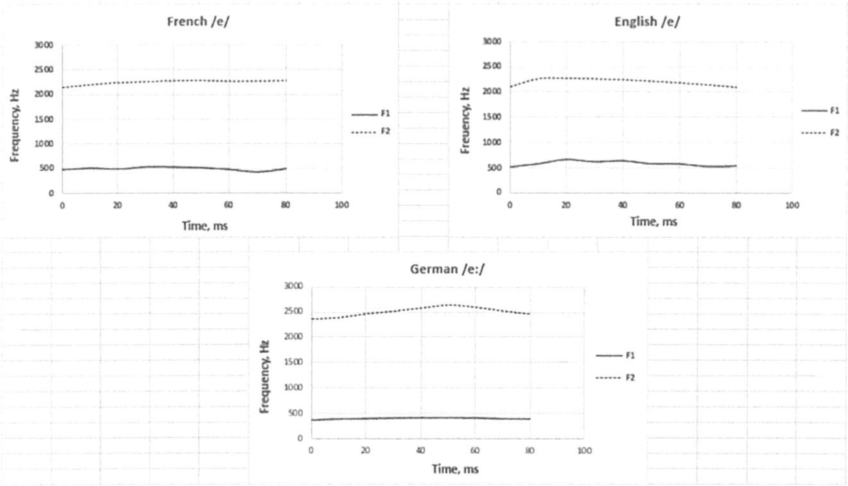

Fig. 3 Averaged plots of the formant trajectories of the vowel /e/ (/e:/) after tip and front consonants in English, French and German

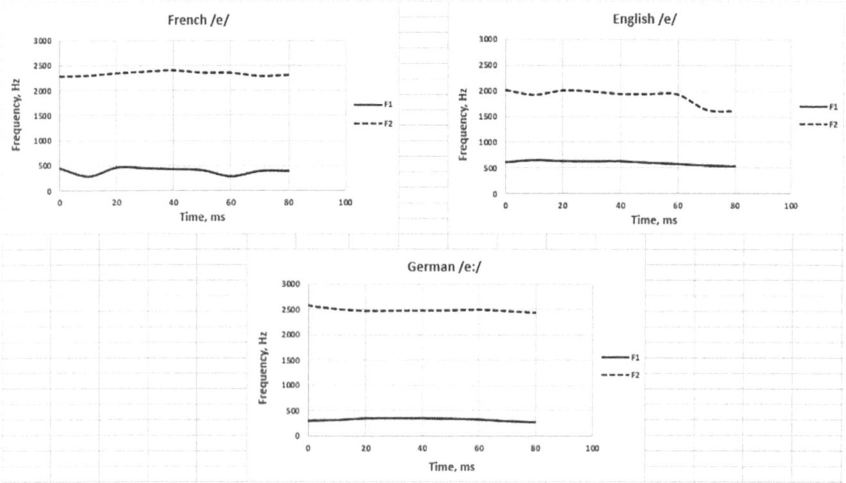

Fig. 4 Averaged plots of the formant trajectories of the vowel /e/ (/e:/) after back consonants in English, French and German

4 The Slopes of Formant Trajectories

To calculate the derivatives of F1 and F2 functions, trend lines were constructed in Excel. The roots of the trend line equations were then identified. These values were plotted in order to illustrate the rate of change of the formant values.

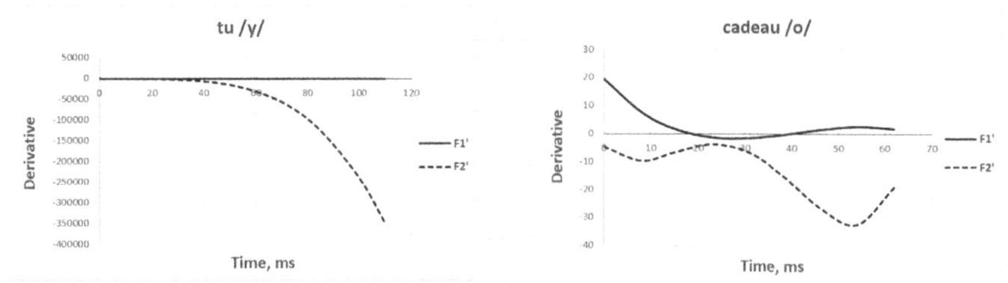

Fig. 5 The slopes of F1 and F2 trajectories of the French vowels /y/ and /o/

The results revealed that F2 slopes were generally higher than F1 slopes in every language (see Figs. 5, 6 and 7). However, the languages differed from each other to a certain extent. Firstly, in English and German, higher slopes were observed in back vowels in all the contexts (see Figs. 6 and 7). On the contrary, in French, front close vowels showed higher slopes. The highest slopes in this language occurred in vowel center or near the end of a formant trajectory (see Fig. 5). In English and German vowels, by contrast, the highest slopes occurred more often in the transition region from a preceding consonant to a vowel (see Figs. 6 and 7).

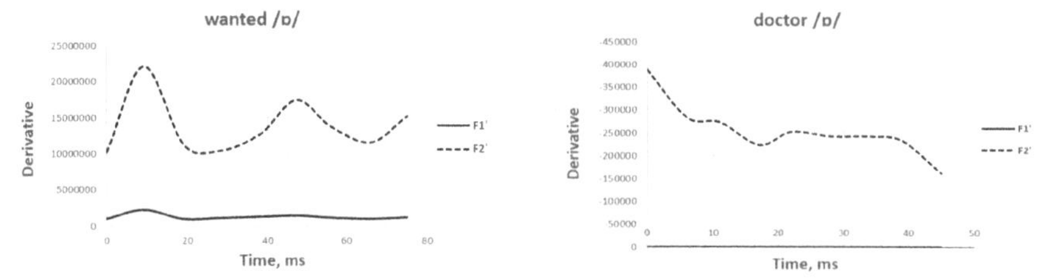

Fig. 6 The slopes of F1 and F2 trajectories of the English vowel /ɒ/

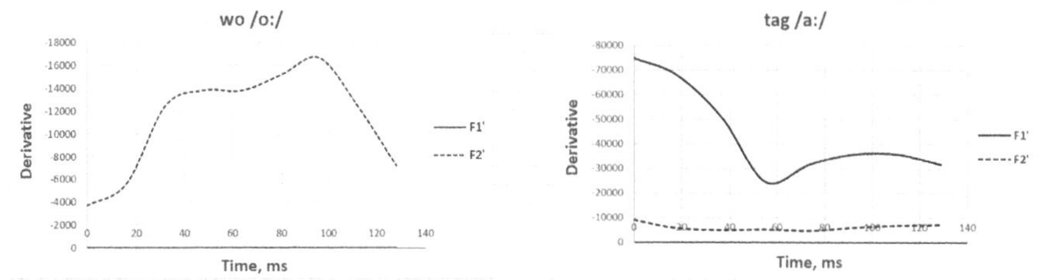

Fig. 7 The slopes of F1 and F2 trajectories of the German vowels /o:/ and /a:/

5 Formant Structure Variability

In order to evaluate the formant structure variability in the monophthongs, the formant values calculated before in Hz were converted into values on the psychoacoustic Bark scale. The following formula was used [15] (Tables 1, 2 and 3):

$$6 * \sinh^{-1}\left(\frac{Hz}{600}\right)^{40} \tag{1}$$

Formant variability was the most significant in F1 of English vowels. Overall, F1 variability was higher than that of F2. Contrary to English monophthongs, German vowels demonstrated the lowest variability.

Table 1 Averaged F1 and F2 values of the French vowel /ɔ/ in labial context given in Hz and Barks

French /ɔ/			
F1		F2	
Hz	Barks	Hz	Barks
694	5.9	1208	8.7
689	5.9	1204	8.7
689	5.9	1216	8.7
684	5.9	1270	9.0
688	5.9	1280	9.0
721	6.1	1380	9.4
717	6.1	1377	9.4
724	6.1	1397	9.5
723	6.1	1329	9.2

Table 2 Averaged F1 and F2 values of the English vowel /ɒ/ in labial context given in Hz and Barks

English /ɒ/			
F1		F2	
Hz	Barks	Hz	Barks
490	4.5	1086	8.1
418	3.9	1091	8.2
582	5.2	1078	8.1
573	5.1	1094	8.2
579	5.1	1105	8.2
538	4.8	1119	8.3
446	4.1	1140	8.4
425	4.0	1144	8.4
555	5.0	1128	8.3

Table 3 Averaged F1 and F2 values of the German vowel /ɔ/ in labial context given in Hz and Barks

German /ɔ/			
F1		F2	
Hz	Barks	Hz	Barks
598	5.3	1013	7.8
646	5.6	1045	7.9
692	5.9	1082	8.1
754	6.3	1099	8.2
735	6.2	1174	8.5
744	6.2	1283	9.0
739	6.2	1326	9.2
730	6.2	1396	9.5
698	6.0	1346	9.3

In addition, English and German back vowels showed less formant variability in comparison with front vowels in these languages. An opposite tendency was observed for French monophthongs. The formant structure variability increased from front to back French vowels.

6 Conclusions

This study has shown that both similarities and differences could be observed in the formant trajectories of English, French and German vowels. Monophthongs differ from each other not only in terms of formant transitions, but also in terms of formant structure variability.

As known from many theoretical works, acoustic features of vowels are determined by their articulatory characteristics [3, 8]. Some findings of this research illustrate this correlation. For example, the formant values of back vowels were more variable than those of front vowels in French. Similarly, the steepness of the first transition regions varied between French rounded and unrounded vowels. It was also revealed that F1 values are overall more variable than F2 values. This implies that tongue position in the oral cavity from back to front changes more frequently than tongue location in the vertical plane. However, the slopes of F2 trajectories appeared to be higher than those of F1 trajectories. This indicates that vowel height generally changes more significantly within monophthongs than backness does.

The indicated differences between languages suggest that automatic language recognition can be based on formant transitions and on the shapes of formant slopes. Formant structure variability can also be used for automatic speech recognition (ASR). For example, Shannon and Paliwal [13] revealed that speech recognition based on the Bark scale demonstrated similar performance as speech recognition based on mel-frequency cepstral coefficients.

Formant trajectories are of importance for ASR systems. Particularly, formant transitions are used for ASR combined with MFCC. MFCC is a method of extracting speech features by obtaining speech spectral power. Then, spectral powers are multiplied by functions that approximate jBark or mel scale. Thus, spectral powers are divided into 20–24 energy values (this number is equal to that of critical bands). After that, a logarithm is applied to convert to decibels. The final step to get the MFCC is an inverse cosine transform [11].

There is evidence that MFCC-based ASR systems can be advanced when formant trajectories are incorporated. In particular, using formant trajectories is likely to improve the performance of forensic voice comparison systems. Forensic voice comparison is needed to define whether a suspect and an offender are the same person or different people on the basis of their speech samples. Enhancing the quality of this process can increase the reliability of evidence provided to courts by forensic experts [7].

References

1. Andruski, J. E., Nearey, T. M.: On the sufficiency of compound target specification of isolated vowels in /bVb/ syllables. J. Acoust. Soc. Am. **91**, 390–410 (1992)
2. Baker, R., Hazan, V.: LUCID: A corpus of spontaneous and read clear speech in British English (2010)
3. Bondarko, L.A.: Osnovy obshhej fonetiki: uchebnoe posobie dlya studentov lingvisticheskikh i filologicheskikh spetsial'nostej [Basics of phonetics—a textbook for students of linguistics and philology]. Moscow (2004)
4. Broad, D.J., Clermont, F.: Target-locus scaling methods for modeling families of formant trajectories. J. Phon. **38**, 337–359 (2010)
5. Carre, R., Mrayati, M.: Vowel-vowel trajectories and region modeling. J. Phonetics **19**(3/4), 433–444 (1991)
6. Foley, M., Hall, D:. MyGrammarLab. Advanced. C1-C2. Book with key and MyEnglishLab, 410 p. Pearson Education Ltd. Harlow (2012)
7. Hughes, V., Foulkes, P., Wood, S.: Formant dynamics and durations of um improve the performance of automatic speaker recognition systems. In: Proceedings of the 16th Australasian Conference on Speech Science and Technology (ASSTA), University of Western Sydney, Australia (2016)
8. Kodzasov, S.V., Krivnova, O.F.: Obshchaya fonetika [General phonetics]. Russian State University for Humanities Press, Moscow (2001)
9. Motta, G.: Wir 3 Lehrerhandbuch. Klett, Stuttgart (2007)
10. Nearey, T. M., Assmann, P. F.: Modelling the role of inherent spectral change in vowel identification. J. Acoust. Soc. Am. **80**, 1297– 1308 (1986)
11. O'Shaughnessy, D.: Acoustic analysis for automatic speech recognition. Proc. IEEE **101**(5), 1038–1053 (2013)
12. Pinson, C., Bourmayan, A., Cros, I. (eds.): Methode de francais. C1 - Livre + DVD-Rom, 168 p. Didier, Paris
13. Shannon, B.J., Paliwal, K.K.: A comparative study of filter bank spacing for speech recognition. In: Microelectronic Engineering Research Conference, vol. 41, pp. 310–312 (2003)
14. Stachurski, M., Summers, R.J., Roberts, B.: The verbal transformation effect and the perceptual organization of speech: influence of formant transitions and F0-contour continuity. Hear. Res. **323**, 22–31 (2015)

15. Wang, S., Sekey, A., Gersho, A.: An objective measure for predicting subjective quality of speech coders. IEEE J. Sel. Areas Commun. **10**(5), 819–829 (1992)
16. Watson, C.I., Harrington, J.: Acoustic evidence for dynamic formant trajectories in Australian English vowels. J. Acoust. Soc. Am. **106**, 458–468 (1999)

Russian Backchannel Vocalizations: Approaches to Description

Daniil Vasiliev and Elena Shamina

Abstract The paper offers a concise description of Russian discourse elements extracted from the SibLing Corpus of Russian Dialogue Speech. Only vocalizations that have no lexical meaning and function as backchannel cues are considered. The approaches to analysis embrace establishing their occurrence frequency, sound quality, and prosodic features with the help of computer acoustic tools. Russian backchannel vocalizations are shown to be of two recurrent types and to contain sounds outside the phoneme inventory of the Russian language. They are typically pronounced with a rising tone and are easily recognized by Russian speakers as backchannel responses even out of context. Certain discourse markers that are used by the speaker and seem to trigger backchannel vocalizations from the listener have been observed. The findings lead to the conclusion that Russian dialogue discourse is strictly organized and systematic.

Keywords SibLing dialogue corpus · Backchannel vocalizations · The Russian language

1 Introduction: Backchannel Vocalizations

Backchannels are short conventional speech signals such as Russian aga (uh-huh) or da nu (really?) produced by the listener. They signify that the message conveyed by the speaker is received and understood and thus encourage the person who has the turn to continue with his or her story without actually relinquishing the turn [1, 6, 9].

It should be noted that although the discourse elements described in the paper fall into the same category with what is typically known as backchannel responses in a way that they also respond to the contents of the speaker's utterance, are optional

D. Vasiliev (✉) · E. Shamina
St. Petersburg University, Universitetskaya Emb. 7/9, 199034 Saint-Petersburg, Russia
e-mail: d.vasiliev@spbu.ru

E. Shamina
e-mail: e.shamina@spbu.ru

P. Eismont et al. (eds.), *Literature, Language and Computing*,
https://doi.org/10.1007/978-981-96-0990-1_11

and do not require acknowledgment [7], they lack lexical meaning. Therefore, such signals as tak (right) or khorosho (good) that occur in Russian conversations go beyond the phenomena referred to as vocalizations that constitute the subject matter of the study.

The main objective of the paper is to give a multifaceted description of backchannel vocalizations present in the SibLing Corpus of Russian Dialogue Speech, which includes their listing, establishing their occurrence frequency, and also analyzing their acoustic properties. An attempt to determine their linguacultural nature through an auditory perception experiment has also been undertaken.

The results obtained can provide valuable insights into cooperation strategies used by native Russian speakers in dialogue discourse. They can also be applied to improve the methodology of teaching Russian as a second language and to develop speech recognition and synthesis programs.

2 Materials and Methods

The backchannel vocalizations analyzed in the paper have been extracted from the SibLing Corpus of Russian Dialogue Speech. The corpus was developed at the Department of Phonetics of Saint Petersburg State University in 2020 by a group of linguists supervised by T. Kachkovskaya. It includes dialogues recorded under studio conditions when native speakers of Russian, male and female siblings aged 23 to 40, were asked to complete two speaking tasks [4]. The fact that the speakers were not able to see each other was supposed to trigger conversational cooperation and the use of backchannel responses. The backchannel vocalizations analyzed in the paper have been extracted from 5 dialogues between 6 females and 3 males (56 min of the recording). The task performed by the interlocutors involved guiding a partner through a set of schematic maps. One of the female respondents participated in two dialogues which explains the uneven number of speakers.

Close observation of discourse strategies applied by Russian speakers in the corpus material helps to formulate the approaches to describing backchannel vocalizations. Their analysis is performed in several steps. The first stage involves auditory and expert analyses of the context resulting in allocation of a signal perceived into the category of vocalizations. The second stage of analysis which includes the use of computer speech analysis tools (Praat and Wave Assistant) is aimed at giving an accurate phonetic transcription and acoustic description (F0, duration) of the discourse elements identified. The data validity is assessed in a perception experiment. Finally, the data obtained is statistically analyzed.

3 Results and Discussion

3.1 General Characteristics: Types and Occurrence Frequency

As a result of contextual analysis of the material presented above, 85 backchannel vocalizations have been identified. The majority of them are produced by female speakers (92%). Notwithstanding the impressive difference between their occurrence frequency in men's and women's speech, the fact does not seem to allow generalizations. Yet the analysis of three dialogues featuring two male, two female, and two different sex speakers suggests that male speakers can be generally more reluctant to use supportive conversational means than females. For example, in the research material two male native speakers of Russian have only produced 5 backchannel vocalizations in a 12-min-long conversation, whereas two female interlocutors have used three times as many discursive elements in a conversation of the same duration. In a 10-min conversation between two interlocutors of different gender, the female speaker produced 20 vocalizations, while there were only two discursive elements that belonged to her male counterpart. The rate at which the discursive elements in question are used can be socially and culturally predetermined (as well as subject to individual variation) and further analysis of non-related interlocutors' conversations can provide a more accurate insight into the matter.

Russian backchannel vocalizations identified fall into 2 types, roughly represented by conventional spellings aga (uh-huh) and ugu (mm-hmm). Both of them consist of two open syllables. The first syllable is unstressed and usually starts with a glottal plosion that is followed by either a bilabial nasal syllabic sonorant or a central mid-open vowel, while at the beginning of the stressed syllable speakers produce either a velar or glottal voiced fricative which is followed by either a bilabial nasal syllabic sonorant or a back open vowel (Fig. 1). It is worth noticing that Russian backchannel vocalizations not only slightly vary in form, but contain sounds that go beyond the phoneme inventory of the Russian language. For example, the usually voiced glottal fricative only occurs as a facultative variant of /g/ in a limited number of contexts [13].

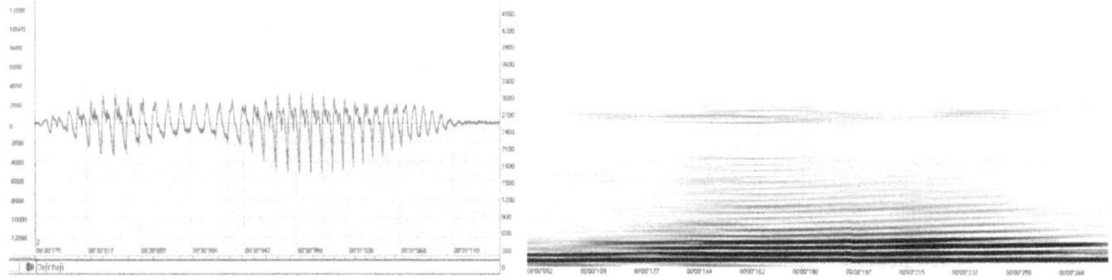

Fig. 1 Oscillogram and spectrogram of [0294–0266 mm] vocalization

The discursive elements under study occur in the research material with different frequency: of [0294–0266 mm] in 59% and [0294–0266 mm] in 41% of the cases, so the former seems to be predominant. Although O. Gerasimenko in her article suggests that there is a wider variety of backchannel responses in Russian speech [9], a closer look at the discursive elements identified by the linguist shows that they should be referred to as incipient speakerships (which also fall into the category of backchannel responses) [3] rather than vocalizations. Therefore, it can be concluded that the number of recurrent Russian backchannel vocalizations is rather limited.

3.2 *Prosodic Characteristics*

Further instrumental analysis of the Russian backchannel vocalizations identified reveals that their mean duration varies between 281 for [0294–0266 mm] and 397 ms for [0294–0266 mm]. It also shows that both discursive elements are frequently (in 82% of the cases) marked by falling-rising or rising intonation (Fig. 2). Similar results (66%) have been obtained in the research conducted by Guseva [10].

The diapason of F0 changes in backchannel vocalizations with a rising tone ranges from 1 to 4 semitones. The flat tone is used by native speakers of Russian in about 12%, whereas the falling tone in only 5% of the cases.

The melodic contour of the vocalization depicted in Fig. 3 above shows a rise in the F0 which is localized on the stressed syllable. The global F0 maximum equals 227 Hz, whereas its global minimum is 207 Hz. The pitch change interval constitutes 2 semitones.

In **Fig. 4**, the second most frequently occurring F0 change pattern of backchannel vocalizations in the Russian language can be seen. The unstressed syllable of [0294–0266 mm] is marked by a F0 fall whose interval equals 3 semitones. The stressed syllable, on the other hand, is characterized by a 2-semitone pitch increase.

Although falling and flat tones are rarely produced by native speakers of Russian to mark backchannel vocalizations, the cases of their use should also be exemplified in

Fig. 2 Intonation types in Russian backchannel vocalizations

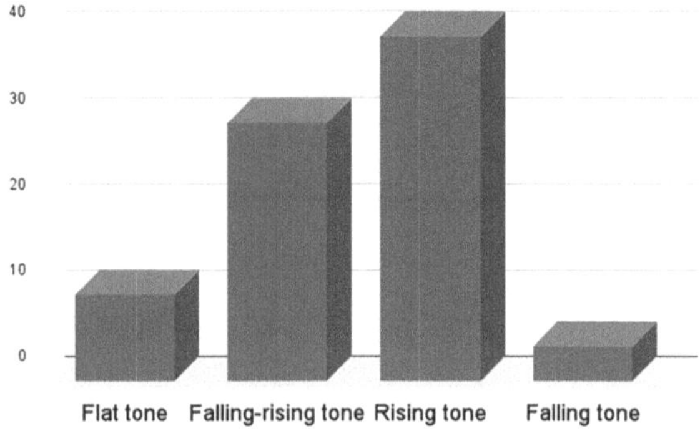

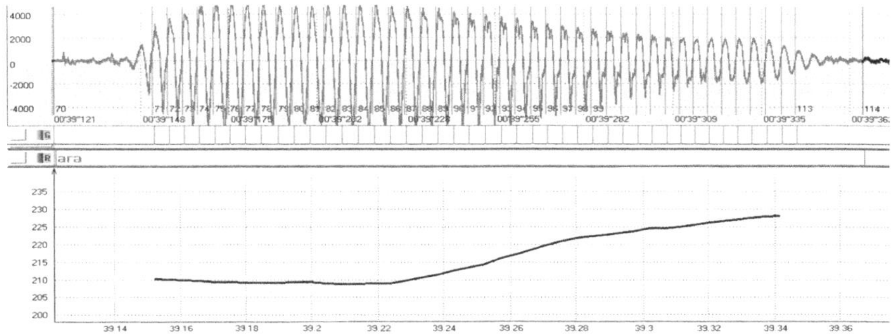

Fig. 3 Rising tone in [0294–0266 mm] vocalization (female speaker)

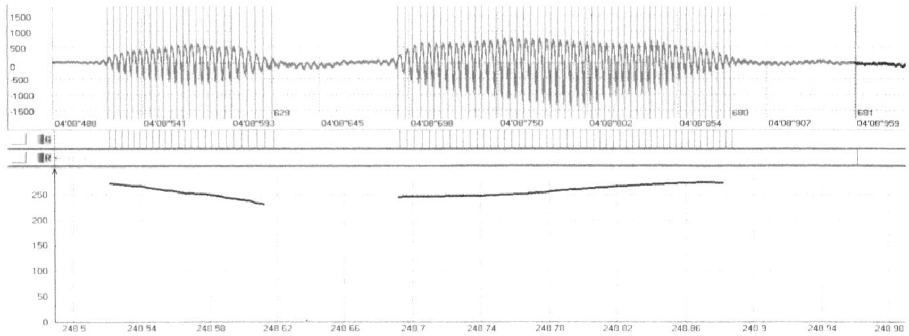

Fig. 4 Falling-rising tone in [0294–0266 mm] vocalization (female speaker)

the paper. Figure 5 above demonstrates a falling pitch change occurring in a discursive element [0294–0266 mm] uttered by a female speaker. The F0 is decreasing throughout the whole duration of the signal until it reaches the global minimum at 195 Hz. The pitch fall interval constitutes 3 semitones. No fluctuations of F0 in backchannel vocalization [0294–0266 mm] can be observed in Fig. 6 below.

3.3 Perception

An auditory perception experiment has been carried out as one of the approaches to backchannel vocalization study. The respondents, 71 native speakers of Russian of different age, occupation, and social status, were asked to listen to six backchannel vocalizations (2 Russian, 2 English, and 2 Japanese) and guess what meaning each of them could convey. The choice of the auditory stimuli can be explained by the fact that the analysis presented in this article constitutes a part of a wider study of backchannel vocalizations in Russian, English, and Japanese. The questionnaire in Russian (alongside its translations into English and Japanese) was uploaded onto

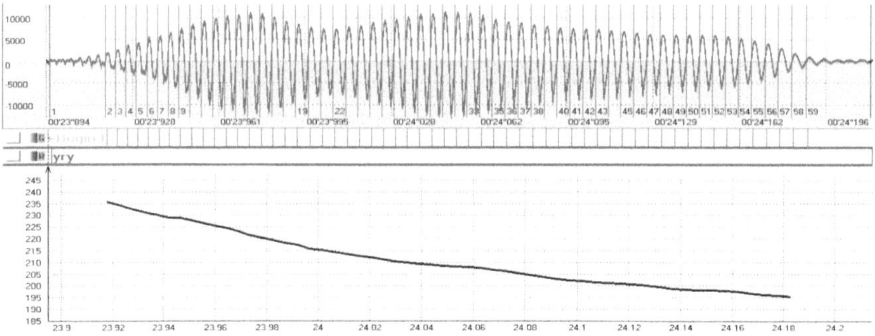

Fig. 5 Falling tone in [0294–0266 mm] vocalization (female speaker)

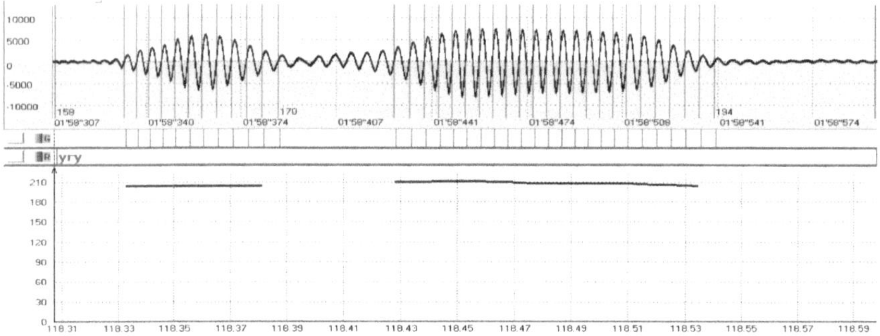

Fig. 6 Flat tone in [0294–0266 mm] vocalization (female speaker)

Google Forms, with only audio stimuli presented to the informants and no restriction was given on the number of times one could listen to the signals.

The results obtained imply a systematic use of backchannel vocalizations in the dialogue discourse as native speakers of Russian easily identify those used in their native tongue even out of context. Discursive elements [0294–0266 mm] and [0294–0266 mm] have been recognized as such by 85% and 92% of Russian respondents respectively.

4 Evidence of Communicative Adaptation

Evidence of communicative adaptation on the prosodic level has also been gained in the study. Native speakers of Russian follow communicative adaptation strategies, which manifests itself in their backchannel vocalizations being always lower in intensity than other stretches of speech. Instrumental analysis of speech segments preceding backchannel vocalizations reveals that F0 fluctuations can also be made

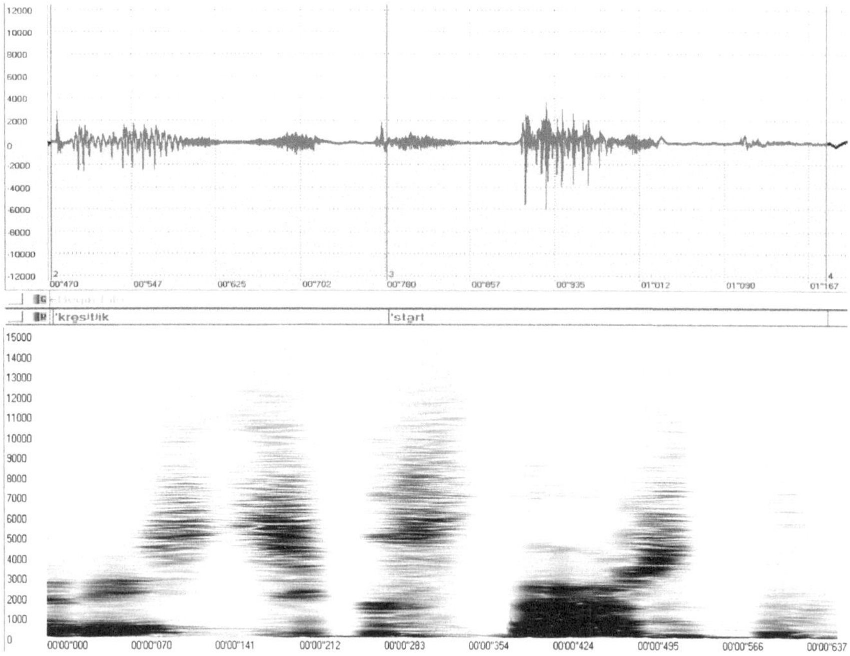

Fig. 7 Creaky voice spectrogram (female speaker)

use of to achieve a higher level of communication effectiveness [11]. Utterances marked by a rising tone (Russian Intonation Patterns 3 and 4 [8]) are followed by discursive elements characterized by similar melodic contours (in 74% of cases). It can signify that listening is an active process that involves adjusting the listener's vocalizations' prosodic characteristics to those of the speaker.

Although F0 fluctuations have proven to be a more frequent means of prosodic communicative adaptation, female native speakers of Russian can also revert to creaky phonation [12]. Segments marked by such voice quality modulations can be used to signal the end of an utterance and thus incentivize the listener to produce a backchannel vocalization. Figure 7 contains a spectrogram with visible irregular low-frequency periods of F0 fluctuations, which constitutes a clear case of creaky voice.

5 Conclusion

Backchannel vocalizations are a relatively new subject of linguistic research. They are discursive elements that function in dialogue discourse as quasi-verbal or speech signals conveying the listener's understanding and interest and encouraging their counterpart to continue speech production. A successful description of a linguistic phenomenon which has not yet been thoroughly studied requires a particular attention from the researcher with as many approaches to its description and cataloging as possible. Several approaches are suggested and implemented in the paper for description of Russian backchannel vocalizations: establishing occurrence frequency, sound quality and variation, prosodic features, as well as determining perception/recognition probabilities.

The data suggest that the use and perception of backchannel vocalizations is socially and culturally dependent. Still, the methods employed in the paper seem to be valid for description of similar discursive elements in other languages.

The results obtained by the authors can provide valuable insights into communication cooperation strategies are preferred by native speakers of Russian in dialogue discourse. They can also be used to improve the methodology of teaching Russian as a second language and to develop speech recognition and synthesis applications.

References

1. Allwod, J., Nivre, J., Ahlsén, E.: On the semantics and pragmatics of linguistic feedback. J. Semant. **9**, 1–26 (1993)
2. Benus, S., Gravano, A., Hirschberg, J.: The prosody of backchannels in American English. In: Proceedings of 16th International Congress of Phonetic Sciences, pp. 1065–1068. Saarbrücken (2007)
3. Jurafsky, D., Shriberg, E., Fox, B., Curl, T.: Lexical, prosodic, and syntactic cues for dialog acts. In:. Proceedings of the Workshop on Discourse Relations and Discourse Markers, pp. 114–120. Montreal (1998)
4. Kachkovskaia, T., Chukaeva, T., Evdokimova, V., Kholiavin, P., Kocharov, D., Kriakina, N., Mamushina, A., Menshikova, A., Zimina, S.: SibLing Corpus of Russian Dialogue Speech Designed for Research on Speech Entrainment. In: Proceeding of the 12th Conference on Language Resources and Evaluation (LREC 2020), pp. 6556–6561. Marseille (2020)
5. Schiffrin, D.: Discourse Markers. Studies in International Sociolinguistics 5. Cambridge University Press, New York (1988)
6. Yngve V.: On getting a word in edgewise. In: Papers from the Sixth Regional Meeting [of the] Chicago Linguistic Society, 1970, pp. 566–577
7. Ward, N., Tsukahara, W.: Prosodic features which cue back-channel responses in English and Japanese. J. Pragmat. **32**(8), 1177–1207 (2000)
8. Bryzgunova E.A.: Zvuki i intonaciya russkoj rechi [Sounds and intonation of Russian speech]. Russkij yazyk, Moskva (1977)
9. Gerasimenko O.A.: Funkcii chastic obratnoj svyazi v telefonnom dialoge (na primere leksem a, aga i gm) [Functions of feedback particles in telephone dialogue (using the example of lexemes a, aha and gm)]. In: Proceedings of the International Conference on Computer Linguistics and intellectual technologies "Dialog 2012», p. 103–108 (2012)
10. Guseva, D.D.: Proyavlenie kommunikativnoj adaptacii v prosodicheskikh kharakte-ristikakh replik-reakcij [Manifestation of communicative adaptation in prosodic characteristics of replica reactions]. In: Foneticheskij licej 6, 10–18 (2021)
11. Kachkovskaya, T.V.: (Otv.red.) Kommunikativnaya adaptaciya v dialoge: vzglyad fonetista [Communicative adaptation in dialogue: a phonetic perspective]. SPb.: Izd-vo SPBGU (2022)

12. Krivnova, O.F., Andreeva, A.M.: Laringalizaciya v ocenochnykh replikakh russkogo dialoga [Laryngalization in evaluative remarks of the Russian dialogue]. In: Trudy Mezhdunarodnogo seminara DIALOG'2005 po komp'yuternoj lingvistike i eyo prilozheniyam. Moskva (2005). http://www.philol.msu.ru/~otipl/SpeechGroup/publications/krivnova-2005-2006/andreevaa_krivnova_d-2005.doc, last accessed 01.05.2023
13. Popov, M.B.: Fonetika sovremennogo russkogo yazyka [Phonetics of the modern Russian language]. SPb. 304 s (2014)

Phonetic Realisation of the High Rising Terminal in English Dialects (A Case of Belfast and Newcastle Dialects)

Kira Sypacheva

Abstract The paper attempts to describe the realisation of the High Rising Terminal (HRT) in different English dialects. Only declarative utterances have been analysed. The material for the research includes phrases containing HRT produced by local radio show hosts from Belfast and Newcastle. The research findings have revealed that there is considerable similarity between the intonation contours used by the speakers of both dialects.

Keywords High rising terminal · English intonation · English dialects · Belfast English · Newcastle English

1 Introduction: High Rising Terminal

Although a substantial amount of research has been devoted to segmental phonetic differences between dialects of English, which has provided extensive evidence of intra-dialect variation in their phonological systems of phonemes [e.g. 10], intonational variation across English dialects is still largely unexplored. This is not to say that intonational differences are minor and virtually negligible to native speakers of English. On the contrary, speakers of different dialects habitually encounter communicative failures due to these differences. Hence there is considerable variation between English dialects on both segmental and suprasegmental levels.

However, some intonational differences may be particularly salient to native speakers compared to others. For example, it is reported that the speakers living in northern cities of Great Britain (Birmingham, Liverpool, Glasgow, Belfast, etc.) tend to use rising tones more extensively than the speakers living in other parts of the UK [3]. This noticeable variation could be attributed to Irish influence since the northern area of the UK was either in Ireland or had experienced immigration from Ireland [3]. In such dialects as Belfast English and Tyneside English (Newcastle English), declaratives are typically pronounced with a rise instead of a fall, as is typical for

K. Sypacheva (✉)
St. Petersburg State University, Saint-Petersburg, Russian Federation
e-mail: k.sypacheva@gmail.com

P. Eismont et al. (eds.), *Literature, Language and Computing*,
https://doi.org/10.1007/978-981-96-0990-1_12

most dialects of English [7–10]. This is likely to cause misunderstanding between speakers of the aforementioned dialects and those of Southern British English in a conversation. Additionally, it is not only the difference in meaning of the rising tone in Belfast and Tyneside that attracts attention of speakers of other varieties of English, but also the differences in the phonetic shape of the tone.

In some languages it is the prosodic features of a language variety that can help speakers to differentiate it from the other varieties [11]. This assumption has not been confirmed for English dialects, as there has not been a single large study on this subject.

Some studies have suggested that the rising tone in Belfast English consists of a nuclear rise followed by a plateau [7–9]—such intonation patterns are not observed in southern varieties, e.g. Cambridge, where a rising tone is represented by a steady rise [7–9].

As this area is the least investigated in dialectology, it seems reasonable to divert cross-dialect investigation from less distinctive intonation features to more prominent ones which are likely to cause misunderstanding between the speakers of different English varieties and, consequently, are easier to acknowledge. Thus, the unique use of the rising tone in regional dialects noted by investigators and native speakers of different English varieties has been chosen as the subject of this study.

The aim of the study is to analyse the intonational differences between the two regional varieties of English (Belfast English and Tyneside) by observing the phonetic realisation of HRT in declaratives in order to reveal any possible distinctive intonation features of these dialects. While it has already been stated that the use of the rising tone in these dialects is unique, it remains to be seen whether the rise also has a unique shape or it is similar to that of RP.

Since it has been observed that this intonation contour has a similar use in modern Southern British English varieties (e.g. RP) [12, 14, 16], a comparison with RP is also made.

The research findings will contribute to further investigation of intonational variation between different varieties of English.

2 Materials and Methods

When analysing intonation, many conflicting factors come into play, so it is essential to create such conditions which would ensure directly comparable data. In this study, the groups of native speakers of Belfast and Newcastle English have been controlled for dialect, speaking style, age and gender. Most of the speakers of Belfast English and those of Newcastle were born in Belfast and Newcastle respectively or have lived there for a substantial amount of time, and have graduated from a local university. The speaking style has been determined by the communicative situation of a radio show. The recorded shows are characterised by their informal style and friendly atmosphere, and feature dialogues between hosts, interviews with guests and listener participation.

Since both dialects have been singled out for their frequent use of rising tones in declaratives [7–9, 14], only declarative utterances have been acoustically analysed. Differentiating declarative utterances from declarative questions has not been without difficulty, as both communicative types were possible in some of the contexts. For the purpose of providing near-homogeneous data, the phrases referring to either utterance type were excluded from the material.

The utterance type for each phrase containing HRT has been asserted from its pragmatic context. For example, the phrase "Class start of the Saturday show" has been defined as a declarative because it was a text message from one of the radio listeners read by the radio host. The host's additional comment "I must have just missed that. Apologies." suggests that the text message was understood so the phrase is not a declarative question:

I got a text which says 'Class Start of the Saturday show'. I must have just missed that Apologies.

The material, which includes 63 recordings of declarative utterances in Belfast English[1] and 22 declaratives in Newcastle English,[2] has been acoustically analysed with the help of the computer program Praat [2], which allows to estimate such acoustic characteristics as fundamental frequency, melodic peaks and the pitch range.

The recordings have been sorted by speaker, the shape of rising intonation patterns and dialect. For each intonation contour the location of the nuclear accent has been determined, as well as the number of syllables following the nucleus in order to describe the shape of the rising tone in full detail.

3 Results and Discussion

3.1 Prosodic Characteristics of HRT in Belfast English

Nuclear tones are said to contribute most to the meaning of utterances so the most prominent acoustic information is concentrated within nuclear accents.

Nearly half of the declaratives (30 out of 63) containing HRT produced by the radio presenters from Belfast ended in the nuclear syllable with no syllables following it, so the rising movement of the tone was realised only within the final syllable. Figure 1 shows a typical realisation of the nuclear tone within the final syllable of the phrase.

There has not been much variation observed in the way HRT was realised in the final syllable of the phrases. The intonation contours in such phrases were represented by a steady rising movement of pitch. However, the pitch range within the nucleus fluctuated from speaker to speaker, ranging from 5 to 23 semitones, which may be explained by the individual characteristics of the speaker's voice quality and their preferred way of speaking.

---

[1] https://disk.yandex.ru/d/8umPVvbDXMnl_g.

[2] https://disk.yandex.ru/d/xZ_zqhprwRCuEA.

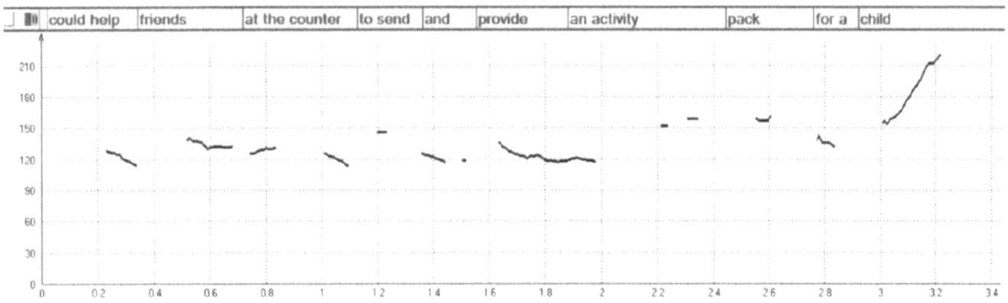

Fig. 1 Fo-contour of the phrase "could help friends at the counter provide an activity pack for a child"[3]

Additionally, if the nucleus takes a middle position in a phrase, the pitch level continues to rise steadily to the end of the phrase. The rest of the phrases (33 out of 63) showed the same rising pattern as the previous group of phrases.

Such results lead to the hypothesis that the increasing number of syllables after the nucleus would result in the increase in the pitch range. The hypothesis was later tested with nuclear pitch ranges being contrasted in the two types of utterances (with and without syllables following the nucleus) produced by the same speaker. For this purpose one of the speakers who had more phrases with HRT compared to others was chosen.

The comparison revealed no correlation of such kind, as the mean value of the HRT pitch range was roughly the same regardless of the number of syllables following the nucleus. For example, the HRT pitch range in all utterances produced by one of the speakers varied from 5 to 13 semitones in the phrases containing no syllables after the nucleus and from 6 to 13 in the phrases with one and more syllables following the nucleus.

Some of the samples had an unusual realisation of HRT with a low-level tone on the nuclear syllable followed by a rising pattern within the rest of the syllables placed after the nucleus. The phrase demonstrated in Fig. 2 could be described as having a double rise with two nuclei "birthday" and "tomorrow" pronounced with a low rising tone and HRT respectively.

It has also been observed that the last prenuclear syllable can have an additional rise in pitch (a step-up). Figure 3 shows an example of such a contour in which the last prenuclear syllable (the first syllable of the word "degrees") has an additional rise of approximately 30 Hz (2 semitones).

3.2 *Prosodic Characteristic of HRT in Newcastle English*

Similar intonation contours have been observed in the phrases with HRT produced by the speakers of Tyneside (Newcastle English). In most of the phrases, HRT was

[3] 'Belfast High Rises—sound file 1': https://disk.yandex.ru/d/8umPVvbDXMnl_g.

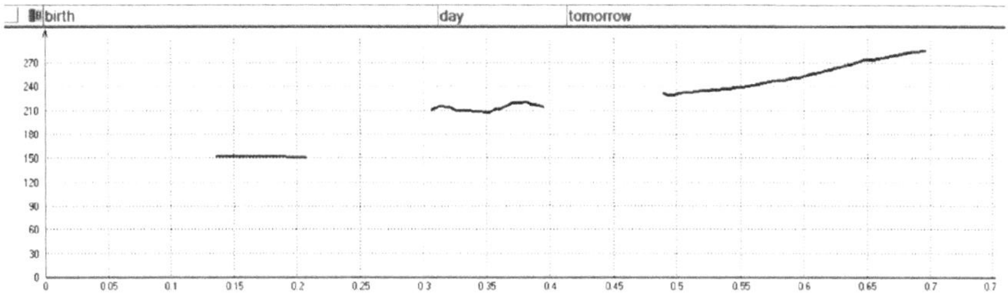

Fig. 2 Fo-contour of the phrase "birthday tomorrow"[4]

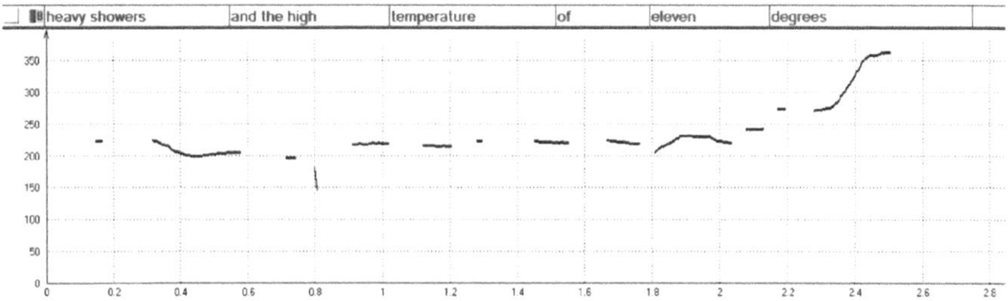

Fig. 3 Fo-contour of the phrase "heavy showers and the high temperature of 11 degrees"[5]

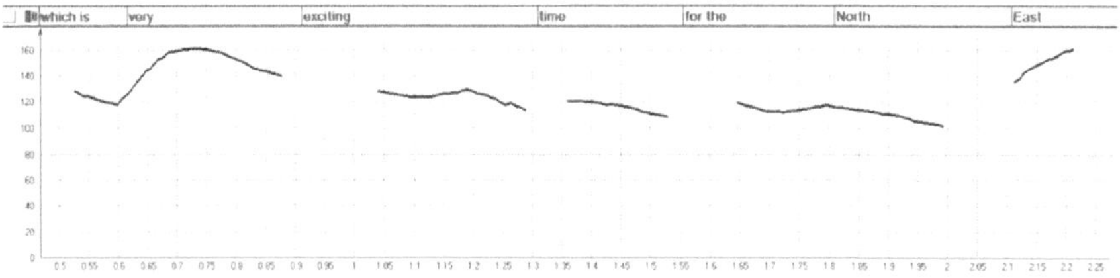

Fig. 4 Fo-contour of the phrase "which is a very exciting time for the North East"[6]

represented by a steady rising movement starting from the beginning of the nuclear syllable and continuing to the end of the syllable, if the nucleus was the final syllable of the phrase, or the end of an utterance if there were more syllables following the nucleus.

Figures 4 and 5 demonstrate examples of a steady rising movement spreading over the nucleus (the final syllable "East"), and the nucleus and the proceeding syllables ("optimistic ending").

---

[4] 'Belfast High Rises—sound file 10': https://disk.yandex.ru/d/8umPVvbDXMnl_g.

[5] 'Belfast High Rises—sound file 9': https://disk.yandex.ru/d/8umPVvbDXMnl_g.

[6] 'Newcastle High Rises—sound file 1': https://disk.yandex.ru/d/xZ_zqhprwRCuEA.

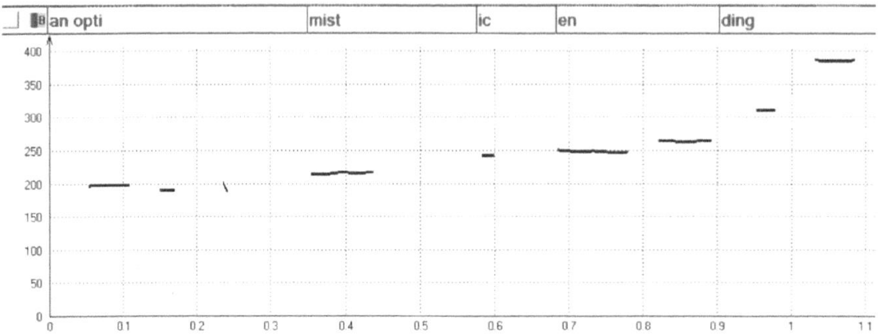

Fig. 5 Fo-contour of the phrase "an optimistic ending"[7]

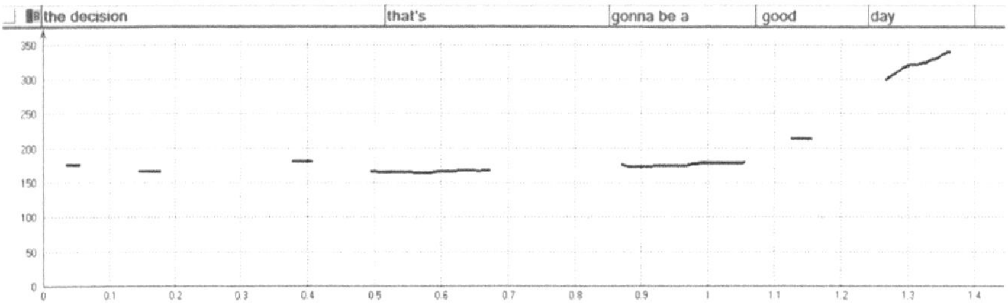

Fig. 6 Fo-contour of the phrase "the decision that's gonna be a good day"[8]

In some of the utterances, the last prenuclear syllable had an additional increase in pitch level. For example, in Fig. 6 the last prenuclear syllable "good" was pronounced with an additional rise in pitch of just about 30 Hz (from approximately 170 Hz to 210 Hz, 3 semitones).

It is interesting to note that some of the phrases also contained inclination, i.e. the rising pattern of pitch spreading over the prenuclear part of an utterance. Figure 7 demonstrates a step-up on the final prenuclear syllable of the phrase (the first syllable of the word "together") similar to the one in Belfast dialect observed earlier (see 3.1), as well as an additional rising pattern on the preceding syllables.

3.3 *Comparative Analysis of HRT in Both Dialects and RP*

RP has been one the most investigated English varieties to date with first detailed descriptions appearing at the end of the nineteenth century. There is a range of prosodic annotations that have been proposed for this English variety [3–6, 13, 16].

---

[7] 'Newcastle High Rises—sound file 2':https://disk.yandex.ru/d/xZ_zqhprwRCuEA.

[8] 'Newcastle High Rises—sound file 3':https://disk.yandex.ru/d/xZ_zqhprwRCuEA.

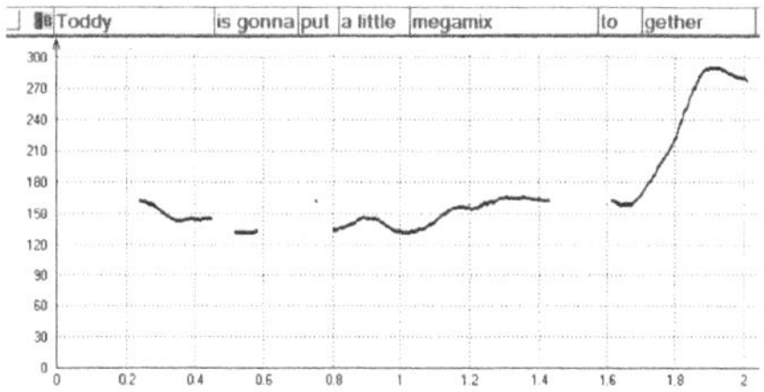

Fig. 7 Fo-contour of the phrase "Toddy is going to put a little megamix together"[9]

The system of tone groups suggested by O'Connor and Arnold [13] in the second half of the last century is considered one of the most successful and is still used at practical English phonetics lessons.

The equivalent of HRT is the High Rise, which is part of the intonation system of RP. This tone is used in the tone group titled *The High Bounce*. The tone group consists of high-pitched prenuclear syllables and a nucleus produced with a high-rising tone. If there are one or more proceeding syllables, the rising contour is realised within the nucleus and the following syllables. In another variation of the High Bounce the nuclear syllable is pronounced with a middle-level tone, and the high-rising contour is realised on the proceeding syllables.

It is also worth noting that all modern dialects are subject to change, as is every modern language variety. In recent decades, researchers of the pronunciation changes in Standard British English (RP) have observed a new use of the High Rising Terminal contour, which ends in a High Rise nuclear tone. Being normally associated with declarative questions (questions with declarative sentence word order), this tone started to occur in declaratives more frequently to convey that the speaker is seeking the hearer's encouragement and approval of his words [12, 14, 16]. This new use of the intonation contour came to be known as the high-rising terminal (HRT), Upspeak and Uptalk [12, 14, 16].

The results of this study on realisation of HRT in the two regional dialects suggest that there are many similarities concerning the shape of the intonation contour of this tone between the regional dialects and RP. However, it should be noted that the prenuclear syllables of an utterance can have an additional rise in the regional dialects (a step-up), which is not characteristic of the High Bounce used in RP. A compound tone (a double rise) has not been observed in RP either.

Since only the grammatical meaning of HRT has been considered, little can be said about the attitudinal function of the tone. However, it could be hypothesised that some of the functions of the tone can overlap with those of Upspeak—a relatively recent use of the High Bounce observed in the speech of young speakers of RP and its modern varieties (Southern Standard British pronunciation). To answer this question, further analysis of the pragmatic context of the phrases is required as well as the evaluation of native speakers' perception of the tone. The meaning of HRT other than grammatical is beyond the scope of the present paper.

[9] 'Newcastle High Rises—sound file 4':https://disk.yandex.ru/d/xZ_zqhprwRCuEA.

4 Conclusion

The research findings have revealed a number of similarities regarding realisation of HRT across English dialects. Firstly, it has been shown that HRT is mainly represented by a steady rising movement, which is normally continuous up until the end of an utterance and is close in its shape to the High Bounce (the High Rise) used in RP. Secondly, a few unusual intonational contours have been observed in both Belfast and Tyneside dialects. It is noteworthy that these new types of intonation contours have been found in both dialects, with the exception of the pattern of the double rise, which was produced exclusively by the speakers of Belfast English.

The correlation between the length of the sequence of syllables following the nucleus and the HRT pitch range has not been found, which means that the HRT pitch range remains the same and is spread evenly among the nucleus and the proceeding syllables.

Considering all of this evidence, it can be concluded that English intonation is subject to intra-dialect variation. It should be investigated further to establish more correlations between the intonation patterns, their cross-dialect similarities and differences, and their meanings. The evidence of this study may be applicable to various linguistic areas. From a theoretical perspective, it may shed some light on the types and scope of interlanguage variation. Pragmatically, the evidence may be used in the development of didactic materials designed for English intonation teaching as well as contribute to better intelligibility between speakers of English since learners will become more aware of non-standard intonation patterns. The data could also be implemented in speech technology, which, in the long term, may require more knowledge of the dialectal differences to improve the effectiveness of the human–computer interface.

References

1. Arvaniti, A., Atkins, M.: Uptalk in Southern British English. In: Proceedings of Speech Prosody, University of Boston, US (2016)
2. Boersma, P., Weenik, D. Praat: doing phonetics by computer [Computer program], Version 5.3.59. 2013. – URL: http://www.fon.hum.uva.nl/praat/
3. Cruttenden, A.: Intonation, Cambridge Textbooks in Linguistics, 2nd edn. Cambridge: Cambridge University Press (1997)
4. Cruttenden, A.: Gimson's Pronunciation of English, Eighth Edition. Routledge (2014)
5. Hirst, D., Cristo, A.: Intonation systems. A Survey of Twenty Languages, Cambridge (1998)
6. Hughes, A., Trudgill, P., Watt, D.: English Accents and Dialects, 5th edn. Routledge (2013)
7. Grabe, E.: Intonational variation in urban dialects of English spoken in the British Isles. In: Gilles, P., Peters, J. (eds.), Regional Variation in Intonation. Tübingen, NiZemeyer, pp. 9–31 (2004)
8. Grabe, E., Post, B.: Intonational variation in the British Isles. In: Proceedings of the Speech Prosody, pp. 343–346. Aix-en-Provence (2002)
9. Grabe, E., Post, B., Nolan, F., Rarrar, F.: Pitch accent realisation in four varieties of British English. J. Phonet. **27**, 161–185. Cambridge (2000)

10. Jarman, E., Cruttenden, A.: Belfast Intonation and the Myth of the Fall. University of Manchester (1976)
11. Leyden, K., van, Heuven, V.J.: On the Prosody of Orkney and Shetland Dialects, Phonetica, vol. 63, pp. 149–174. Leiden University, Leiden (2006)
12. Lindsey, G.: English after RP. Standard British Pronunciation Today, pp. 107–108. Palgrave Macmillan, London (2019)
13. O'Connor, J.D., Arnold, G.F.: Intonation of Colloquial English, 2nd edn. Longman Group Ltd., London (1973)
14. Warren, P., Uptalk in English varieties. In: Uptalk: The Phenomenon of Rising Intonation, pp. 69–96. Cambridge University Press, Cambridge (2016)
15. Wells, J.C.: Accents of English, vols. 1–3, Cambridge, CUP (1982)
16. Wells, J.C.: English Intonation. Introduction, Cambridge University Press, p. 37. Cambridge (2009)

Unveiling the Power of Hesitation: Exploring Vocalizations in the Speech of Introverts and Extroverts

Daria Gorbunova, Kristina Zaides, and Natalia Bogdanova-Beglarian

Abstract This study investigates vocalized hesitations, specifically filled pauses, in the spontaneous speech of individuals with varying levels of introversion and extroversion. The primary objective is to examine the potential correlation between psychotype and the frequency of vocalized hesitations, thereby elucidating distinct speech patterns associated with introversion and extroversion. Through a rigorous analysis of statistical data and correlation measures, this study aims to contribute to our understanding of the intricate interplay between personality traits and verbal communication. Research suggests that introverts tend to exhibit a higher rate of vocalized hesitations, possibly serving as cognitive processing strategies during speech production. In contrast, extroverts are hypothesized to display fewer vocalizations and prioritize more fluid speech output, reflecting their inclination for externalized thought processes. By uncovering the underlying mechanisms of vocalized hesitations and their relationship to introversion and extroversion, this research enhances our knowledge of how psychotypes manifest in spontaneous speech. The findings have implications for psycholinguistic theories and provide valuable insights for researchers and practitioners working in the fields of psychology, communication sciences, and psycholinguistics.

Keywords Vocalized hesitations · Introverts · Extroverts · Psychotype · Personality traits · Speech patterns · Spontaneous speech · Psycholinguistics

---

N. Bogdanova-Beglarian
St. Petersburg State University, Universitetskaya Emb. 7/9, 199034 Saint-Petersburg, Russia
e-mail: n.bogdanova@spbu.ru

D. Gorbunova (✉) · K. Zaides
Independent Researcher, Saint-Petersburg, Russia
e-mail: dgorbunova2@gmail.com

P. Eismont et al. (eds.), *Literature, Language and Computing*,
https://doi.org/10.1007/978-981-96-0990-1_13

1 Introduction

For human speech activities, there are phenomena that indicate various difficulties faced by speakers during the process of spontaneous speech generation. The reason for such difficulties is elementary: deficit during speech production. For example: "in real communication conditions, during natural spontaneous dialogue, the production of a text (utterance) essentially occurs in 'extreme conditions'—with a time deficit and the absence of the possibility to carefully plan a strategy" ([21]: 162),"the process of speech generation is closely intertwined with the process of thought generation, forming a unified speech-thought process implemented by mechanisms of speech thinking" ([20]: 110). Wilhelm von Humboldt described the speech act as a spontaneous struggle, a dramatic conflict between thought and its verbal embodiment: "For even the most everyday feeling and the deepest thought, language turns out to be insufficient, and people regard this invisible world as a distant country to which only language leads them, never reaching the destination. Every speech, in the truest sense of the word, is a struggle with thought, in which one feels both strength and weakness" ([19]: 378), "The gap between thoughts and language... is observed in speech fluctuations, false starts, and reformulations that abound in everyday speech. Interestingly, both introspection and speech failures show that people constantly compare their thoughts with their verbal expression and other possible variations of this expression. Clearly, people engage in mental monitoring of verbal variants that can be used to organize and express their thoughts, weighing different possibilities" ([10]: 64).

In "extreme conditions," human speech cannot be smooth and "polished"; it inevitably contains various signs of spontaneity known as hesitation phenomena (HP). These phenomena manifest in different ways and, in some manner, slow down the speech. Previously, these phenomena were studied in disciplines unrelated to linguistics, as they were considered external speech defects. However, in recent decades, they have become the foundation of an interesting and promising field that emerged at the intersection of linguistics, psychology, medicine, and the theory of probabilistic processes [24]. The linguistic study of these phenomena falls under the domain of colloquialistics [13, 30].

Hesitation phenomena have been widely investigated in linguistics in recent years [1, 9, 11, 12, 15, 22, 23, 25, 27], and others; see also [32] for a comprehensive review). The concept of hesitation phenomena is broader than that of hesitation pauses (HPa). In a narrow sense, HPa refers only to physical pauses, which occur when the speaker selects a word to fill a specific position within the syntactic structure of the utterance [26]: 147). In a broader sense, hesitation phenomena include both filled and unfilled pauses, as well as other forms of hesitation such as vocalizations, sound elongations, self-repairs, repetitions, and more.

Vocalizations are considered the most universal way of filling hesitation pauses in any language. They are non-speech or speech-like sounds that serve as a form of speech disruption, causing a break in the smooth unfolding of the speech flow. Vocalizations provide the speaker with a pause to prepare for the next portion of speech and, in combination with correction, contemplate possible ways to correct the preceding portion [27].

Taking into account the universality of vocalizations discussed in this article, we will focus on a specific psychological dimension, extroversion-introversion. The main psychological groups studied are introverts and extroverts.

An introvert is understood as a person prone to introspection, calm, restrained, introjective and somewhat pessimistic, appreciating order, in need of a clear plan of action.

An extrovert is understood as an impulsive, aggressive, optimistic and cheerful, outward-oriented personality, devoid of deep control of emotions.

Our objective is to demonstrate the inseparable connection between extroversion and vocalized hesitations. Previous research has indicated that introverts tend to exhibit a higher frequency of hesitations in their spontaneous speech [17], albeit without a detailed examination of specific hesitation types. By investigating the relationship between vocalizations and extroversion/introversion, we aim to gain valuable insights into how personality influences speech production and communication styles.

2 Vocalized Hesitations and Their Classifications

The task of studying hesitation pauses was first initiated by English and American researchers in the 1950s, with the main objective of understanding the causes of their occurrence. The investigations were conducted based on audio recordings of spontaneous English speech and reading. Researchers such as Maclay and Osgood [23], as well as Goldman-Eisler [16], discovered a connection between hesitation pauses and the process of lexical selection in the English language. By examining the overall proportions of pauses in spontaneous speech and reading, they noticed that pauses are more related to content rather than the structure of the utterance: "These results show that at the time of uttering fluent speech the speaker's pausing is under control and that it is relatively well-integrated into the syntactic structure, that pauses serve the function of communication rather than being symptomatic of internal processes" ([16]: 83). Conversely, in disfluent speech, pauses are less controlled and reflect internal planning processes.

All types of hesitation pause in spontaneous speech (including but not limited to vocalizations) can arise due to a variety of factors that operate collectively and interrelatedly:

1. Physiological: such as interruptions in breathing or health-related difficulties like asthma.
2. Linguistic: including the selection of or search for an appropriate pronunciation, word choice, and consideration of morphological and syntactic relationships.
3. Psycholinguistic: such as temperament type, habitual speech rate, anxiety levels, vocabulary knowledge, and depth of understanding of the topic.

4. Sociolinguistic: including the level of speech competence, language proficiency, speech culture, professional background, educational level, and age.
5. Extralinguistic: such as communicative conditions and the degree of speech preparedness.

Maclay and Osgood also extensively examine vocalized hesitations, devoting significant attention to the role of anxiety as a prominent factor in the process of pause filling: "If anxiety is a tension-producing phenomenon, vocalization is likely to be tension-reducing. This implies that a subject in an anxiety state as he begins to talk will show an initially high rate of hesitations followed by a decreasing rate as speech continues. The level of hesitations may increase again as a result of external factors or as a consequence of the content of his own utterances" [23].

According to Aleksandrova [1], hesitation in spontaneous speech can be a cause of communication failures as it hinders the understanding of the intended meaning and negatively affects the emotional state of the interlocutor. Therefore, in effective communication, all elements of hesitation should be reduced to unfilled pauses. A simple experiment conducted by researchers in St. Petersburg provided grounds to disagree with this statement: the removal of hesitations filled with non-speech sounds from spontaneous monologues led to a decrease in expert evaluations of these texts, sometimes by two points on a 7-point scale (see: [5]). Analyzing a large corpus of spontaneous monologues recorded from speakers of the Russian language allowed to conclude that vocalizations as a type of fillers in hesitations generally indicate a high level of speaker proficiency, while lexical or verbal fillers indicate a low level ([4]: 99).

In a comprehensive examination of the factors contributing to hesitations, Bortfeld et al. [7] conducted an analysis of recorded task-oriented dialogues. Their findings revealed that the roles played by participants, specifically whether they were describing images or attempting to find matching images, had a significant impact on the frequency of hesitations, particularly fillers. This effect was observed irrespective of the length or complexity of the utterances.

Although the argumentation below seems to emphasize the significance of vocalizations, it is important to distinguish between fillers and vocalized hesitations in terms of terminology. Both fillers and vocalized hesitations indicate moments of hesitation or uncertainty in speech, but vocalization appears to be a specific type within the category of fillers. While vocalized hesitations refer to audible sounds produced during speech, fillers encompass units that may have their lexical meaning "bleached," undergo processes of grammaticalization and pragmaticalization, and serve specific functions in speech, cf.:

(1) *ya vot segodnya* **(e-e)**[1]*/mne predlozhili* **(e-e)***/ya vot seychas ochen'* **(m-m)** *zanyat*[2] (S125, m., 52, extr.)[3]—vocalization, hesitation pauses filled with audible sounds;
(2) **(m) vot***/oni stoili voobshche iznachal'no* **(e) vot** *yesli priti v obychnyy magazine/ dve dve s polovinoy tysyachi* (S121, w., 28, intr.)—short vocalized hesitations extended with filler *vot*.

The functions of vocalizations largely coincide with the functions of other hesitational phenomena in spontaneous speech. They serve to demonstrate speech hesitation, buy time for considering the next word or continuation of speech, make corrections if something said is unsatisfactory to the speaker, and can be considered a form of speech manipulation.

Hesitation pauses, as well as vocalizations, could even assist in the ongoing process of understanding. For example, Howell and Young [18] found that utterances with self-repairs were rated as more comprehensible when preceded by pauses. In an online task where participants had to select one of three geometric shapes, Brennan and Schober [8] observed that the fastest identifications occurred when the interruption included a filler or a silent pause of the same duration. With the help of vocalizations, the speaker not only fills a pause of hesitation and gives themselves time to find the right word, but also can maintain the listener's attention and prevent their intervention in the dialogue until their own utterance is complete [6]. Moreover, some of them—notably, vocalizations—may be a part of the speaker's expressive armory, which can be further categorized according to psychotype.

3 Data and Processing Procedure

The research material was sourced from the "One Day of Speech" corpus, which was created with the purpose of studying the speech behavior of Russian language speakers throughout a day using the 24-h recording method.

To collect data for the "One Speech Day" corpus, the principle of "casting a wide net" was utilized, involving the collection of a wide range of language speaker data, which then became the subject of multidimensional analysis ([31]: 68). The corpus comprises over 1 million word occurrences in transcriptions, recording speech from 128 speakers and over 1000 of their interlocutors in various communicative situations.

---

[1] Vocalizations and fillers are marked in all examples as follows: vocalizations are underlined and bold, filler is bold.

[2] The transcribing texts from the corpus "One Day of Speech" include special symbols of discourse transcription:/— short physical pause; // — long physical pause; () — short hesitation pause; (...) — long hesitation pause; (e-e) — vocalized pause; - — prolongation of sounds; ... – break, etc. (on the rules of transcription, see: Russian Language of Everyday Communication 2016: 242-243).

[3] In the brackets after the example, we write the speaker's code, gender, age, and psychological group (extravert or introvert).

Table 1 Quantitative characteristics of the subcorpus by gender

Gender	People	Words	Number of contexts
Male	30	106,547	277
Female	20	69,821	227

The data for the study consists of speech produced by 50 Russian speakers, where vocalizations were annotated. Gender differences analysis was obtained before the psychological analysis, so all 50 informants were considered valid (see Table 1).

The psychological basis for the study relies on the results of two psychological tests—FPI and EPI—using only the extroversion/introversion scale to explore correlations between the poles. Ambiverts, by definition, alternate between both levels of arousal or may remain at an optimal level, which can be considered average and lacking specific characteristics, making their interpretation challenging.

A further comparison of the results from the two tests on the "introversion/extroversion" scale revealed a coincidence rate of 64.6%. Informants whose test results did not align between the two questionnaires were excluded from the final sample. The most representative data for further analysis came from only 26 speakers. In total, the final psychological sample for further analysis consisted of 16 extroverts and 10 introverts. Exclusions were not only made due to a lack of psychological data; several speakers were also excluded due to poor recording quality or inadequate transcription, as well as very short speech episodes. The distribution of speakers by psychotype was found to be insufficiently uniform to claim psycholinguistic balance. The higher number of extroverts, as indicated by the test results, can be attributed to the fact that psychological testing took place after the recordings and was not a determining factor in selecting or inviting specific speakers to participate in the experiment.

After obtaining all the necessary information about the speakers' psychological type, there was a need for cleaning, normalization, and quantitative assessment of the textual data in the corpus. To qualitatively evaluate the correlations between psychological types and vocalizations, as well as to calculate basic statistics, it is necessary to know the exact word count in the "speech day" of each informant represented in the final psychological sample. Since the transcriptions contain not only the words of the speakers but also the utterances of all interlocutors they interacted with during the "speech day," one of the stages of normalization involved the automatic recognition and removal of words spoken by all interlocutors.

Thus, the final user subcorpus consisted of 433 contexts with vocalizations extracted from the speech of 26 informants. Out of these, 10 were introverts and 16 were extroverts. The total volume of the material analyzed reached 95,543 words, with introvert informants contributing 29,380 words and extrovert informants contributing 66,163 words (see Table 2).

Table 2 The final quantitative characteristics of the pilot subcorpus

Psychological group	People	Words	Number of contexts
Introverts	10	29,380	191
Extroverts	16	66,163	242

4 Vocalizations in the Speech of Introverts and Extroverts

The current research has been carried out with the integration of all the criteria required for the successful application of quantitative linguistic methods in both practical and theoretical domains. Although quantitative linguistic methods are typically associated with practical applications, their utilization in this study allows for a substantial expansion and modification of our scientific understanding of the entire language system and its functional capacities ([3]: 39).

As the original dataset contained more than 100,000 words, traditional manual methods with standard text editors were inadequate for processing such a large volume of data. Consequently, all further analysis was performed using computer methods, specifically leveraging the Python programming language and libraries such as NumPy and Pandas,[4] which are designed for analyzing extensive data arrays.

Upon reviewing Table 1, it becomes clear that women use more vocalizations than men, despite the overall corpus data indicating that women hesitate less. This suggests that the frequency of vocalizations cannot be solely attributed to hesitations or pauses in speech. Other factors, such as communication style, expressiveness, cultural norms, or social expectations, may contribute to the observed difference. Further analysis and investigation are required to gain a comprehensive understanding of the underlying factors influencing the higher occurrence of vocalization.

As can be seen from Table 2, there are nearly twice as many vocalizations in the speech of introverts compared to extroverts, despite the higher number of the latter. This disparity in the frequency can be attributed to inherent differences in communication styles and cognitive processing. Introverts tend to engage in more introspective thinking, carefully considering their words before speaking. On the other hand, extroverts typically exhibit more spontaneous and outgoing speech. Extroverts tend to use vocalizations in conjunction with other hesitation units and fillers, demonstrating prolonged and thorough hesitation when they choose to do so. In contrast, introverts use vocalizations less frequently in chains, but insert single hesitations frequently, after nearly every word.

These results are highly consistent with the findings of the Dewaele and Fernham [14] experiment, in which 25 Flemish students were presented with speech tasks under stressful (formal) and relaxed (informal) conditions. The results revealed a negative correlation between the proportion of vocalization *er* and the level of extroversion in formal situations. The researchers put forward a hypothesis that introverts,

[4] All software used in this study is free and distributed as open source: https://pandas.pydata.org/, https://numpy.org/.

Table 3 Top 5 most frequent vocalizations in the speech of speakers with different psychotypes

Psychotype	Vocalization	Number of contexts
Introverts	e	60
	e-e	60
	m-m	28
	m	15
	e-m	11
Extroverts	m-m	99
	e-e	79
	a-a	29
	e	26
	m	2

being more anxious and less stress-tolerant, are expected to exhibit a higher frequency of hesitations compared to extroverts, cf.:

(3) ***vot*** **(e-e)** *ya tol'ko chto slyshal* **(m-m)** *(...) chto u Poltavchenko/syn* (S122, m., 33, extr.);

(4) ***(e-m) (e) (m)*** *pretenzii byli takie/vo-pervykh znachit yey nuzhno bylo chtoby *V za nikh ne tsep'yalas' yeyo Stesha% ne drala ikh* (S125, m., 52, extr.);

(5) ***(e-e)*** *to est' na samom dele v nashem predstavlenii/nu/skazhem tak/bol'shinstva/****(eh-m)*** *mnenie o tom chto svad'ba dolzhna byt' v belykh tonakh/eto* ***(e-e) (n-n)*** *nu vot traditsionnost' takaya nekaya/da* (S121, w., 28, intr.);

(6) *chto/nu konechno* ***(e-e)*** *eto oche... eto provokatsiya ochen' legko* ***(e-e)*** *znachit* ***(e)*** *otdavat' tekh kto ne osobenno znachit tsennen/ponimaesh' da?* (S130, w., 74, intr.)

The findings regarding the usage of single vocalizations and vocalization chains are further supported by frequency list (see Table 3). Interestingly, while for introverts the short single vocalization *(e)* places the first rank in frequency list, for extroverts the rank is as low as fourth.

5 Conclusion

The analysis of transcriptions, quantitative data, and comparative observations revealed an uneven distribution of vocalizations among different psychotypes. Specifically, it was found that introverts tend to use vocalizations twice as frequently as extroverts, both as isolated instances and within chains. This indicates inherent differences in how introverts and extroverts incorporate vocalizations into their speech patterns. Furthermore, a closer examination of vocalizations within speech contexts highlighted distinct behaviors exhibited by introverts and extroverts. Introverts showed a tendency to insert single hesitations more frequently throughout their speech, while extroverts had a higher likelihood of using vocalizations in chains with other hesitation units. Additionally, when we were comparing vocalization frequencies based on gender, intriguing findings emerged. Despite having fewer overall hesitations in the corpus, women tended to utilize more vocalizations compared to men. This suggests that gender may play a role in the frequency and usage of vocalizations within speech. These findings emphasize the importance of considering individual differences, such as psychotype and gender, when studying language use and communication patterns. To gain a deeper understanding of the observed variations in vocalization patterns, further research could explore the underlying psychological and sociolinguistic factors driving these differences. Moreover, investigating the impact of cultural and contextual variables on vocalization usage would contribute to a more comprehensive understanding of this phenomenon.

Acknowledgements The presented research was partially supported by Saint Petersburg State University, project #94033528 "Modeling of Russian Megalopolis Citizens' Communicative Behavior in Social, Speech and Pragmatic Aspects Using Artificial Intelligence Methods".

References

1. Aleksandrova, O.A.: Speech-Communicative Status of the Oscillation Pause PhD Thesis. Veliky Novgorod (2004) (in Russian)
2. Alexandrova, O.A., Ivanitsky, V.V.: Oscillation pause—a complex phenomenon of modern communication. In: Novgorod State University Herald, 25, 95–101 (2003) (in Russian)
3. Baranov, A.N.: Introduction to Applied Linguistics: a Textbook. Moscow: Editorial URSS (2001)
4. Bogdanova, N.V.: On the syntactic correlates of differentiation of the levels of speech culture. In: Living Word in Russian Speech of the Kama Region. Perm: Perm State University press, 92–100 (1993) (in Russian)
5. Bogdanova, N.V.: The level of speech competence as a real social characteristic of the speaker, defining his speech. In: Proceedings of the XXXVIII International Philological Conference. Iss. 22. Field Linguistics. Integral Modeling of the Sound Form of Natural Languages. St. Petersburg: Faculty of Philology and Arts of St. Petersburg State University, 29–40 (2010) (in Russian)
6. Bogdanova-Beglarian, N.V.: Final vocalization in oral discourse as a method of speech manipulation (the effect of deceived expectation). In: Analysis of Colloquial Russian Speech (AR3–2023). Proceedings of the Tenth Interdisciplinary Seminar. St. Petersburg. In Print (2023). (in Russian)
7. Bortfeld, H., Leon, S.D., Bloom, J.E., Schober, M.F., Brennan, E.: Disfluency rates in spontaneous speech: effects of age, relationship, topic, role, and gender. Lang. Speech **44,** 123–147 (2001)
8. Brennan, S.E., Schober, M.F.: How listeners compensate for disfluencies in spontaneous speech. J. Memory Lang. **44**, 274–296 (2001)
9. Cenoz, J.: Pauses and Communication Strategies in Second Language Speech. http://www.librarything.com/author/cenozjasone (2013).
10. Chafe, W.: On the Way to Linguistics Based on Thinking. In: Language and Thought: Modern Cognitive Linguistics. Languages of Slavic Culture, Moscow, pp. 60–88 (2015) (in Russian)
11. Clark, H.H., Fox Tree, J.E.: Using *uh* and *um* in spontaneous speaking. Cognition **84**, 73–111 (2002)
12. Corley, M, Stewart, O.W.: Hesitation disfluencies in spontaneous speech: the meaning of *Um*. Lang. Linguist. Compass **4**, 1–18 (2008)
13. Devkin, V.D.: German Colloquial Speech: Syntax and Vocabulary. International Relations, Moscow (1979). (in Russian)

14. Dewaele, J.M., Furnham, A.: Personality and speech production: a plot study of second language learners. In: Personality and Individual Differences, vol. 28, pp. 355–365 (2000)
15. Fehringer, C.: Hesitation Phenomena in the Language Production of Bilingual Speakers: the Role of Working Memory. http://www.llc.manchester.ac.uk/subjects/german/fgls/conference2007/Fileuploadmax10Mb,99794,en.doc (2007)
16. Goldman-Eisler, Frieda: Psycholinguistics. Experiments in Spontaneous Speech. Academic, London (1968)
17. Gorbunova, D.A.: Pragmatic markers in Russian spoken discourse: correlation with speaker's Psychotype. (PhD Thesis). 275 p (2022)
18. Howell, P., Young, K.: The use of prosody in highlighting alteration in repairs from unrestricted speech. Quart. J. Experi. Psychol. **43**(A), 733–758 (1991)
19. von Humboldt, W.: On the difference in the structure of human languages and its influence on the spiritual development of mankind. In: W. von Humboldt. Selected Works on Linguistics. Progress, Moscow, pp. 37–297 (1984) (in Russian)
20. Katsnel'son, S.D.: Language Typology and Verbal Thinking. Nauka, Leningrad (1972) (in Russian)
21. Levitskiy, Y.A.: To the question of the second communication. In: Erofeeva, E.V. (ed.) Problems of Socio- and Psycholinguistics. Iss. 15. Perm Socio-Psycholinguistic School: Ideas of Three Generations, to the 70th Anniversary of Alla Solomonovna Stern: Collected Articles, Perm, Perm State National Research University Publ., 159–167 (2011) (in Russian)
22. Lounsbury, F.G.: Pausal, juncture and hesitation phenomena. In: Psycholinguistics, pp. 96–101. Waverly Press, Baltimore (1954)
23. Maclay, H., Osgood, C.E.: Hesitation phenomena in spontaneous English speech. Word **15**(1), 19–44 (1959)
24. Nikolaeva, T.M.: A new direction in the study of spontaneous speech (on the so-called speech oscillations). Prob. Linguist. **3**, 117–123 (1970) (in Russian)
25. O'Connell, D.C., Kowal, S.: Uh and um revisited: are they interjections for signaling delay? J. Psycholinguist. Res. **34**(6), 555–576 (2005)
26. Phonetics of Spontaneous Speech, Svetozarova, N.D. (ed.). Publishing House of Leningrad State University, Leningrad (1988) (in Russian)
27. Podlesskaya, V.I., Kibrik, A.A.: Correction of failures in oral spontaneous speech: the experience of corpus research. In: Computational Linguistics and Intellectual Technologies: Proceedings of the International Conference "Dialogue'05". RGGU, Moscow. http://www.dialog-21.ru/media/2416/podlesskaya-kibrik.pdf (2005) (in Russian)
28. Russian Language of Everyday Communication: Features of Functioning in Different Social Groups: Collective Monograph, Bogdanova-Beglarian, N.V. (ed.). LAIKA, St. Petersburg (2016) (in Russian).
29. Shriberg, E.E.: Preliminaries to a theory of speech disfluencies. PhD Thesis. University of California at Berkeley (1994)
30. Skrebnev, Yu.M.: Introduction to Colloquialistics. Saratov State University Press, Saratov (1985). (in Russian)
31. Sound Corpus as a Material for Analysis of Russian Speech: Collective Monograph. Part 1. Reading. Retelling. Description, Bogdanova-Beglarian, N.V., (ed.). St. Petersburg State University, St. Petersburg, Philology department (2013) (in Russian)
32. Yakovleva, E.B.: Speech hesitations: formal and functional aspects: analytical review. In: Nagornaya, A.V., (ed.), RAS INION. Center for Humanitarian Scientific Information Research. Department of Linguistics. Series: Theory and History of Linguistics. Moscow (2016) (in Russian)

Communicative Interfaces

This Robot Smiles So Nicely, I Don't Trust Him—The Effect of Robot's Smiles on User's Trust

Anna A. Zinina, Artemiy A. Kotov, and Nikita A. Arinkin

Abstract In two consecutive experimental studies we evaluate the influence of robot's smiles on user's trust to the facts, reported by the robot. In each experiment, two F-2 robots reported "hard to believe" facts and the user had to indicate, if he trusts the received information. In the first experiment ($N = 54$) one robot smiled after the utterance, while the other robot did not. Robot's smile increased subjects' reaction time, but did not affect the level of trust. In the second experiment ($N = 24$), smiling behavior was updated: robot was rotating its head, skewing its gaze direction to the user and rising its eyebrows. People loved this robot and preferred it to the other, non-smiling robot. At the same time, the level of user's trust to this robot dropped: people noted its smile and reduced their level of confidence to the reported facts.

Keywords Social robots · Human–Machine interaction · Robot companion · Nonverbal behavior · Nonverbal cues

1 Introduction

Human smile is a complex socio-cultural phenomenon, it has numerous functions in communication and generally lies at the center of modern human behavior code. Depending on its form and context, a smile can express positive emotions, like *pleasure*, *joy*, *amusement*, *contentment* [1], serve as a marker of *mockery*, *neglect*, *irony*, as well as express *schadenfreude*, *embarrassment*, *frustration*, and even *suffering*.

A. A. Zinina · A. A. Kotov · N. A. Arinkin
National Research Center "Kurchatov Institute", Moscow, Russia
e-mail: zinina_aa@nrcki.ru

A. A. Zinina · A. A. Kotov
Russian State University for the Humanities, Moscow, Russia

A. A. Zinina · A. A. Kotov (✉) · N. A. Arinkin
Moscow State Linguistic University, Moscow, Russia
e-mail: kotov@harpia.ru

P. Eismont et al. (eds.), *Literature, Language and Computing*,
https://doi.org/10.1007/978-981-96-0990-1_14

Fig. 1 F-2 companion robot

Smile is a social cue to be used in many communicative situations, like *greeting*, *goodbye*, *approval*, *agreement*, etc. Smiles are usually considered as emotionally or socially associated with the user's trust. For example, when subjects are presented with photos of the same person with or without a smile, smiling photos are more likely to be trusted [2]. There are evidences that facial expression has a strong correlation with user's trust and with the perceived trustworthiness of the author of the message. Specifically, a smile, along with attractiveness, significantly influences trustworthiness, even for short-term exposure (as little as 100 ms) [3]. A neutral (computer generated) face is evaluated as trustworthy, depending on its similarity to prototypical expressions of happiness or anger [4], since these expressions signal the addressee to approach or avoid a person. Moreover, a face that looks happy is perceived as trustworthy, whereas a face that looks angry is perceived as untrustworthy [5]. In other studies, it is noted that a virtual agent's smile has no noticeable effect on its assessment but provokes a smile in interaction partners [6]. In our study we rely on the findings in interpersonal commutation, suggesting, that a human smile, rated as genuine, increases trust and allows a game player to entrust a higher sum to the "smiling" counterpart [7]. In our work, we test the assumption that robot's smile increases the level user's trust to the information, reported by the robot. In the experiment, we used F-2 robot (Fig. 1).

2 Methods and Experiments

In our study we have conducted two consecutive experiments, trying to increase the pleasantness of the robot's smile. In each experiment we used a pair of F-2 companion robots, located in front of the user on the table. Robots were in turn announcing statements (facts) and the user had to evaluate each utterance as "true" or "false" immediately after by pressing a button on a monitor, located in front of the user. Robots were indicated by "triangle" and "square" marks, located on their bodies.

The acoustic representations for the utterances were generated using the Yandex voice synthesizer, which is now the default F-2 robot voice. During the utterance, each robot made some addressive gesture, like moving a hand toward the listener. In all other time intervals, robots we maintaining "inactive behavior"—were slightly moving their hands and head, like imitating breathing, and were slightly changing their gaze direction.

The study used 28 "hard to believe" statements—real, but "unbelievable" facts (50%) and false statements (50%). For example, *Sixty people become millionaires every day*. The procedure reminded a game *Do you believe that...?* Within each experiment, robots reproduced the utterances in random order: all 28 utterances were presented to each participant, but one particular utterance could be represented by different robots in interactions with different participants. The degree of confidence in these statements was evaluated in a preliminary experiment (N = 30, mean age 22, 7 males), where subjects were asked to indicate whether a statement was true or false by pressing *Believe* or *Don't believe* button on the screen. It was shown that there was some general bias toward trust to the information, but there was no significant shift in evaluation of each particular fact.

2.1 First Experiment

In the first experiment (N = 54, mean age 20, 9 males), one of the robots smiled after each statement (mouth was getting a smiling shape on the monitor, where the face is projected), while the other robot only declared the statement and continued with inactive behavior. A human interacted with each of the two robots consecutively—Fig. 2. After each statement, declared by any robot, the participant had to indicate, whether the statement is "true" or "false", by pressing a graphic button on a monitor with the mouse. The choice and speed of the answer were recorded. After the end of the experiment each participant filled out a questionary, indicating, in particular, which robot was more attractive and which robot was more trustworthy.

2.2 Initial Results

There are significant differences in the proportion of trustworthiness to each fact between the "no robots" condition (preliminary experiment), the "robot with a smile" condition, and the "robot without a smile" condition ($\chi^2 = 0.76$, $p < 0.01$). Thus, we can conclude that the presence of a physical companion robot does affect the degree of user's trust. According to the results, no significant differences were found in the degree of confidence to the information coming from the robot with the smile and the robot without a smile. A Two-Way ANOVA analysis of the response rate also showed no significant effects of smiling behavior type and "true/false" response. However, a significant interaction between the two factors was found—participants much faster

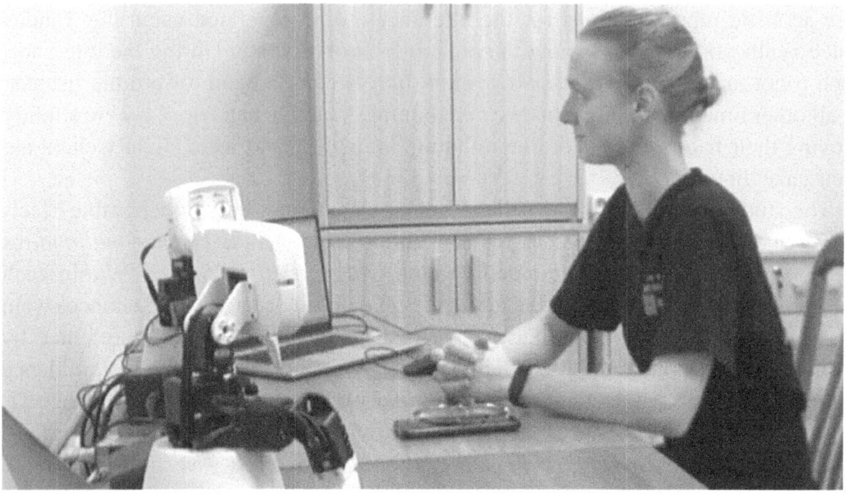

Fig. 2 The experimental situation

responded "true" to the robot with a neutral facial expression, as compared to the "false" response, while to the smiling robot they responded "true" and "false" at the same speed ($F(1, 5) = 147{,}500$). We can suggest, that robot's smile implies the mechanisms of interpersonal interaction that slow down the response, as people are required to analyze robot's facial expression, which can be confusing in assessing the plausibility of the judgment.

We have also suggested that insufficient articulation of smile can reduce the influence on the participant. For the second experiment we analyzed the patterns of articulated smiles in the multimodal corpus, and executed the second experiment with the same robots on the same sets of judgments, but different in the pattern of smile.

2.3 Pattern Analysis for Smiles

Based on the results of the first experiment, we decided to update the smile patterns for the robot to make them more articulated: more visible and attractive. A smile can be analyzed, based on its duration [8], geometry—in computer vision systems, or physiology—from the point of view of facial muscle movements—via EMG or with annotation in FACS [9]. At the same time, the face of F-2 robot is rather simplified: it does not operate in FACS instruction space and does not allow smooth transitions of mouth pictures. To develop the new patterns, we analyzed smiles and their contexts in the multimodal corpus REC [10]. Within the corpus, people often display a closed smile, similar to compressed lips, without raising the corners of the mouth (Fig. 3a). This pattern corresponds in the corpus annotation to the communicative function *compensation*, where a person loses his social face in the dialogue and

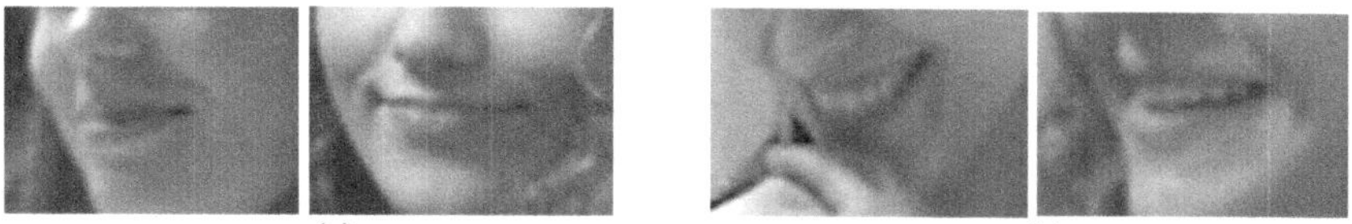

(a) (b)

Fig. 3 Variants of smiles in REC corpus: **a** smiles, expressing compensation; **b** smiles directed at the influence (controlled smile)

"compensates" it with post-factum lip compression. This smile can be considered as a push-reaction, invoked by an internal state of the speaker and not intended for the emotional influence. A voluntary smile in the corpus is often quite wide, open across the entire mouth (Fig. 3b).

Within the pattern of voluntary smile, subjects use other behavioral movements: they frequently turn their head sideways or downward while still maintaining eye contact with the listener, that results in skewing gaze direction. They also, sometimes, tilt their head toward the shoulder, and raise their eyebrows. In this way, they combine a smile with the *request of feedback* movements—as head-turning and eyebrow rising are annotated in REC. For the second experiment we have updated smile pictures, to make mouth opening more evident, and combined smiles with head-turning, head-lowering and eyebrow-rising—see Fig. 4. As we expect, these means should make the smiles more articulated in the second experiment. Head tilting was not used due to the kinematic model of the robot: its head has only 2 degrees of freedom and cannot tilt aside.

In dynamic behavior, informants in the corpus also use other means of feedback requests together with voluntary smiles: they address the opponent with gestures (move open palm to the opponent), tap on the table or move their fingers in the air (as if in impatience), squint, wrinkle their nose or stick out tongue. These more compound patterns were not implemented in the experiment, as they may further influence the perception of the robot.

(a) (b)

Fig. 4 Extension of the basic smile pattern (on F-2 robot 3D simulator): **a** "flat" smile with closed mouth, **b** open smiles with head rotation and eyebrow rising

2.4 Second Experiment

The second experiment (N = 24, mean age 22.5, 5 males) was executed on the same robots and on the same list of sentences, with the only difference—a more expressive smile pattern was used on the "smiling" robot. 18 people (75%) indicated, that they noticed the difference between robots, but only 9 (40.9%) managed to describe this difference in the final survey—here we considered free responses, where people indicated, that the smile of the robot with "square" *was expressive* or *emotional*, or, at least, was different in its *facial expressions*. One person noted distinct head rotations by the robot with "square", not his smiles.

The core parameter was the level of trust to the robot with smiles (marked with "square). People were evaluating trust to the robot on a scale from 1 to 5 (where 1—*don't trust*, 5—*completely trust*), average score was 3.4 (average trust to the robot without smiles was 3.7). We also asked them to choose the robot they trusted more. From the results, we can see that the scores on the semantic differential scales are consistent with the subjects' choices ($F(4, 36) = 24.252$, $p < 0.01$)—Fig. 5.

In their answer to the question *Which robot you liked more?* 6 people preferred the smiling robot (with square) and 2 people preferred non-smiling robot (with triangle), while 16 people did not express any preference—they liked both robots equally. At the same time, trust to the robot with smiles among those, who chose this robot, is rather low—only 2.5 on average. According to factor analysis ($F(4, 36) = 5.2188$, p < 0.01) we can conclude that preference for a particular robot can be considered as

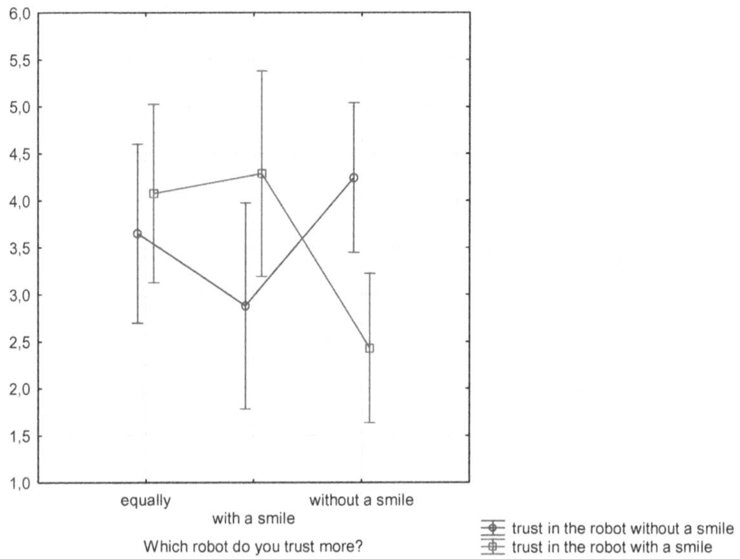

Fig. 5 Assessing trust in robots using semantic differential scales and selecting the robot that subjects trust more

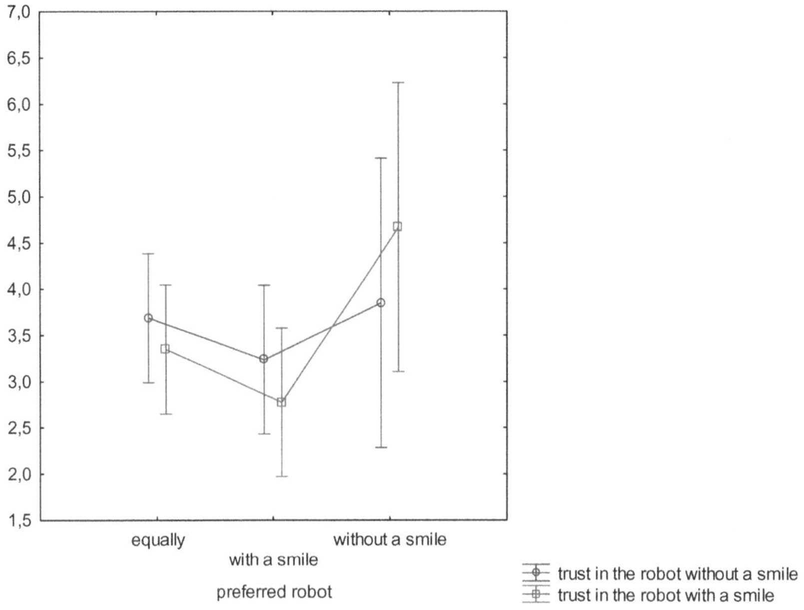

Fig. 6 The effect of preferring a particular robot on the level of trust to robots

a factor related to trust to the robots. Thus, Fig. 6 shows that the robot with a smile is less trusted overall.

Although we have expected, that a smile makes a speaker more attractive and does maintain trust between the counterparts, the results seem quite different. We see the following tendency: people, who evaluate trust to the robot with smiles as "low" (set 2 or 1 on this scale), also loved this robot more. Those, who prefer the robot with smiles (marked with "square"), also evaluate trust to this robot as low as 2.5 (and give 3.3 for the non-smiling robot). This also correlates with the explicit recognition of the differences between the robots: people, who noticed the difference, evaluate trust to the smiling robot as 2.7 on average (3.3 for the non-smiling robot). As we can assume, a more expressive smile has some contradictory influence on the user. On the one side, smile makes a positive impression on the user, making him love this robot. On the other side, smile forces the user to question the words of the robot, lowering the level of user's trust. There were also those subjects who labeled the robot with the smile as *sarcastic*, not *trustworthy*. Thus, people predominantly noticed the difference in the behavior of the two robots. However, some people considered such smiles as a cute expression of emotionality, while others considered them more like a negative mockery. Both these groups did not trust the robot with smiles.

The results can be linked to a wider cultural context, as suggested in [11]: for example, societies with a high level of corruption have lower trust to smiling people. However, in a recent study, the authors were not definitive on the impact of smiling on the trust level to a person; they noted that it is a combination of factors, like *gender*, *attractiveness*, *skin color*, etc., that is important in the cumulative evaluation of the trust [12]. While the robot is free from different human characteristics, the communication with robot, and in particular, the possibility to distinguish *trust* and *attractiveness* of the addressee—may be greatly influenced by cultural stereotypes and communication practices.

3 Conclusion

The first experiment showed that the presence of an anthropomorphic robot affects the level of trust to the information: the same utterances, presented on the screen and reported by the robot, get different degree of trust. The presence of the robot increased the subjects' trust to the facts. In the first experiment, robot's smile decreased the speed of the "true" response. At the same time, a faint smile had no significant influence on user's trust. A more articulated smile, combined with head rotation and eyebrow rising, had a very interesting and rather contradictory influence on the listener. On the one side, this smile made people prefer this robot and like this robot more. On the other side, this smile made people question the words of the robot, reducing the level of trust to the reported information. This represents a contradictory nature of smile, where the attractiveness diverges with the trust, forcing people to question, why the robot smiles at the end of its sentence.

Acknowledgements The research was carried out under the state assignment of the Ministry of Science and Higher Education of the Russian Federation, registration number—124122200011-0.

References

1. Ekman, P.: Emotions Revealed: Recognizing Faces and Feelings to Improve Communication and Emotional Life. New York (2003)
2. Scharlemann, J.P., Eckel, C.C., Kacelnik, A., Wilson, R.K.: The value of a smile: game theory with a human face. J. Econ. Psychol. **22**(5), 617–640 (2001)
3. Willis, J., Todorov, A.: First impressions: making up your mind after a 100-Ms exposure to a face. Psychol. Sci. **17**(7), 592–598 (2006)
4. Oosterhof, N.N., Todorov, A.: The functional basis of face evaluation. Proc. Natl. Acad. Sci., USA **105**, 11087–11092 (2008)
5. Said, C.P., Sebe, N., Todorov, A.: Structural resemblance to emotional expressions predicts evaluation of emotionally neutral faces. Emotion **9**, 260–264 (2009)
6. Krämer, N., Kopp, S., Becker-Asano, C., Sommer, N.: Smile and the world will smile with you—the effects of a virtual agent's smile on users' evaluation and behavior. Int. J. Hum. Comput. Stud. **71**(3), 335–349 (2013)
7. Centorrino, S., Djemai, E., Hopfensitz, A., Milinski, M., Seabright, P.: Honest signaling in trust interactions: smiles rated as genuine induce trust and signal higher earning opportunities. Evol. Hum. Behav. **36**(1), 8–16 (2015)

8. Si, M., McDaniel, J.D.: Creating genuine smiles for digital and robotic characters: an empirical study. In: 2015 IEEE Games Entertainment Media Conference, GEM 2015 (2016). https://doi.org/10.1109/GEM.2015.7377231
9. Ugail, H., Aldahoud, A.A.A.: Facial Emotional Expressions. Computational Techniques for Human Smile Analysis. SpringerBriefs in Computer Science. Springer, Cham (2019). https://doi.org/10.1007/978-3-030-15381-6_1
10. Kotov, A., Budyanskaya, E.: The Russian emotional corpus: communication in natural emotional situations. Comput. Linguist. Intel. Technol. **11**(18), 296–306 (2012)
11. Krys, K., Melanie Vauclair, C., Capaldi, C.A., Lun, V.M.C., Bond, M.H., Domínguez-Espinosa, A., Yu, A.A.: Be careful where you smile: culture shapes judgments of intelligence and honesty of smiling individuals. J. Nonverbal Behav. **40**(2), 101–116 (2016)
12. Wilson, R.K., Eckel, C.C.: Attributions of trust and trustworthiness. Polit. Behav. 1–23 (2023)

The Botik of Peter the Great: Creating a Virtual Assistant for the Applicants to St. Petersburg State University

Olga Mitrenina, Maria Ladushina, and Anastasia Kolpashchikova

Abstract The article provides a summary of our research on designing a conversational interface for the Admissions Committee of St. Petersburg State University, with a focus on reflecting the university's values and brand. The primary aim was to go beyond simple text-based responses and useful links, and instead, employ a virtual assistant persona embodying Peter the Great to resonate with the modern youth audience and align with the university's historical legacy. To ensure linguistic authenticity, a comprehensive study of Peter the Great's personal correspondence and relevant pedagogical texts of the early eighteenth century was conducted. Based on these sources, a collection of expressions was curated as a preliminary version of the chatbot's responses. Subsequently, testing was conducted among a group of students to gauge the understandability of the language. Furthermore, a series of studies were carried out to balance the stylistic elements with the requirements of usability. The CAILA platform was used to develop "The Botik of Peter the Great" chatbot, employing language that captures the essence of the Peter the Great era while maintaining an engaging, informative, and user-friendly approach. The chatbot was launched as a widget on the Admissions Committee's website and made available on the Telegram messenger platform.

Keywords Virtual assistants · Chatbots · Conversational interface · Language stylization · Usability requirements · Middle Russian

O. Mitrenina (✉) · A. Kolpashchikova
St. Petersburg University, Universitetskaya Emb. 7/9, 199034 Saint-Petersburg, Russia
e-mail: o.mitrenina@spbu.ru

M. Ladushina
National University of Science and Technology "MISIS", Leninskiy Pr. 4, 119049 Moscow, Russia

P. Eismont et al. (eds.), *Literature, Language and Computing*,
https://doi.org/10.1007/978-981-96-0990-1_15

1 Introduction

Dialogue systems are becoming a mandatory attribute of every organization and company that involves interaction with its users. They reduce the workload of customer service employees, as well as make it easier for visitors to find information and reduce the amount of face-to-face interaction. Besides, some users *prefer* using a virtual assistant because they can take their time and ask for information over and over "without feeling like they're 'bothering' a human agent" [1].

Our task was to create a Russian-speaking virtual assistant for the applicants to St. Petersburg State University as an addition to the admissions website. The chatbot must act as a widget on the site pages and as an assistant in Telegram messenger. Its main task is to assist in navigating the site. At the same time, its tasks do not include being a conversation expert, chit-chat bot or similar; its tasks were narrowed down to providing the user with a short textual reply or a useful link.

When developing the bot, it was necessary to combine two contradictory tasks: to be understandable to the modern youth audience, but at the same time to convey the spirit of the oldest Russian university located in the cultural capital of Russia.

2 Selection of Assistant's Personality

2.1 Why Peter the Great

The first task was to specify a personality for the chatbot.

When developing modern virtual assistants (voice, text, and others), there is a strong tendency to personalize them, giving them traits of a specific personality (chatbot personality, chatbot persona). A personalized virtual assistant begins to fulfill the functions of a company or organization's logo: promoting personalization and distinguishing the marketing object from a myriad of other similar marketing objects, and ideally, visually expressing the main direction of the company's activities and the philosophy of its brand. Unlike an "inanimate" logo, a virtual assistant can interact with visitors, influencing them not only through direct recommendations but also through its speech style.

Saint Petersburg State University is the oldest university in Russia, and Peter the Great is the founder of both the university and the city of Saint Petersburg itself, one of the names of which is "the City of Peter". These facts made it practically inevitable for us to choose Peter the Great as a virtual impersonation of the assistant for aspiring university students. Furthermore, we wanted the chatbot's personality to set a specific tone of communication and prepare students for studying in the oldest university in the country with a rich academic tradition, in the "northern capital", renowned for its cultural and historical landmarks, in the most beautiful city of Russia. By making this choice, in construction of our chatbot persona we could use well-known facts about Peter I, primarily him being a great patron of university education, knowledge, and progress in general. The assistant itself quickly acquired the name "The Botik of Peter the Great", given that the word "Botik" in Russian is ambiguous: it means not only the famous boat of Peter the Great, but also a small (chat-)bot.

2.2 Balance Between Past and Future

In the responses of the virtual assistant, we made an effort to adhere to the stylization of the vocabulary and syntax to Peter the Great's era (additional details are discussed in the next section). However, it was necessary to take into account that the bot interacts with a young audience in the twenty-first century [2]. This determined its "personal characteristics".

- It is polite. More often than not, much more polite than its real-world interlocutors.
- It is "from another era".
- It is aware that it is a robot ("my technology is still imperfect"/"my achievements are modest, but knowledgeable people tirelessly work on me" [in order not to overload the article, we provide approximate translations of Russian sentences into English]).
- It is scholarly and educated, as evidenced by its rich vocabulary, "bookishness", and a certain eloquence in its speech.

To ensure linguistic authenticity, we consulted authentic texts of Peter the Great's personal correspondence, as well as experts in the history of Peter the Great's era. However, it should be noted that our goal was not to strictly adhere to the language stylization. The very fact that the persona of "Virtual Peter" exists in the modern world and deals with contemporary tasks allowed us to approach the stylization with a certain degree of freedom. In his "backstory", we had to make the assumption that Virtual Peter has familiarized himself with the realities and terminology of the modern era, in order not to impair the user-bot interaction and the success of the user experience. For example, the opening phrase is: *Privetstvuyu Vas, budushchij student! Ya Vash virtual'nyj pomoshchnik s dushoj Petra I, pokrovitelya nauk i vsyacheskogo ucheniya. Rad budu Vashej milosti otvety na voprosy predostavit.* (*'Greetings to you, future student! I am your virtual assistant with the soul of Peter the Great, patron of sciences and various learning. I shall be honored to guide you on your journey, ask your questions'*). Furthermore, due to the nature of the requested information, it is necessary for the virtual assistant to be familiar with concepts such as telephone, email, website, personal applicant account, and others.

We made an effort to ensure that the content the user seeks is not obscured by archaic speech. Department names, lists of required documents, and similar types of information were conveyed in a modern neutral language. Considering the specific nature of the information (for example, a user's question might require a large table of specialties or a link to a document with admission conditions), the virtual assistant often responds with a link to a website page, allowing for seamless stylization of the assistant's introductory and concluding statements. The only category we considered potentially affected by such a communication style is foreign students, so in the reply to them, the assistant answers in English first, providing them immediately with the link to the English version of the university website. The message for international students is initially provided in English and without stylization, as we assumed that this group of applicants may experience difficulties in understanding the chatbot.

Subsequently, creating texts for the bot became a separate important task, which was further complicated by the potential conflict between the proposed character and the target audience. Peter the Great is a historical figure, an authoritative personality with established views, a person of his time, from whom we do not expect a mastery of the modern language. In other words, he is a conversational partner who may not be easily accepted by a diverse target audience consisting of applicants. Here, we are not only referring to the diversity in age, knowledge level, and professional skills, but also to the fact that the admission process is often an anxious moment. Therefore, the virtual assistant must not only have a distinct personality but also be comfortable to communicate with, informative, and easily understandable.

3 Language Fine-Tuning

3.1 *Outline*

The language used by the virtual assistant is crucial in representing its unique characteristics and advantages. The linguistic features should always be aligned with the functions of the bot and serve its main purpose.

The process of finding the optimal language solution was conducted in three stages. The first stage involved selecting the main language references and preparing quotations that vividly expressed the peculiarities of the language during Peter the Great's era. The second stage consisted of composing a set of phrases that included stylized responses to address all the key questions outlined in the bot's scenario. During this stage, the initial tests of the virtual assistant's performance were conducted. Based on the results of these tests, the main objective for the third stage became clear—it was necessary to create a balanced language for the chatbot where the stylistic elements would not hinder the fulfillment of its main function. Further details regarding each stage are provided below.

3.2 *First Stage: Research*

Information was gathered on the language characteristics of Peter the Great's era (the early eighteenth century).

Firstly, an active use of borrowings from foreign languages [3], both lexical and syntactic, was a typical feature of the language during this period. These borrowings were employed to name both new objects and phenomena, as well as familiar ones, much like we currently use terms such as "computers" and "messages".

Another characteristic was the stylistic diversity and even variety, as indicated by numerous researchers [4]. Thanks to these features, we were able to incorporate various elements into the virtual assistant's language, even if they may seem unfamiliar.

Secondly, the frequent use of Slavicisms was prevalent during the early eighteenth century [4], including words taken from Church Slavonic or constructed according to its model. The stylistic variety was further enriched by their combination with Old Russian words, which were not distinguished by any particular "style" at that time. These words serve as recognizable markers of a different era, and their inclusion became an evident part of our stylization.

As references, we selected Peter the Great's letters [5], as well as the literary and pedagogical monument of the early eighteenth century, "Honest Mirror of Youth, or a Testimony to Social Intercourse Collected from Various Authors" (second part) [6]. The choice of letters was a reference to the prototype of a virtual assistant, while the second source was taken as an example of Peter the Great's era text, which was created for a wide range of readers, as it contained guidelines for the behavior of "*yeonglings*" and noble girls.

In the letters, the main objective was to identify phrases that could be utilized in the virtual assistant's responses for the following situations:

- Greeting
- Response to a request
- Expression of gratitude
- Response to failure
- Response to the interlocutor's aggression
- Message indicating a lack of understanding of the request.

Here are examples of phrases from the letters:

Pis'mo Vashe prinyav, otvetstvuyu: … ('Upon considering your missive I came to the following conclusion…'. Letter 395 to Feodor Apraksin)—For the situation "I understand you, here is the link and an answer to your question".

Pis'mo Vashe ya prinyal, no ne vyrazumel, zasim proshu o tom zhe otpisat' mne inache ('Petition of yours rendered me rather confused. Deliver your request in a different manner. Based on a letter 407 to Boris Sheremetiev).—As an example of a classic phrase for a chatbot, "Sorry, I do not understand you".

Pri sem milosti Vashej zhelayu vsyakogo dobrogo zdraviya ('Hereupon I bid you farewell'. Letter 379 to Feodor Apraksin).—Successful assistance or farewell.

The distinctive speech features visible even in the provided examples include archaic words, independent and auxiliary parts of speech (*zasim, vyrazumel, otvetstvuyu, zelo*), outdated morphemes (*pomoshchiyu, zachinat'*), and word forms (*nadeyusya*), adverbial participial constructions often found at the beginning of sentences, inverse or unfamiliar word order for modern ears (the definition after the determined word: *pis'mo Vashe*), the placement of the predicate at the end of the sentence). Additionally, it is noteworthy to mention the spelling of certain words, characteristic of a time when modern orthographic norms were still being established (*est' li*).

Interestingly, during this period, what can now be referred to as the official-business style was beginning to take shape, even evident in the letters of Peter I. Some phrases that may currently appear excessive or humorous could have been considered normal for official correspondence in the first half of the eighteenth century, and this was also decided to be utilized for stylization.

Unfortunately, suitable examples for responding to the interlocutor's aggression were not found in the letters. This can be attributed to both the genre of the letters and their nature of complementarity, as well as the temporal and spatial distance from the interlocutor.

The reference to the second source, "Youth as an Honest Mirror" [6], provided an understanding that through sentence structure and the incorporation of specific words, one can create the feeling of the language used in the early eighteenth century without burdening the phrase with obscure terminology.

3.3 A Sample of a Lexical Study

In order to maintain the chosen style, it is necessary not only to add elements that create an impression of eighteenth-century language but also to remove words and expressions that appear out of place in the context of all the dialogues and which Peter the Great could not have used.

The "backstory" of the bot assumes that the virtual assistant has learned modern words and understands contemporary realities. This is necessary for the chatbot to remain understandable and useful, as well as able to provide accurate information (about the website, admissions office phone number, document submission method, etc.). However, replacing words that are not directly related to the admissions and education process at the university seems acceptable. Currently, a list of such words is being compiled, and sometimes research into the history of a word is required to determine whether it should be included in this list.

One of such controversial words is the word "*information*". On the one hand, it may seem too modern for the eighteenth century. On the other hand, it has a characteristic Latin appearance, and according to researchers' observations, the number of borrowed Latin and Polish words increased significantly during Peter the Great's era [3].

The eighteenth-century Russian language dictionary does indeed include the word "*information*" with a note that it is a new word, and with a first occurrence date of 1702, as expected, it indicates its Latin origin and borrowing through Polish (*informacyja*), Ukrainian, and Belarusian (*informaciya*) languages. However, the definition the dictionary provides differs from what is expected: "*message, notification; report*" (*And as soon as I receive the information, I will send it to Resident Kaster with a special courier.* AB IV 28). It can be assumed that the modern meaning (for example, in "The Great Explanatory Dictionary": 1. *Information.* 2. A report on the state of affairs somewhere, on certain events, processes, etc. 3. Specialized. Information about the state of affairs in the surrounding world, its properties, ongoing processes, etc.) developed later.

Therefore, in the dialogues of the virtual assistant, the word "information" will have to be replaced.

3.4 Second Stage: Testing the Utterances

Based on Peter the Great's letters, simplified sets of expressions were compiled. For each scenario branch, it was necessary to select several phrases in order to diversify the speech of the virtual assistant. This is required for cases where we anticipate that the user may ask the same question multiple times or begin a conversation with the bot on multiple occasions.

At this stage, the phrases taken from the letters were reworked as follows [7]:

- The syntax of the phrases was simplified, indicating the obvious connection between parts of the sentence and reducing the use of participle constructions. However, the inverted word order for noun + adjective/participle phrases and the placement of the predicate at the end of the sentence were retained.
- The length of the phrases was reduced in order to ensure that the message format does not distract the user from the content.
- Some words have been replaced with more understandable ones. For example: *ponyal* instead of *vyrazumel.*
- Religious fragments, which are often found in letters, have been removed: … *predaya Vas vo vsemogushchestvo Bozhie ('...commending you to the omnipotence of God'), s Bozhieyu pomoshchiyu ('with God's help').*

For the remaining parts of the script, utterances in modern language were prepared, after which the word order was changed, outdated words and words with outdated morphemes were added. As a stylistic device, the use of familiar words in atypical positions was also chosen*: **Takie** dokumenty […] predostavit' potrudites' ('Be so kind as to furnish the following documents')* instead of *eti.*

In addition, it was necessary to come up with response options for obscene language. Users tend to use offensive language toward chatbots more frequently than toward real people, and it was assumed that they would behave the same way even toward a bot in the form of a tsar. In real life, one can end a conversation with an offender or respond sharply, but a bot should maintain the conversation. Therefore, the following formulations were devised as responses to obscene language:

A Vy, ya vizhu, v drevnerusskoj leksike sil'ny! No ezheli Vy zdes' ne za potekhoj, a za znaniem, to izvol'te voproshanie vybrat' ('I gather you have mastered some Russian spells of the days of yore! Yet should you yearn not for amusement but for knowledge, ask your questions with decency').

The intermediate version of the chatbot was tested on a sample of 10 students from the Faculty of Philology and 10 students from the Faculty of Management. After testing, both logs with information about where the user did not want to continue the dialogue and feedback from the students were collected.

The test results showed that in most cases, the chatbot's speech is perceived normally, for example, it is sufficient for it to provide a link. However, some utterances remain unclear, which creates discomfort in communication, even if the necessary information was obtained in the response. There was also a comment about the bot making spelling mistakes in relation to the utterances where outdated spelling of words was used *(est' li).*

3.5 Stage Three: Simplification of the Bot's Language

Considering the test results, the bot's responses were simplified. The utterances were revised to ensure that elements that clearly contributed to the archaic style of speech were retained, but did not cause significant difficulties during testing.

The following stylization methods were preserved:

- Placing the predicate at the end of the sentence;
- Inverting the word order for noun + adjective/participle phrases, although not consistently applied in every sentence;
- Outdated vocabulary mainly retained in the form of function words (e.g. *ezheli, sej, pokuda*, and a conjunction *da*);
- Outdated vocabulary may be used if the utterance contains no more than two such words and the meaning of the phrase is clear from the context, e.g. *Ne dlya kazhdoj special'nosti potrebno sdavat' dopolnitel'noe vstupitel'noe ispytanie. No dlya nekotorykh nuzhno tvorcheskoe ili professional'noe zadanie vypolnit', ili zhe portfolio predostavit'.* ("Not every trade requires another trial. Yet some do: be so kind as to provide the full account of your merits and good deeds (portfolio). Otherwise, mayhap, withstanding a creative challenge is in order");
- The use of familiar words in atypical positions (e.g. *takoj dokument* instead of *etot dokument*);
- Incorporation of idiomatic expressions that are atypical for formal communication to maintain a diverse style, e.g. *Obshchezhitiya **vo vsej krase raspisany** na stranice sej* ("Our students' abode is vividly presented hither **in all its beauty**").

4 Technical Implementation

The virtual assistant was created on the Just AI Conversational Platform (JAICP platform) [8], developed by Just AI. It allows the creation of dialogue systems using developing bot scripts and machine learning. JAICP Domain Specific Language (JAICP DSL) was used for some basic requests of the user. It is based on tags and uses the patterns that describe keywords and expressions. For example, here are two of the patterns that attribute the user request to the state "WhatCanYouDo":

```
q!: * {как* вопрос* * [я] мо* [$you] зада*} *
q!: * {$what * $you * (мож*|уме*)} *
```

The main functionality of the bot was implemented using the CAILA (Conversational AI Linguistic Assistant) module [9]. Unlike rule-based approaches that require writing patterns using special syntax, CAILA is based on Natural Language Understanding, including the "self-learning" function on training phrases. This allows, even if just to a certain extent, not to hard-code user phrases but to rely on semantic similarity in user's prompts recognition.

Below is an example of training phrases for the intent of displaying a list of bachelor's programs:

- What are the available majors?
- Find a bachelor's program.
- What exams do I need to take?
- Where can I apply?
- What is the competition for the program?
- How many spots are available for the program?
- I want to study linguistics.
- Choose a suitable program for my studies.
- Where can I read about the programs?
- Where can I get accepted to mathematics and computer science?
- I passed physics and chemistry, where can I apply with them?
- Find a program based on my results in the Unified State Exam (USE).
- I'm applying to the Faculty of Geography, what USE subjects do I need?

The technology works in such a way that the user is redirected to this intent when entering similar (but not exact) phrases. The CAILA evaluates the system's probabilities for different intents.

The most frequent questions were presented in the form of *Chastye voproshaniya* ("Oft-inquired matters (FAQ)") buttons, which are displayed to the user at the start of the dialogue and after each iteration.

We based our decision on the following advantages of using buttons in text chatbots:

- Buttons significantly reduce the number of failed interactions.
- "User care" is the main principle of UX design: clicking a button is more convenient and/or faster than typing text.
- Buttons are particularly useful when users know what they are interested in but cannot formulate it precisely (e.g., they do not know that all admission campaign events and their dates are referred to as "admission calendar").
- Similarly, buttons help when a dialogue participant does not know what questions other users ask and/or what questions can already be asked, i.e., is not aware of all available information options.

Let us explain the last point: every time a new stage of the admission campaign occurred (the exam schedule was posted, lists of document submitters were published), we added the corresponding question to the top row of the FAQ, thereby simultaneously notifying users about the start of this stage and the availability of information about it.

In the FAQ, we decided not to have a unified syntactic form, formulating questions in a way that a real user might type them into a search engine (some using noun phrases, others using interrogative questions). This was done to mimic the formulations of real users, albeit at the expense of some unity. Later on, we found that frequent user phrases are indeed structured in this way—some queries consist of a phrase for a search engine, while others are in the form of a question.

Following the logic described in the section on language peculiarities of the bot, we decided not to stylize the language in the FAQ. The final list of "Oft-inquired matters" looked like this:

- Lists of applicants
- Examination schedule
- Browse undergraduate programs
- Applicant's personal account
- Documents required to apply
- Application dates and deadlines
- Contact the Admission committee
- Browse graduate programs
- Accommodation
- Admission of international students

Since the launch of the bot on June 11, 2023, the developers have constantly analyzed the logs of user conversations and tuned up the system so that it more accurately understands the intentions of the interlocutors. The tuning included correcting tags in JAICP DSL and new trainings for the CAILA using additional training phrases.

5 The Results of the First Admission Campaign

"The Botik of Peter the Great" was available in the summer of 2023 during the University admissions campaign as a widget on the Admissions Committee's website [10] and on the Telegram messenger platform @SPBU_Petri_bot.

During the period from June 22 (launch of the chatbot) to September 1, 11,950 unique users communicated with the bot, excluding empty sessions. The total number of messages was 59,573 (excluding empty messages). The average duration of one session was 5 messages per user. The use of the FAQ in form of buttons proved to be justified — in the first two weeks of the bot's operation, 58% of user sessions started with the FAQ button. Phrases from the FAQ were used in 68% of all user prompts, and only 32% of messages were written by users in a free form.

User requests such as "Can you speak English" and "English, please" accounted for 30 messages out of approximately 60,000, which is 0.05%.

Below are the examples of some off-topic phrases:

Questions like "who are you/what can you do"	575 times
Question "how are you doing"	25 times
Obscene language	24 times
Phrases like "stupid bot"	10 times
Phrases of gratitude ("thank you", etc.)	137 times
Politely said goodbye to the bot	6 times

Cases of bot responses like "I didn't understand you" account for only about 7% of the total number of messages (3973 messages out of 59,573). This is a very high response rate.

6 Conclusion

In conclusion, our work on designing a conversational interface for the Admissions Committee of St. Petersburg State University has successfully achieved its objectives. By selecting Peter the Great as the virtual assistant's persona, we were able to not only provide users with concise textual responses and relevant links but also reflect the university's values and brand.

Through an in-depth study of Peter the Great's personal correspondence and pedagogical text from the early eighteenth century, we ensured linguistic authenticity of the virtual assistant's language. The collection of expressions derived from these historical sources was tested among a group of students to ensure understandability.

Balancing the stylistic elements with usability requirements posed additional challenges, but through careful research and analysis, we achieved a harmonious blend of historical language and user-friendly interaction. The use of the CAILA platform enabled us to develop the "The Botik of Peter the Great" chatbot, which captures the essence of Peter the Great's era while remaining engaging, informative, and accessible.

The successful implementation of the chatbot as a widget on the Admissions Committee's website and availability on the Telegram messenger platform further demonstrates the effectiveness of our language solution in meeting users' needs.

Overall, our research showcases the significance of designing a conversational interface that not only provides practical assistance but also embodies the values and spirit of an institution. The findings from this project contribute to the field of conversational interfaces and serve as a reference for similar endeavors in utilizing historical personas and language to create engaging and user-centric virtual assistants.

Acknowledgements The authors would like to express their gratitude to Andrey Grebenyuk and Evgenii Sokolov for their help with archaic forms of language. The present study was supported by the grant of St. Petersburg State University (project No. 124032900006-1 "Modeling the communicative behavior of residents of a Russian metropolis in social, speech and pragmatic aspects using artificial intelligence methods").

References

1. Pearl, C.: Designing Voice User Interfaces: Principles of Conversational Experiences. O'Reilly Media, Inc. (2016)
2. Saerbeck, M., Schut, T., Bartneck, C., Janse, M.: Expressive robots in education: varying the degree of social supportive behavior of a robotic tutor. In: Proceedings of the 28th International Conference on Human Factors in Computing Systems, vol. 3, pp. 1613–1622 (2010)
3. Sanbaiyar, V.: Inoyazychnaya leksika v putevykh zapiskakh Petrovskoj epokhi [Foreign vocabulary in travel notes of the Petrovsky era. In: Knowledge. Understanding. Skill, no. 1, pp. 154–159 (2007)
4. Mayorov, A.P.: Slavyanizmy v delovom yazyke 1-y poloviny XVIII veka [Slavonicisms in the business language of the 1st half of the 18th century]. In: Philological Sciences, no. 4, pp. 29–36 (2009).
5. Bychkov, A.F. (ed.): Pisma i bumagi imperatora Petra Velikago [Letters and Papers of Emperor Peter the Great], vols. 2–4. Gosudarstvennaya Tipografiya, Saint Petersburg (1893–1900)
6. Yunost chestnoe zertzalo ili Pokazanie k zhitejskomu obkhozhdeniyu, sobrannoe ot raznykh avtorov. Napechatasya poveleniem Tzarskogo velichestva [Honest Mirror of Youth, or a Testimony to Social Intercourse Collected from Various Authors. Published by the Decree of His Majesty the Tsar]. Khudozhestvennaya Literatura, Moscow (1976)
7. Babaeva, E.A., Zapolskaya, N.N.: Yazykovoj kontinuum Petrovckoj epokhi: obzor grammaticheskikh traktatov pervoj chetverty XVIII veka [Language continuum of the Petrovsky era: an overview of grammatical treatises from the first quarter of the 18th century]. Studies in Slavic historical linguistics. In: Khaburgaev, G.L. (eds.) Memory of Professor, pp. 188–206. MSU, Moscow (1993)
8. JAICP Homepage.https://just-ai.com/platforma-jaicp. Accessed 1 July 2023
9. CAILA Documentation. https://docs.caila.io/docs/ru/. Accessed 1 July 2023
10. The website of St. Petersburg State University Admissions committee. https://abiturient.spbu.ru/. Accessed 1 July 2023

RuOHQA: Creating QA Corpus in Russian Based on Oral History Archives

Liudmila Bukreeva, Daria Guseva, Mikhail Dolgushin, Vera Evdokimova, and Vasilisa Obotnina

Abstract The work described in this paper is aimed to enable better analysis of oral history archives. Our objective was to turn many facts and stories from Holocaust survivors into more accessible forms. We focused on Russian oral history archives, namely on the spoken interviews collected by the Yad Vashem Foundation, transcribed and summarized these valuable data sources automatically as well as manually by experts. We created the new Russian question–answer corpus (ruOHQA) that represents a labeled data-collection of oral history archives containing over 1,555 entries. Structure of SQuAD was used as a base approach for data organization. This paper discusses the detailed creation process, linguistic characteristics, strengths, and weaknesses of the corpus. We compare the ruOHQA with the SberQuAD dataset in order to clearly demonstrate our contributions and the potential for further research in this area. Particular attention was paid to the potential of the corpus for training neural network models. Hence, we present the annotated task-oriented corpora of Holocaust testimonies in Russian.

Keywords Question answering · Corpora · Visual history archives

1 Introduction

Oral history is a method of preserving historical records [1] as well as conducting an interview with people who participated in historically significant events. In this case, the interview affords insights into the narrator's memories so that the narrator could share their personal story and subjective vision of history. As a result, the researchers attain spoken accounts kept in the form of audio and video recordings that become an invaluable source of data. The further goal is to transcribe and summarize oral history archives in order to enable their analysis and interpretation.

The large amount of oral history data in Russian spans over multiple topics. For example, The Visual History Archive of Holocaust testimonies compiled by the

L. Bukreeva · D. Guseva · M. Dolgushin (✉) · V. Evdokimova · V. Obotnina
St. Petersburg State University, Universitetskaya Emb., 7-9, Saint-Petersburg 199034, Russia
e-mail: dolgushin.m@iias.spb.su

P. Eismont et al. (eds.), *Literature, Language and Computing*,
https://doi.org/10.1007/978-981-96-0990-1_16

USC Shoah Foundation [2] possesses over 7,000 multimedia recordings in Russian where approximately 200 are annotated with keywords. Apart from that, the Yad Vashem Foundation provides 25 freely available interviews with Holocaust survivors in Russian [3]. Most of the videos contain manually typed subtitles. Despite the stable interest in materials of such kind [4–6], there is no collected tagged-corpus for the presented records.

Annotated interviews can be gathered into a Question–Answer corpus and further used as the dataset to train neural network models for the question answering task. In this paper we present the Russian QA Corpus based on the interviews from the Yad Vashem Foundation. The corpus contains over 2,000 automatically gathered entries, further manually aligned and abelled by experts.

In Sect. 3, we describe the principle of creating the corpus, the stages of its creation and the difficulties we encountered. Section 4 presents a preliminary analysis of the linguistic characteristics of the corpus. The conclusion, potential, and possible usefulness of the proposed corpora for further research are described in Sect. 5.

2 Related Work

In recent years, multiple researches on the processing of corpora based on the material of the Archives with visual history data have been presented to attempt its application in the QA problem. The international project MALACH (Multilingual Access to Large Spoken Archives) [7] was launched in 2003 for the purpose of creating a system for automatic selection of keywords in the multimedia materials of the Shoah archive. As a result, speech recognition systems with sufficient accuracy to highlight keywords were created in many languages: English, Hungarian, Czech, Slovak, Russian [8–11]. Based on the MALACH project, transcribed corpora were created and published in English and Czech [12, 13].

The article [4] estimates the culturally significant task of recognizing the highly emotional speech of Holocaust witnesses based on the data of the MALACH corpus. Following the practice of the previous article [4], the developments in [5] are intended toward expanding speech recognition of the Holocaust witnesses in Czech as well as in English.

The study [14] describes crafting of a rule-based dialogue system formulating queries specified by an expert for obtaining answers to questions from the history applications archive based on the MALACH corpora. The previously mentioned paper [6] develops a QA model that would allow formulating queries in a natural language; however, the resulting accuracy turns out to be very limited due to the colloquial form of speech in the researched mMQA corpus with 8914 entries of questions and answers. The results of experiments show that further research of oral history data remains relevant.

The main dataset for developing and testing models in Russian to solve the QA problem is SberQuAD [15]. It was created in accordance with the methodology used for the development of the English SQuAD corpus [16, 17]. It contains about 50,000 question–answer pairs.

The paper [18] presents an automatically tagged corpus based on the Russian Wikipedia with 160 thousand ruGPT-3 records remaining after processing, and 3.4 million records generated by ruT5.

Our task focuses explicitly on creating the QA dataset and considers its further applied usage following the practice of earlier works published.

3 Method

Our data-gathering process started from collecting video recordings of interviews with Holocaust survivors from the Yad Vashem Foundation [3]. A recording could be added to our corpus only if it contained manually added subtitles. Interview recordings with automatic subtitles (4 out of 25) were not added to the corpus due to the error prone process of speech recognition technology. Thus, we collected 21 transcribed recordings with the total duration of approximately 26 h. The size of the corpus containing unpreprocessed subtitles reached 20,200 entries.

Video recordings and subtitle files were indexed with unique codes identifying them. The videos were divided into smaller parts according to the start and end marks obtained from the subtitles. All the video materials were kept in order to further clarify the controversial points during the corpus annotation, which arose when the interviewer and the narrator spoke simultaneously.

Since punctuation in subtitles was kept as in original in most cases, we decided to conduct a preliminary automatic annotation of the corpus, thereby dividing the interviewer's speech from that of the narrator's. The context of the expected replies to the questions was automatically extracted based on the assumption that the answer would follow an interrogative sentence. However, in some cases it led to the false selection when questions followed one another (e.g. 'Kak ee zvali? Vy pomnite?'—'What was her name? Do you remember?') as well as to the false detection of questions when the narrator's answer speech contained rhetorical questions or questions within the context of a story (e.g. 'i emu govoryat: "Slushaj, ty ehtogo mal'chika znaesh'?" On govorit ...'—'and they say to him: "Listen, do you know this boy?" He says ...'). As a result of the initial automatic preprocessing, 4228 pairs of question–answer contexts were selected with the preservation of the index from the subtitles. The spoken form of the interviews, the age of the narrators, and the roughness of automatic preprocessing made it difficult to select correct phrases directly related to the question. We decided to annotate our gathered material manually using an expert assessment of four people.

The next phase of our work turned out to be the most challenging and time consuming. According to the results, many errors made by the automatic annotation were corrected along with constructing the specialized format of our corpus. New question entries were also added in case they were inaccurately assigned to the context of the answer. If necessary, the missing punctuation was added to the text

Table 1 Corpus sample with translation

Id	Question	Answer	Context
353_ 686	Vash dom zhe stoit ili vam negde zhit'?	Net. On stoyal, no on ves' byl razvorovannyj. Tam nichego ne bylo	Net. On stoyal, no on ves' byl razvorovannyj. Tam nichego ne bylo. I mama ne poshla tuda zhit' bol'she. Mama. Potomu chto, vsekh rasstrelyali. I mama poshla v kvartiru, gde ee dvoyurodnaya sestra s tremya devochkami, tozhe rasstrelyali, i my poshli v ehtu kvartiru
353_ 686	Was your house standing or did you have nowhere to live?	No. It stood, but it was all plundered. There was nothing there	No. It stood, but it was all plundered. There was nothing there. And mom didn't go there to live anymore. Mom. Because everyone was shot. And my mother went to the apartment where her cousin and three girls were also shot, and we went to this apartment

in accordance with the syntactic rules, grammatical and orthographic mistakes were corrected as well. The possible interviewer's remarks were removed from the context of the answers. As a result, we annotated 1327 entries and composed them into the Russian Oral History Question Answering dataset (ruOHQA). An example of the record with translation into English is presented in Table 1.

We followed the same structure for every entry in our corpus. The first column contains unique indexes of the interrogative speech from the subtitles. The second column is the interviewer's question to the narrator. The third column includes only those answers of the narrator that are directly related to the interviewer's question. Finally, the fourth column contains the context of the answer with all the details provided by the narrator within their story during the interview.

4 Data Analysis

To illustrate the contribution of the ruOHQA dataset, in Table 2 we compare it to the similar Russian QA corpus SberQuAD.

Several important statistics include the average question, answer and context length in both QA corpora. Table 2 clearly shows that the average question length is similar in both datasets, while the average answer length differs considerably. The longer average length of answers in the ruOHQA corpus can be explained by the fact

Table 2 Statistics of the ruOHQA and SberQuAD datasets

Dataset	Total number of samples	Avg. question length (words)	Avg. answer length (words)	Avg. context length (words)
ruOHQA	1,555	7,076	5,444	22,858
SberQuAD	50,364	8,613	2,433	98,666

that the narrators often go into the details about the cases making their speech more extended, although less concise.

To reflect word frequency usage in the ruOHQA corpus, we counted 30 most common tokens in its question and answer parts. Our preliminary processing involved the lemmatizing procedure. We used the Python library pymorphy2 [19] for this purpose. After the lemmatization we removed stop words including prepositions and conjunctions so that we get only the tokens necessary to our query. The graphs of token frequency in Figs. 1 and 2 were finally obtained with the use of the natural language processing library in Python—nltk [20].

The solid curve in Fig. 1 depicts 30 most frequent lemmatized words found in questions from our corpus. The following words reflect specific topics discussed during the interviews: the words related to Holocaust, e.g. 'vojna' (war), 'pomnit'' (remember), 'evrej' (jew) as well as the words connected with family or relatives, e.g. 'mama' (mom), 'papa' (dad), etc. Pronouns and interrogative words also serve as the most common tokens expressing an interviewer's appeal to narrators in the

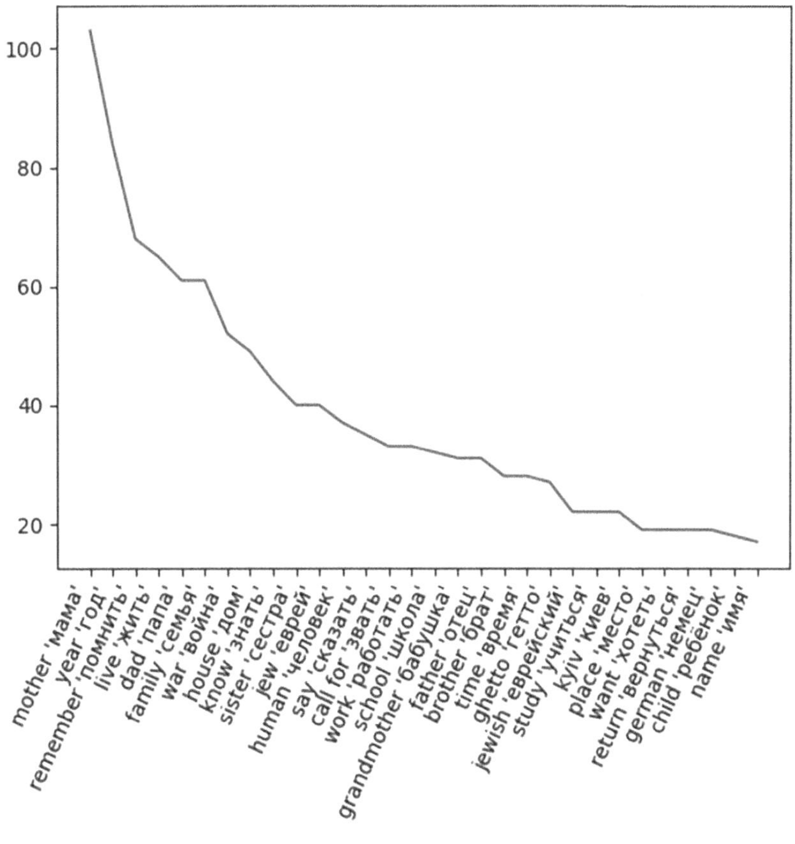

Fig. 1 Frequency distribution for 30 most common tokens in ruOHQA questions

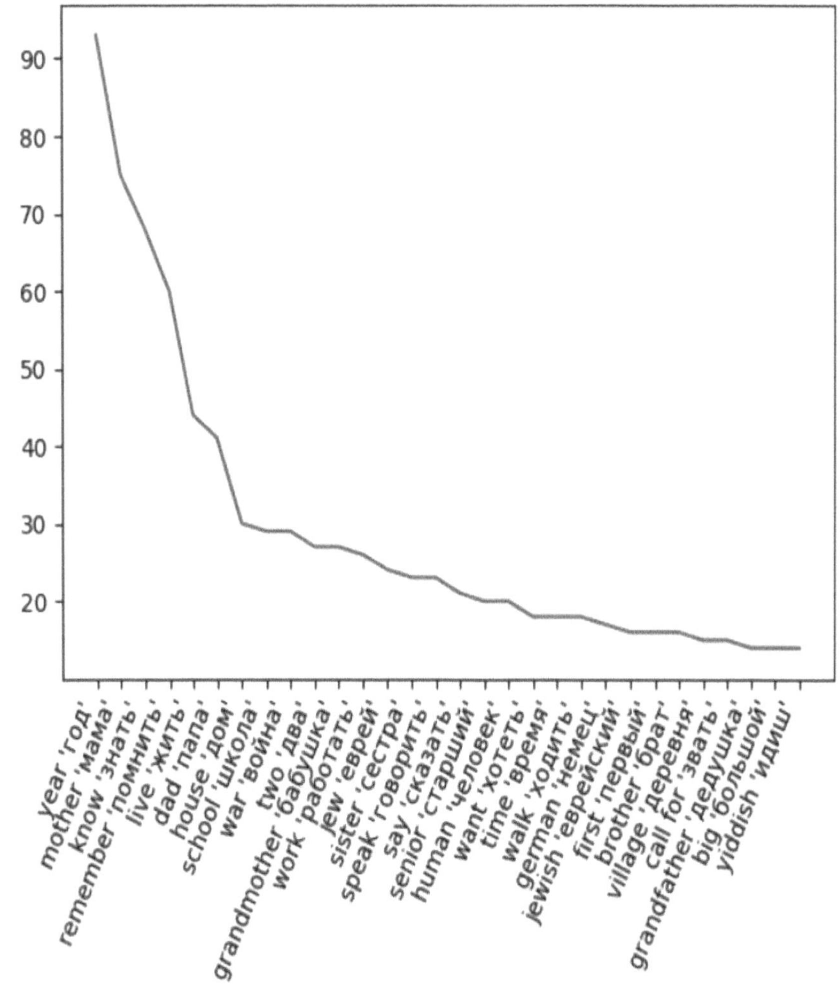

Fig. 2 Frequency distribution for 30 most common tokens in ruOHQA answers

questions' frequency list. The frequency usage is quite representative for material based on interviews with Jewish Holocaust survivors.

The chart in Fig. 2 represents the 30 most common lemmatized words found in answers of the ruOHQA corpus. Here, as in questions, verbs associated with memories are frequently used, e.g. 'znat'' (to know), 'pomnit'' (to remember), and nouns related to family members are spotted, e.g. 'mama' (mom), 'papa' (dad), 'babushka' (grandma), etc. One more specific frequently used word in this corpus showing the nationality of the narrator is 'evrej' (jew).

The chart in Fig. 3 represents the 30 most common lemmatized words found in context of the ruOHQA corpus.

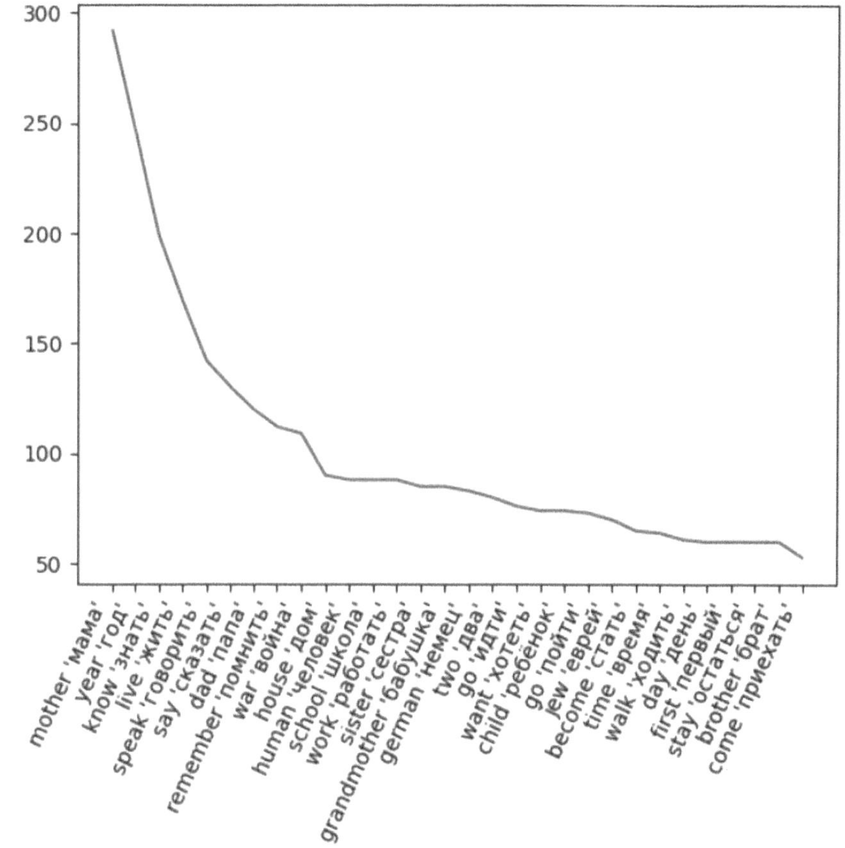

Fig. 3 Frequency distribution for 30 most common tokens in ruOHQA context

5 Conclusion

This article presents a new question–answer corpus based on interview material with Holocaust survivors. The historical significance and complexity of developing such a corpus is described, since speech in the presented corpus initially has an oral form and is largely influenced by the emotional state and age of the respondents, which is clearly spotted in the text. The method according to which the tagging was carried out and the statistical characteristics of the resulting dataset were presented.

In future research, it is scheduled to expand the corpus by processing other materials from oral history archives, such as the Shoah Foundation [2], containing about 7,000 video recordings of people who survived the Holocaust and were interviewed in Russian with no annotated text presented. It is also planned to train a question–answer neural network model based on this material, which would make it possible to obtain answers to questions of interest asked in natural language directly from the interview document.

References

1. Abrams, L.: Oral History Theory. Routledge, London (2016)
2. USC Shoah Foundation. https://sfi.usc.edu/
3. YouTube playlist of Holocaust survivors testimonies by Yad Vashem foundation. https://www.youtube.com/playlist?list=PLanQ0TFmIYBTV8sRAkSDWQLZNhbM v1xp
4. Picheny, M., Tüske, Z., Kingsbury, B., Audhkhasi, K., Cui, X., Saon, G.: Challenging the boundaries of speech recognition: the MALACH corpus. Interspeech **2019**, 326–330 (2019)
5. Psutka, J.V., Pražák, A., Vaněk, J.: Recognition of heavily accented and emotional speech of english and czech holocaust survivors using various DNN architectures. In: Karpov, A., Potapova, R. (eds.) Speech and Computer. SPECOM 2021. Lecture Notes in Computer Science(), vol 12997. Springer, Cham (2021)
6. Chýlek, A., Švec, J., Šmídl, L.: Initial Experiments on Question Answering from the Intrinsic Structure of Oral History Archives. In: Karpov, A., Potapova, R. (eds.) Speech and Computer. SPECOM 2021. Lecture Notes in Computer Science(), vol 12997. Springer, Cham. (2021)
7. MALACH project (2006). https://malach.umiacs.umd.edu/
8. Byrne, W., et al.: Automatic recognition of spontaneous speech for access to multilingual oral history archives. IEEE Trans. Speech Audio Process. **12**(4), 420–435 (2004)
9. Mihajlik, P., Fegyó, T., Németh, B., Tüske, Z., Trón, V.: Towards automatic transcription of large spoken archives in agglutinating languages—Hungarian ASR for the MALACH project. In: TSD 2007. LNCS (LNAI, (ed.) Matoušek, V., Mautner, P, vol. 4629, pp. 342–349. Springer, Heidelberg (2007)
10. Psutka, J., Ircing, P., Psutka, J.V., Hajič, J., Byrne, W., Mírovský, J.: Automatic transcription of Czech, Russian and Slovak spontaneous speech in the MALACH project. In: Eurospeech 2005, pp. 1349–1352. ISCA (2005)
11. Ramabhadran, B., Huang, J., Picheny, M.: Towards automatic transcription of large spoken archives—English ASR for the MALACH project. In: ICASSP 2003, p. I (2003)
12. Ramabhadran, B., et al.: USC-SFI MALACH Interviews and Transcripts English. In: LDC2012S05. Web Download. Philadelphia: Linguistic Data Consortium (2012)
13. Psutka, J., Radová, V., Ircing, P., Matoušek, J., Müller, L.: USC-SFI MALACH Interviews and Transcripts Czech. In: LDC2014S04. Web Download. Philadelphia: Linguistic Data Consortium (2014)
14. Chýlek, A., Šmídl, L., Švec, J.: Question-answering dialog system for large audio-visual archives. In: TSD 2019. LNCS (LNAI, (ed.) Ekˇstein, K, vol. 11697, pp. 385–397. Springer, Cham (2019)
15. Efimov, P., Chertok, A., Boytsov, L., Braslavski, P.: SberQuAD – Russian Reading Comprehension Dataset: Description and Analysis. In: Experimental IR Meets Multilinguality, Multimodality, and Interaction, 11th International Conference of the CLEF Association, CLEF 2020, Thessaloniki, Greece, September 22–25, 2020, Proceedings, pp. 3–15 (2020)
16. Pranav Rajpurkar, Jian Zhang, Konstantin Lopyrev, Percy Liang.: SQuAD: 100,000+ questions for machine comprehension of text. In Proceedings of the 2016 Conference on Empirical Methods in NaturalLanguage Processing, pages 2383–2392, Austin, Texas, November. Association for Computational Linguistics. (16) (PDF) Data Augmentation with Masked Aspect Language Modeling for Aspect Term Extraction (2016)
17. Rajpurkar, P., Jia, R., Liang, P.: Know What You Don't Know: Unanswerable Questions for SQuAD. In: Proceedings of the 56th Annual Meeting of the Association for Computational Linguistics (Volume 2: Short Papers), pp. 784–789, Melbourne, Australia. Association for Computational Linguistics (2018)

18. Dina Pisarevskaya, Tatiana Shavrina.: WikiOmnia: filtration and evaluation of the generated QA corpus on the whole Russian Wikipedia. In Proceedings of the 2nd Workshop on Natural Language Generation, Evaluation, and Metrics (GEM), pp. 125–135, Abu Dhabi, United Arab Emirates (Hybrid). Association for Computational Linguistics (2022)
19. Morphological analyzer pymorphy2. https://pymorphy2.readthedocs.io
20. NLTK documentation. https://www.nltk.org

Corpora in Teaching and Translation

Contrastive Analysis to Identify Cross-Linguistic Correspondences for Translation Purposes

Adelya K. Abdulmanova, Ekaterina K. Vyunova, and Irina A. Lekomtseva

Abstract The article focuses on how we can use contrastive analysis for translation purposes, i.e. search for and identify cross-linguistic correspondences, variants in translation. To find cross-linguistic variants, we used parallel texts matched in subject domain and text type. The cross-linguistic correspondences are viewed as functionally complete units that are natural and idiomatic for each language. These units were analysed by the theoretical language-independent model of the lexico-semantic set, both in the paradigmatic and syntagmatic dimensions. Cross-linguistically, they were compared across the semantic, language-independent categories. The results of the contrastive analysis were used as possible translation choices to achieve functional equivalence. To mark the difference between the polar types of translation equivalence, we used machine-based translation and functional translation. Contrastive analysis provides a wide range of idiomatic and natural language choices for translation.

Keywords Cross-linguistic correspondences · Lexical contrastive studies · Translation equivalence

1 Introduction

The advent of computer technologies has had the tremendous impact on what contrastive analysis is concerned with and how it can be used for translation purposes. In the past, contrastive analysis was chiefly concerned with comparisons of abstract systems across languages, with phonology and grammar in the centre. Today, a growing interest in real-life communication has shifted the focus away from the earlier preoccupation with abstract language (sub)systems in the direction of natural discourse and empirical data as evidence for intra-linguistic, cross-linguistic, and translation observations, with a special emphasis on lexically oriented approaches to contrastive analysis [2, 5]. The cross-linguistic lexical studies are predominantly

A. K. Abdulmanova · E. K. Vyunova · I. A. Lekomtseva (✉)
St. Petersburg State University, Saint-Petersburg, Russia
e-mail: i.lekomtseva@spbu.ru

P. Eismont et al. (eds.), *Literature, Language and Computing*,
https://doi.org/10.1007/978-981-96-0990-1_17

corpus-based studies and the focus of contrastive analysis is therefore language use, rather than language systems. In this regard, the results of corpus-based contrastive analysis can be used for translation purposes.

The aim of this paper is, then, to identify cross-linguistic variants, or cross-linguistic correspondences, i.e. alternative ways of rendering a particular meaning or function in the source and target languages, to use them as possible translation equivalents. To this end, we used parallel texts found on the Internet that served as comparable corpora. The study was carried out as part of a student translation project during the popular-science translation classes at St. Petersburg University.

Our emphasis is not so much on developing the large-scale lexical database of cross-linguistic correspondences which would include a comprehensive description of how language-independent, or logical or semantic, categories are expressed in languages, but rather on the need to preliminary outline the scope and develop a methodology of how to use parallel texts to find cross-linguistics variants as possible translation choices. The main outcome of our study, as we see it, should be an awareness of the need for a larger-scale corpus-based contrastive analysis for translation.

Although the idea to examine patterns of language across texts and consider the relationship between languages was previously expressed both in Russia [8, 24] and beyond [10, 12], there are still few attempts of contrastive analysis for translation purposes [1, 9, 11]. The functional approach to linguistic and cross-linguistic phenomena in translation studies with particular application for translation solutions will enable us to reconsider basic categories of translation studies (e.g. equivalence, translation techniques, etc.) in prescriptive, rather than descriptive dimension. The present paper just provides such an emphasis. This is the focus of the scientific novelty of the paper.

Traditional linguistic approach to translation studies heavily relies on viewing language as a system: a set of words (dictionaries) and a set of rules (grammar). Although dictionaries provide large-scale databases, nevertheless the resulting lexicons tend to be inadequate for translation purposes, especially when it comes to establishing functional equivalence [23], i.e. making a target text seem like an original in the target language, especially in terms of syntagmatic relations as they are highly language-specific. Such contextual patterning of words may consist of several words and these multiword units tend to be stable in form, both lexically and grammatically. Even collocation dictionaries provide little information of this kind.

If we rely only on dictionaries as a source of linguistic data for translation, the translations tend to retain traces of the source language [6], or "translationese", as Chesterman puts it [4]. Particularly, it can be seen in a general tendency, or a universal of translation, to contain fewer "unique items" than comparable non-translated texts [4, pp. 3–13]. A unique item is one that is in some sense specific to the target language and is presumably not so easily triggered by a source-language item that is formally different. Unique items thus tend to be under-represented in translations.

Cross-linguistically, by studying parallel texts we discover idiomatic and natural language choices in each language. In recent studies, linguistic units that are in the focus on contrastive analysis are referred to as functionally complete units of meaning [3]. The notion of functionally complete units of meaning heavily relies on the assumption that words are not isolated but found in semantic and functional relationship with other words. We can characterise functionally complete units of meaning in the following way: they involve collocational (lexical) and colligational (grammatical) choices and cannot be defined solely in lexical or grammatical terms; they are syntagmatic units in that they interrelate with other words and form a multi-word unit which becomes available as a single choice on the paradigmatic axis [3, p. 91].

In Russian translation studies, the notion of functionally complete units is closely related to a notion of cross-linguistic correspondences/variants/synonyms that are idiomatic, stable, natural for each language [21] The idea that such units function lexically and syntactically as a single choice was also proposed by Retsker as far as 1950s. He proposed a notion of "structural-semantic nodes" that make up a single conceptual entity and cannot be defined solely as lexical or grammatical units [20].

The advantage of using parallel texts to identify cross-linguistic correspondences as functionally complete units to choose from during translation is that they are idiomatic and natural in each language. This ensures the translation is accessible and readable for the target-language reader and makes the translation seem like an original in the target language [22, p. 10]. Translationally, cross-linguistic insights gained from parallel texts can be viewed in the sub-paradigm of natural equivalence proposed by A. Pym. Cross-linguistic correspondences are presumed to exist prior to translating. In principle, as Pym puts it, "it makes no difference whether you translate from language A into language B or vice versa: you should get the same value both ways". These cross-linguistic correspondences underpin equivalence-maintaining solutions, or translation solutions, proposed by Vinay and Darbelnet [19, p. 6]. The question is how we can find these functionally equivalent cross-linguistic variants.

2 Methodology

The project was carried out as part of the popular-science translation classes at St. Petersburg University. The project involved first-year master's students in literary translation in the spring semester of 2022–23 academic year.

To find cross-linguistic variants, students used the Internet as a corpus of original, non-translated texts [15]. We used a search engine Google and used several search options. Among them were the following: search for the exact word or phrase (put the word or phrase in quotation marks); combining queries (enter the *OR* operator between queries); search for a specific site (type *site:* before the website address or domain); and find sites with similar content (type *related:* in front of the desired web address). The texts were in the English and Russian languages and matched in subject domain and text type. The subject domain was "Arctic sea ice decline". The text type was newspaper popular-science articles published between 2020 and 2023. It is important to note that our aim was to show how we can use parallel texts in the classroom setting to identify cross-linguistic variants as possible translation choices, rather than to perform a comprehensive corpus-based contrastive analysis.

The project had two parts: a contrastive part and a translation part. The contrastive part included the three methodological steps of any contrastive analysis: description, juxtaposition, and comparison. The description included selection of the items to be compared and a preliminary characterisation of these in terms of a language-independent theoretical model, i.e. lexico-semantic set. The juxtaposition involved a search for and identification of cross-linguistic variants. In the comparison proper the degree and type of correspondence between the compared items were specified [2, p. 14]. The translation part was an attempt to use the results of the contrastive analysis for translation purposes and to compare the different translations that we based on the results of the contrastive analysis and on dictionaries.

As we are primarily concerned with translation matter, our starting point in the contrastive analysis was a text to be translated from Russian language into English language [26].

The first step was to identify keywords/lexical units in the source text, i.e. units that refer to key information. Then we found other Russian original texts in the same subject matter and genre to identify intra-linguistic synonymous units. We organised these units into the lexico-semantic set that would serve as a language-independent theoretical model as a basis for contrastive analysis. The units were organised in the set by specific semantic relations on the paradigmatic and syntagmatic axis. To this end, we started from the onomasiological perspective to organise lexical units into the lexico-semantic set and, following Karaulov's approach, used four large semantic, language-independent categories as part of the lexico-semantic set, mainly: nomination; predication; location; and assessment [14]. We also added a semantic category of time. Further, by using a semasiological approach to organising lexical units into the lexico-semantic set, we developed a more accurate and deep structuring of the set by semantic decomposition of the lexical units to reveal semantic zones, i.e. units of meaning within these language-independent categories. These semantic, language-independent categories, along with the semantic zones, served as a basis for comparison—the tertium comparations—to search for and identify cross-linguistic variants in the target language. Also, we identified syntagmatic relation between the lexical units. As a result, we had a complex network of paradigmatic and syntagmatic relationship between the lexical units that varied in terms of fixedness and idiomaticity.

From a contrastive point of view, it does make sense to attempt to combine the paradigmatic and syntagmatic perspectives. As known, the meaning of lexical units can be determined with respect to two linguistic dimensions: the paradigmatic and syntagmatic [2, p. 27]. The paradigmatic dimension reflects how the senses of the lexical units in a language are related to each other. Monolingually, these relations are traditionally described in terms of synonymy, hyponymy and belonging relations, namely: part (details, signs)—whole, object—internal attribute, object—external attribute, and object—locus [14]. The syntagmatic dimension relates words to the linguistic context, lexically, semantically, and grammatically. Syntagmatic phenomena are described in terms of lexical co-occurrence (collocation), or contextual patterning of words. Semantic features of semantic zones representing procedural knowledge will be represented by actant structures: agents, objects, location, instruments, purpose, cause, manner, etc. [7, 14] Cross-linguistically, the use of collocations tends to be highly language-specific and the syntagmatic aspect of lexis is therefore of great importance, both theoretically and practically.

Such complex network of paradigmatic and syntagmatic relationship between the lexical units bridges the gap between the underlying linguistic system and textual practice. In other words, as Karaulov puts it, it represents language in its "pre-speech readiness" [14].

The second step involved a search for and identification of cross-linguistic variants in the English language to be compared across these semantic language-independent categories. We used original, non-translated English texts matched in the subject matter and text type with the Russian original, non-translated texts. The work also resulted in a complex network of paradigmatic and syntagmatic relationship of lexical units, i.e. a lexico-semantic set in the English language.

The third step was to identify the type and degree of correspondence between the cross-linguistic variants. Thus, the contrastive analysis resulted in identifying functionally complete units in each language to be further used in translation.

The translation part involved using the identified cross-linguistic variants as possible translation equivalents to achieve functional equivalence. To mark the difference between the machine-based translations that are mainly based on the assumptions that translation choices are determined by cross-linguistic correspondences derived from contrastive analysis of the language as a system, and the translations that used the results of the functional contrastive analysis, students made two variants of translations: first, they used a machine translation service Google Translate; and second, they used the results of the contrastive analysis to produce a target text.

The project was implemented during two classes (four academic hours). The first class focused on the contrastive part and an attempt to use the results of the contrastive analysis in translation. During the second class, we discussed the results of the contrastive analysis and translations and outlined the possible ways of how we could use the results of the contrastive analysis for translating texts by applying different strategies for translation of newspaper popular-science texts. This approach to translation of newspaper popular-science articles was used for translating texts of other subject domains, too.

3 Results and Discussion

3.1 Contrastive Analysis

Below is an example of lexico-semantic set "Arctic sea ice decline" in the Russian and English languages in contrastive perspective (Table 1).

Table 1 Results of contrastive analysis

Paradigmatic dimension	
Semantic category "Nomination"	
Semantic zone "Ice" led, arkticheskiy morskoy led, ploshchad ldov, ledovaya shapka, obshchaya ploshchad ldov v Severnom Ledovitom okeane, obyem morskogo lda v Arktike, dolya mnogoletnego lda, ledyanoy pokrov	Semantic zone "Ice" Arctic summer sea ice, summertime Arctic Sea ice, a sea ice-free summer Arctic, Arctic Sea ice, polar ice sheets, vast ice sheets at the poles, the ice in this region, polar ice, ice cover
Semantic category "Location"	
Semantic zone "Arctic" Arktika, Severniy Ledovity Okean	Semantic zone "Arctic" Arctic, Arctic Sea, icy regions
Semantic category "Time"	
Semantic zone "Summer" Letnie mesyatsy, leto, bezledniy sezon, bezlednoe leto	Semantic zone "Summer" ice-free summer, summer months, summer, this time of the year
Semantic zone "Referring to when something happens over a period of time" Letom, v letne-osenniy period	Semantic zone "Referring to when something happens over a period of time" During the summer, in summer and autumn
Syntagmatic dimension	
Semantic category "Predication"	
Semantic zone "Melting" Predicate phrases: morskoy led budet ischezat, ldy tayut, ploshchad ldov umenshayetsya, ploshchad ldov sokrashchayetsya, obyem morskogo lda snizilsya, Arktika stremitelno tayet, padayet dolya mnogoletnego lda, Arktika poteryala okolo 40% ledyanogo pokrova, Arktika budet polnostyu osvobozhdatsya ot lda, Arktika budet svobodna oto lda Noun phrases: polnoye tayaniye arkticheskikh ldov, pochti polnoye letneye tayaniye morskogo lda v Arktike	Semantic zone "Melting" Predicate phrases: Arctic summer sea ice could be gone; Summertime Arctic Sea ice sure to vanish, vast ice sheets at the poles will continue to melt away, Arctic Sea ice may soon disappear completely, lose ice cover, icy regions are melting at increasing rates, ice loss each year has been rising steadily
Noun phrases: polnoye tayaniye arkticheskikh ldov, pochti polnoye letneye tayaniye morskogo lda v Arktike	
Semantic zone "Results of Arctic sea ice melting"	Semantic zone "Results of Arctic sea ice melting"
vsya Arktika budet svobodna oto lda v letniye mesyatsy, Arktike predskazali svobodu oto lda, Severniy Ledovitiy okean v letnie mesyatsy budet pochti svoboden oto lda	The Arctic will see ice-free summer, the Arctic may be sea ice-free in summer, the Arctic could go ice-free, the Arctic will have ice-free summers

The contrastive part resulted in the lexico-semantic sets "Arctic sea ice decline" in the English and Russian languages. Linguistically, the set is organized on paradigmatic and syntagmatic axis, and the results are functionally complete units that involve collocational (lexical) and colligational (grammatical) choices. On the paradigmatic axis, the lexical units in each semantic zone are in relation of synonymy as a sense may be linguistically represented by several linguistic units [21].

The set may need deeper structuring by more accurate semantic decomposition of its elements. A deeper and more semantically diverse structure will include more semantic zones depending on what units of meaning we need to analyse in a cross-linguistic dimension. Yet our aim is just to outline the general methodology of how to organise lexical units in the contrastive perspective by the theoretical model of the lexico-semantic set as a set of language-independent categories and lexical units.

Cross-linguistically, these units are cross-linguistic variants, or synonyms. Translationally, the functional complete units can be used as translation equivalents, especially if a translator strives to achieve functional equivalence and make a target text seem like an original, as the functionally complete units have a certain degree of fixedness and idiomaticity that makes them natural for each language.

3.2 Translation

Let us take a sentence from the source text to translate into English. We present two variants of translation: a machine-based translation and a functional translation, i.e. a translation that is based on the results of the functional contrastive analysis.

Source text: Mnogie issledovateli prognoziruyut, chto v techeniye neskolkikh mesyatsev *v letne-osenniy period vsya Arktika budet svobodna oto lda* [26].

Machine-based translation (Google Translate): Many researchers predict that *the entire Arctic will be ice-free for several months during the summer-autumn period.*

Functional translations:

The Arctic may be sea ice-free in summer and autumn, researchers predict.
The Arctic will likely see summer free of ice, researchers predict.
The Arctic could go ice-free in summer, researchers predict.
The Arctic will have ice-free summers, researchers predict.

The machine-based translation tends to contain traces of the source language, especially in the syntagmatic terms. It is important to note that we do not approach the machine-based translations in terms of correct/incorrect paradigm. Rather, we try to show that there are different modes of translation. To this end, there should be a range of cross-linguistic variants as translation choices to implement different translation strategies. The machine-based translations tend to follow the original word for word, the syntactic structure of the target text is evident in the translation, although the translation can read quite fluently at times, whereas the functional translation tends to seem like an original in the target language.

Let us have a closer look at the cross-linguistic correspondence *Arktika budet svobodna oto lda/The Arctic will likely see summer free of ice/the Arctic could go ice-free in summer/the Arctic will have ice-free summers.* Cross-linguistically, these variants are semantically similar and they may be viewed as cross-linguistic synonyms as they belong to the same semantic zone in the lexico-semantic set and therefore express the same unit of meaning. Yet, they are syntactically different and therefore not easily found by students as translation equivalents.

These cross-linguistic variants in the English language may be viewed in terms of the notion of unique items. They are specific to the target language and not so easily triggered by a source-language item as they are formally, or syntagmatically different.

It is important to note that the methodology proposed in this paper can be used in translating only certain types of texts. Following Karl Buhler's theory of language function, Reiss's text typology, and Newmark's text types [16], the methodology can be well applied to the informative texts, but not to the expressive texts, which are characterised by idiosyncratic language.

If a translator has to render the exact contextual meaning of the source text as closely as the semantic and syntactic structures of the target language allow, the machine-based translation, after human editing, can suffice. If a translator should produce a target text that should seem like an original, non-translated text, corpus-based contrastive analysis has much to offer to translators, especially students in translation studies.

This opposition can be viewed as polarities of equivalence: Nida's formal and dynamic equivalence [19]; Newmark's semantic and communicative translation [16]; House's overt and covert translation [13]; Nord's documentary and instrumental translation [17]; Venuti's resistant and fluent translation [27]; Toury's adequate and acceptable translation [25].

As a translation can represent a source text differently, which can be also determined by a translation brief, a translator should be equipped with a wide range of language choices in cross-linguistic perspective to make translation choices. In this regard, cross-linguistic analysis of the language use, rather than language system, can provide such an emphasis.

4 Conclusion

The integration of contrastive analysis that focuses on natural discourse, especially corpus-based lexical studies, and translation can significantly enrich these areas with new approaches to solving fundamental issues both in contrastive analysis and translation studies. From the cross-linguistic perspective, contrastive analysis can be extended to functional analysis of cross-linguistic variation [18] on the level of language use, rather than on the level of language systems. From the translation perspective, contrastive analysis makes it possible to take a fresh look at such fundamental categories of translation studies as equivalence and ways to achieve it and improving the criteria for the quality of translation.

References

1. Achkasov, A.V.: Zhnrovye voprosy perevoda (Genre issues in translation). Vestnik Sankt-Peterburgskogo universiteta. Ser. 9. Vyp 4. In Russian. Izdatelstvo Sankt-Peterburgskogo universiteta, St Petersburg (2016)
2. Altenberg, B., Granger, S.: Recent trends in cross-linguistic lexical studies. In: Lexis in Contrast. Corpus-Based Approaches. John Benjamin Publishing Company, Amsterdam (2002)
3. Bonelli, E. T.: Functionally complete units of meaning across English and Italian: towards a corpus-driven approach. In: Lexis in Contrast. Corpus-Based Approaches. John Benjamin Publishing Company, Amsterdam (2002)
4. Chesterman, A.: What is a unique items? In: Doubts and Directions in Translation Studies: Selected Contributions from the EST Congress, Lisbon 2004. John Benjamins Publishing Company, Amsterdam (2007)
5. Doval, I., Teresa Sanchez Nieto, M.: Parallel Corpora for Contrastive and Translation Studies. New Resources and Applications. John Benjamin Publishing Company, Amsterdam (2019)
6. Duff, A.: The Third Language: Recurrent Problems of Translation. Pergamon Institute of English Press, Oxford (1981)
7. Fillmore, C.: Frames and semantics of understanding. https://www1.icsi.berkeley.edu/pubs/ai/framesand85.pdf
8. Gak, V.G.: O kontrastivnoy lingvistike (On contrastive linguistics). Novoe v zarubezhnoi lingvistike. Vyp. 25. Kontrastivnaia lingvistika. In Russian. Progress, Moscow (1897)
9. Garbovsky, N.K.: Sopostavitelnaia stilistika i metodologiia perevoda (Contrastive stylistics and methodology of translation). Vestnik Moskovskogo universiteta. Ser. 22. Teoriia perevoda, No 1. In Russian. Moscow (2013)
10. Hatim, B., Mason, I.: Discourse and the Translator. Routledge, London (1990)
11. House, J.: Global English, discourse and translation. Linking constructions in English and German popular science texts. In: Munday, J., Zhang M. (eds.) Discourse Analysis in Translation Studies. John Benjamins Publishing Company, Amsterdam (2017)
12. House, J.: A Model for Translation Quality Assessment. TBL-Verlag Narr (1977)
13. House, J.: Translation Quality Assessment: Past and Present. Routledge, London (2014)
14. Karaulov, Y.N.: Lingvisticheskoye konstruirovaniye i tezaurus literaturnogo yazyka (Linguistic construction and the thesaurus of literary language). In Russian. Nauka, Moscow (1981)
15. Mikhailov, M., Cooper, R.: Corpus Linguistics for Translation and Contrastive Studies (Routledge Corpus Linguistics Guides). Routledge, London (2016)
16. Munday, J., Pinto, S.R., Blakesley, J.: Introducing Translation Studies. Theories and Applications, Routledge, London (2022)
17. Nord, C.: Translating as a Purposeful Activity: Functionalist Approaches Explained. St. Jerome Publishing, Manchester (1997)
18. Petrova, E.S.: Sopostavitelnaya tipologiya angliyskogo i russkogo yazykov. Grammatika (Comparative typology of English and Russian languages. Grammar) in Russian. Faculty of Philology, St Petersburg State University, St Petersburg; Academy, Moscow (2011)
19. Pym, A.: Exploring Translation Theories. Routledge, London (2017)
20. Retsker, Y.I.: Teoriya perevoda i perevodcheskaya praktika: ocherki lingvisticheskoy teorii perevoda (Translation Theory and Translation Practice: Essays on the Linguistic Theory of Translation) in Russian. R. Valent, Moscow (2010)

21. Riabtseva, N.K.: Perevodovedeniye v Rossii i za rubezhom. Ch. 2. Analiz empiricheskogo materiala (Translation Studies in Russia and Abroad. Part 2. A Case Study) in Russian. https://iling-ran.ru/riabtseva/translationstudies2.pdf. Accessed 1 May 2022
22. Robinson, D.: Becoming a Translator: An Introduction to the Theory and Practice of Translation. Routledge, London, New York (2019)
23. Salkie, R.: Two types of translation equivalence. In: Lexis in Contrast. Corpus-Based Approaches. John Benjamin Publishing Company, Amsterdam (2002)
24. Schveitzer, A.D.: Kontrastivnaya stilistika. Gazetno-publitsisticheskiy stil v angliyskom i russkom yazykakh (Contrastive stylistics. Newspaper and journalistic style in English and Russian). In Russian. Librocom, Moscow (2020)
25. Toury, G.: Descriptive Translation Studies—and Beyond, Revised edition. John Benjamins Publishing Company, Amsterdam (2012)
26. Uchenyy predpolozhil, kogda arkticheskiye ldy nachnut polnostyu tayat letom (The scientist suggested when the Arctic ice will begin to melt completely in the summer). https://ria.ru/20230211/ldy-1851380640.html
27. Venutti, L.: The Translator's Invisibility: A History of Translation. Routledge, London and New York (1995)

Semantically Bleached Words of Everyday Russian Speech: The Problem of Translation into Other Languages (A Pilot Study Based on the Material of the Buryat Language)

Altana Bazarzhapova

Abstract The paper deals with the problem of translation of peripheral phenomena that actively arise in Russian spontaneous everyday speech. In particular, the words *istoria* (*history*), *tema* (*theme*), *moment* (*moment*) and *fakt* (*fact*), which are often used in meanings not assigned by traditional dictionaries, are considered. In some contexts, taken from language corpora and separate records of everyday speech, these words lose the status of full-fledged significant words and are used as semantically bleached "packaging" words. (*Hod'ba na shpil'kah – ne sil'no poleznaya* ***istoria; Tam artroz kakoj-nibud', vospalitel'naya*** ***tema***). These marginal implementations of the words are not reflected in traditional explanatory and translation dictionaries, however, they require the attention of translators, since, despite their small role in constructing the meaning of the statement, such uses are significant in the context of communication. As part of the study, a pilot experiment was conducted in order to establish methods for translating into the Buryat language the desemanticized word *istoria*, first of all, and semantically bleached *tema*, *moment* and *fakt*. The participants of the experiment are native speakers of the Buryat language who were asked to translate into Buryat a number of Russian utterances, including desemanticized uses of the indicated words. During the analysis of the results, possible ways of translating such uses were identified, and the factors influencing the nature of the translation were described. The involvement of the Buryat language as a target language is connected with the relevance of research into modern Buryat speech and translation issues involving this language.

Keywords Russian everyday speech · Semantically bleached words · Desemanticization · Translation · The Buryat language · Experiment

A. Bazarzhapova (✉)
St. Petersburg State University, Universitetskaya emb. 7/9, 199034 Saint-Petersburg, Russia
e-mail: altanaanatla28@gmail.com

P. Eismont et al. (eds.), *Literature, Language and Computing*,
https://doi.org/10.1007/978-981-96-0990-1_18

1 Introduction

Desemanticization, or semantic “bleaching”, is “one of the most widespread changes in word meaning” [1: 1], implying the partial or complete loss of the meaning of a word. The theory of this linguistic phenomenon was developed in a number of foreign works [2, 3], and now desemanticization and its reflexes remain the subject of many studies devoted to different languages, including the Russian language. Back in the middle of the last century, in the V.V. Vinogradov’s work, special attention was paid to particular nouns that can lose their lexical meaning, come closer in function to pronouns and be used in relation to a practically unlimited number of referents,—these are words *veshch’, delo, shtuka, vopros, fakt* [4]. E.A. Zemskaya, in her research, supplements this series of substitute words with the words *muzyka* and *istoria*, implying the following uses: “*A kuda devat’ etu* ***muzyku****? (of something useless)* < ... > *Ty menya vtravil v etu* ***istoriyu/nu*** *i raskhlebyvaj//*” [5: 37–38]. In addition to the group of nouns, other lexical groups can be subject to desemanticization.

Semantically bleached words occur in different languages (for example, French *machin, chose* and English *thing, stuff*) and, in all likelihood, the existence of such units is a linguistic universal, in as much as pronouns as part of speech are universal. Desemanticized nouns have a wide range of functions, which is clearly demonstrated in one study on the example of words *veshch’, delo, shtuka* [6: 96–102]: (1) pointing to objects seen by communicants (*Daj-ka mne etu* ***shtuku***); (2) substitution of desemanticized words for various nouns and demonstrative pronouns (*Daj-ka mne* ***eto****. = Daj-ka mne etu* ***veshch’*** *= Daj-ka mne etu* ***shtuku*** *= Daj-ka mne eto* ***delo***); (3) cataphoric function, due to which the speaker can hold the listener’s attention and emphasize the importance of certain information (*Bylo takoe* ***delo****: podnyalsya ves’ molodoj soznatel’nyj narod protiv cerkovnyh brakov*); 4) the function of syntactic modification of a sentence in cases where the use of a traditional pronoun is not typical or undesirable (cf. *Iskusstvo –* ***veshch’*** *dorogostoyashchaya/*Iskusstvo – eto dorogostoyashche*). To sum up, according to V.G. Gack’s observations [7], desemanticization, being the limit of the semantic development of a word, turns it into an element that has a structural-organizing or stylistic purpose in the language. The latter, in particular, is expressed in colloquial nature of the desemanticized uses of the mentioned words.

Thus, it is obvious that desemanticized words, or words that are in the process of semantic bleaching, play an important role in oral discourse, and it is noteworthy that there are some additions to the group of such words in modern Russian speech.

2 Recent Additions to the Group of Semantically Bleached Russian Words

The study of everyday speech in various forms has long shown that the actual functioning of a word does not always correspond to its description in dictionaries, and marginal, "non-dictionary" phenomena are often out of our field of attention. This thesis is once again confirmed by observations: an analysis of some uses from the oral subcorpus (OS) of the National Corpus of the Russian Language, sound corpus «One Day of Speech»[1] (ORD) [8], as well as individual recordings of speech (everyday conversations, interviews, lectures, websites, etc.) demonstrates that the words *istoria, tema, moment* and *fakt* are often used in a semantically bleached way, and such usages are not described in traditional dictionaries. Further, each of the 4 indicated words is considered separately.

2.1 Desemanticized Word Istoria

In the study [9], it was found that in modern speech (starting approximately from the mid-late 2010s) the word *istoria* began to be used very widely, went beyond the usual combinability and acquired the ability to "cover" the meanings of words of completely different topics. In such contexts, the word *istoria* can be replaced by more familiar "packaging" words—*veshch', delo, shtuka*—or can be completely removed from the utterance with a slight modification. Such communicative behavior of this word is not described in any of the considered dictionaries [10–15]. Here are some examples:

(1) *Hod'ba na shpil'kah* – ***ne*** *sil'no* ***poleznaya istoria*** (=****ne*** *sil'no* ***poleznaya veshch'/shtuka; chto-to ne*** *sil'no* ***poleznoe; ne*** *sil'no* ***polezno***) ("not a very healthy thing/healthy") (from an interview with a sports doctor);

(2) *Petrushka nichemu ne mozhet pomeshat' v etoj nachinke: ni myasu, ni kartoshke <... > Takaya vot* ***garmonichnaya istoria*** (= **Takaya vot* ***garmoniya***) ("Such a harmonious thing") (from the cooking TV show);

(3) (И45)[2]: *Nu po chetyrem uglam sceny//da tak/chtoby bylo vidno/chto* ***visyat eti istorii//***(Ж1): *to est' ne tak//nu vot diski povesili* (the word *istorii* here means discs as part of a theatrical scenery) (ORD).

These are far from exceptional contexts—during the study, more than 150 similar semantically bleached uses of the word *istoria* were recorded (out of 442 collected uses of this word), which indicates the active process of the semantic bleaching of

[1] Available at: https://ord.spbu.ru.

[2] A capital letter accompanyied by a number (И45, Ж1) is used to designate speakers in the ORD corpus; they are indicated to separate the communicants' remarks. For other features of the orthographic presentation of the ORD material (conventions of discursive transcription), see [16: 242–243].

this unit. It would probably be possible to note more such uses and determine the proportion between the desemanticized realizations of the word *istoria* and its usual, "dictionary" realizations in modern speech, but now this is poorly feasible, since it is difficult to organize a convenient search for the necessary material in corpora. The point is that the OS contains about 6000 occurrences of the word *istoria* and search for desemanticized uses from the entire array would have to be done manually.

However, the current material seems sufficient, since it demonstrates in detail traces of the desemanticization of the word *istoria* and even semantic modifications of other words.

2.2 Desemanticized Word Tema

The following context, which was analyzed in [9] and was primarily interesting due to the semantically bleached use of the word *istoria*, contains another word that functions in a similar way, cf.:

(1) ***Sleduyushchaya istoria*** *komu-to* ***pokazhetsya melkoj****, no ya tak ne privyk – eto amerikanskij dush* < ... > *V Amerike dushevye lejki vsegda zhestko montirovany v stenu ili potolok. Vsegda v otele est' eti vot shapochki dlya dusha, i eta* ***poshla****, kstati,* ***tema iz Ameriki****, potomu chto nevozmozhno pomyt'sya, ne namochiv golovu* ("This thing came from America") (from the video of an urbanist).

In traditional dictionaries, one main meaning of the word *tema* is indicated—"subject of narration, image, research" (for example, *tema doklada, sochinenie na zadannuyu temu*), and this word is also used as a term in the field of music (*tema s variaciyami*) [12: 1313]. However, the use (4) does not correspond to the dictionary description: the word *tema* here has the same vague semantics as the words *veshch', delo, shtuka* and *istoria*. The word *tema* can be replaced by these units without loss of meaning or taken out of context (=**eto poshlo iz Ameriki*). A similar use, however, is noted in the online dictionary of Russian slang [17], the following interpretation is given: "any object, phenomenon, and in general everything that exists in the world (*Ya vchera takuyu* ***temu*** *zamutil, nad nej vse potom ves' den' rzhali!*)".

Other recordings of speech confirm the formulated observation (examples taken from the Internet are given in the author's spelling):

(5) *TYURBAN* ***Eto voobshche tema*** *osobenno dlya devushek u kogo dlinnye volosy* ("It's really cool") (from a blog);
(6) *...tam artroz kakoj-nibud',* ***vospalitel'naya tema*** (=****nechto****, svyazannoe s* ***vospaleniem***) ("something to do with inflammation") (from an interview with a sports doctor);
(7) *Obshchaga* ***takaya sebe tema****, hrapuny ne dlya vsekh ugodny* (=**Obshchaga – eto* ***tak sebe***) ("so-so") (from an online review);
(8) *Ezdit' s otkrytym bardachkom* ***takaya sebe tema*** (=****tak sebe delo***) ("so-so") (from a forum).

The functioning of the word *tema* and the semantically bleached words *istoria, veshch', delo, shtuka* are also similar in the following aspect. Researchers note that the last three words often form phraseological combinations with other units: *delo v tom, chto; pervym delom; ne v tom delo; vsya shtuka v tom, chto,* etc. [6: 96–102]. The word *istoria* also turned out to have great idiomatic potential: for example, *klassicheskaya/tipichnaya/obychnaya/vechnaya istoria; eto ne moya istoria* "about someone or something who/that does not suit the speaker for some reason" [18]. In the same way, the word *tema* tends to become part of fixed expressions (*tak sebe tema* = *tak sebe* "so-so, bad" or "mediocre, nothing special" [19: 677]; *byt' (ne) v teme* "about someone's [un]awareness" [15: 334]; *byt' (ne) v temu* "about the relevance of something < … > or about the inappropriateness, untimeliness of something" [15: 334–335].

The expression *eto (voobshche/real'no) tema* especially brings together the words *tema* and *veshch'* in the sense that both words in their desemanticized form acquire a positive appraisal, cf. *Tyurban – eto voobshche tema* "anything interesting, noteworthy"; *Tochnyak, temu govorish'!* "good idea, good thought" [17]; *Eto veshch'!* "expresses recognition of the significance, importance, value of smth." [12: 124]. Nevertheless, the word *tema* stands out among all its listed analogues due to its distinct belonging to slang.

2.3 *Desemanticized Word* Moment

In the following context (9), the simultaneous use of several semantically bleached units is noteworthy:

(9) *Chto kasaetsya naneseniya masla na kozhu golovy, eto voobshche* ***otdel'naya istoria*** ("It's a different **story**"). < … > *Esli uzhe konchiki posechennye, to tam uzhe* < … > *my tol'ko sostrigaem* ***vsyo eto delo***. ("We have to cut **the whole thing**") < … > *Kogda proizvoditel' pishet "shampun' protiv posechennyh konchikov, lomkosti", dazhe protiv zhirnosti – vot eshchyo odin takoj* ***moment*** ("another **thing**"), *kotoryj besit vsekh specialistov* < … > *Mozhet byt' po tipu kozha zhirnaya, no ona obezvozhennaya. Mozhet byt' shelushenie, zud, tam razlichnye vot takie* ***momenty*** ("different **things** like this"), *no eto ne menyaet sam tip kozhi golovy* (from an interview with a trichologist).

In the same context, two words we have already considered are presented—*istoria* and *delo*, and, in addition, the word *moment*, which, apparently, also underwent a significant semantic modification, is used twice. Originally having the meaning of time, this word acquired an expanded meaning "a separate aspect of any phenomenon or circumstance, accompanying condition" [10: 295]. This stage of desemanticization of this word is noted in traditional dictionaries. However, in the context (9), as well as in examples (10) and (11), it is probably worth talking about the next stage of desemanticization, since the word *moment* loses the component of its meaning "part or condition of some object or phenomenon" and begins to denote this object or phenomenon itself. This is the reason why the given word can be replaced by similar desemanticized words or extracted from the utterance:

(10) [*Muzh*] *pomogaet, k primeru – mashinu otremontirovat', rezinu pomenyat', tekhosmotr projti... nu vot takie kakie-to* ***momenty*** (=****veshchi***) (something like this, "and so on") (from a forum);

(11) *Pompejskij amfiteatr uglublen. Snaruzhi on nevysokij, a vnutri on glubokij. Vhody dlya samih gladiatorov i dlya pochetnyh zritelej idut vniz. Eto takoj* ***moment ekonomii****. Potom oni perestali ekonomit'* (=**Eto* (*takaya*) ***ekonomiya***) ("It's due to economy") (from a virtual tour with an archaeologist).

2.4 *Desemanticized Word* fakt

Finally, the last of the words mentioned as semantically bleaching in modern everyday speech is the word *fakt* that is used at the junction of clauses as part of a complex sentence in combinations "verb + *tot fakt* + *chto*" (e.g. *hochu obratit' vashe vnimanie na* ***tot fakt, chto****...*). Such uses are analyzed in detail in [20]. It is shown here that the unit *tot fakt chto* functions as a connector (see about the concept of a connector: [21]) and is an analogue of a connector *to chto* (cf.: *hochu obratit' vashe vnimanie na* ***to, chto****...*), but differs from the latter in that it is usually used in official public speech. The fact that the word *fakt* acquires the status of a connector as part of a construction is a reflex of the grammaticalization of this word, and desemanticization is traditionally considered as one of the first stages of grammaticalization. The desemanticization of the word *fakt* is obvious when the connector *tot fakt chto* is used not quite correctly, namely, "in cases where the predicate in the main part does not require or does not allow object" [20: 29], for example, *znat'/videt'/pochuvstvovat' tot fakt, chto...* etc. The fact that the word *fakt* in a desemanticized form acquires a special syntactic and stylistic function is not accidental and correlates with V.G. Gak's observations mentioned in Introduction.

2.5 *The Problem of Translating Semantically Bleached Words*

There is no doubt that semantically bleached words are a separate lexical group. Desemanticized uses of the words *istoria*, *tema*, *moment* and *fakt* are not reflected in traditional academic dictionaries, as they do not belong to the realm of the literary language. Nevertheless, it would be wrong to ignore such uses of the words. While these lexical items do not add anything to the semantic content of the utterances, they have undeniable communicative significance, because they can indicate that the speaker views the current communicative situation as informal [9] and serve as speech characteristics of a linguistic personality. Semantically bleached words can often become "parasite words" in the speech of individual language users or, in the case of a slang word *tema*, be signs of speech "nonchalance" and markers of social belonging.

The significance of these words in the discourse is especially increased when it is necessary to translate such uses into another language. According to V.N. Komissarov, translation is a type of linguistic mediation, the hallmark of which is "its special purpose to serve as a full-fledged communicative replacement for the original" [22: 58]. The English translation of the desemanticized word *istoria* as *history*, *story* or as *event*, *incident* can hardly be considered a full-fledged communicative replacement. With such a translation, not only are communicative nuances missing, but the very logic of the statement is lost. Dictionaries do not offer any other potential English equivalents [23: 1049, 24]. The same applies to the translation of the semantically bleached word *tema*, whose typical English translations—*subject*, *theme*, *topic*—also cover only the nuclear, "dictionary" meanings of this word.

3 Pilot Translation Experiment

Within the framework of this study, we attempted to solve this problem on the basis of Russian-Buryat translations of some contexts. The choice of the Buryat language as the target language is due to the fact that the Buryat language is the second native[3] language for the author of this article, and this, to one degree or another, guarantees the correct analysis of the received translations. In addition, considering the Buryat language as an object of study is in line with the current linguistic trend to study minority languages.

At first, the Buryat-Russian parallel corpus[4] was taken, which is a part of the National Corpus of the Russian Language and has 400 thousand words. However, this corpus includes only literary texts, and almost all texts belong to the pre-war and post-war Buryat literature of the twentieth century, i.e., they hardly contain the usages that are investigated in this paper. Thus, this source is not suitable for solving the problem. The solution was to conduct a pilot translation experiment, the content and results of which are described below.

[3] According to N.B. Vakhtin, the concept of *native language* "is not an exact sociolinguistic term and does not have a clear empirical referent" [25: 78]. This concept may mean the language of family communication, the language that a person mastered the earliest, or the language whose name corresponds to the name of the nationality of the respondents. In the context of this article, the concept *native language* is invested with the criterion of national and cultural identity, and the definition *second* indicates the sequence of its acquisition by the author.

[4] Available at: https://ruscorpora.ru/search?search=CgkyBwgFEgNidWEwAQ%3D%3D.

3.1 Content of the Experiment

A group of 8 bilinguals translated contexts with some semantically bleached words into the Buryat language. Among the participants, there were people with different social and professional backgrounds.[5] The heterogeneity of the group of translators (T) was an important condition, since it was important for the study to get a response from different native speakers, including those for whom language and literature are not part of their professional activities. Of course, as noted by Grosjean [26], not all bilinguals are born translators, despite the fact that it is quite logical to expect translation abilities from a bilingual person. However, it is possible to track on a wider group of bilinguals, not limited to professional translators, whether native speakers feel the semantic change of some words.

The material for the translation was 25 contexts taken from the already mentioned oral subcorpus of the NCRL, the corpus "One Day of Speech" and separate recordings of speech. 13 out of 25 contexts were fillers and contained "dictionary" uses of the word *istoria*, and the remaining 12 included the desemanticized implementations of this word, as well as of the words *tema*, *moment*, *fakt*, *delo*. Here are these 12 contexts:

(1) ***Sleduyushchaya istoria*** *komu-to* ***pokazhetsya melkoj****, no ya tak ne privyk – eto amerikanskij dush < ... > V Amerike dushevye lejki vsegda zhestko montirovany v stenu ili potolok. Vsegda v otele est' eti vot shapochki dlya dusha, i eta* ***poshla****, kstati,* ***tema iz Ameriki****, potomu chto nevozmozhno pomyt'sya, ne namochiv golovu* (from the video of an urbanist);

(2) (I): *ot etih koshek u menya allergiya/chesotka vsyu noch'...* (II): *slushaj chto ty govorish' nakaplivaetsya?.. chto ty mne s...* ***rasskazyvaesh'*** *tut* ***istorii*** (ORD);

(3) *Pompejskij amfiteatr uglublen. Snaruzhi on nevysokij, a vnutri on glubokij. Vhody dlya samih gladiatorov i dlya pochetnyh zritelej idut vniz. Eto takoj* ***moment ekonomii****. Potom oni perestali ekonomit'* (from a virtual tour with an archaeologist);

(4) ***Slozhnaya istoria*** *u menya* **s** *etim* ***zdorov'em*** *i s etim* ***kureniem****/voobshche chyort ego znaet!* (ORD);

(5) *Chto kasaetsya naneseniya masla na kozhu golovy, eto voobshche* ***otdel'naya istoria****. < ... > Esli uzhe konchiki posechennye, to tam uzhe < ... > my tol'ko sostrigaem* ***vsyo eto delo****. < ... > Kogda proizvoditel' pishet "shampun' protiv posechennyh konchikov, lomkosti", dazhe protiv zhirnosti – vot eshchyo odin takoj* ***moment****, kotoryj besit vsekh specialistov < ... > Mozhet byt' po tipu kozha zhirnaya, no ona obezvozhennaya. Mozhet byt' shelushenie, zud, tam razlichnye vot takie* ***momenty****, no eto ne menyaet sam tip kozhi golovy* (from an interview with a trichologist);

[5] Participants of the experiment/Translators (T): (1) a retired nurse (60 years old, female); (2) university teacher (45 years old, female); (3) doctor (60 years old, female); (4) school teacher (45 years old, female); (5) school teacher (43 years old, female); (6) university teacher (35 years old, female); (7) university teacher (25 years old, male); 8) university teacher (35 years old, female).

(6) *Esli temperatura v moshonke povyshaetsya, otsyuda i vse problemy u muzhchin. poetomu hodit' v banyu tozhe nuzhno ne kazhdyj den'* < ... > *podogrev sideniya – eto* ***takaya istoria****, kogda ty sogrelsya i vyklyuchaj* (from an interview with an andrologist);

(7) *Eshchyo ya znayu* ***tot fakt*****,** ***chto*** *ona vozmozhno po lipovym dokumentam poluchaet pensiyu* (from a forum);

(8) *Bilety za poltory tysyachi – vpolne* ***pod"yomnaya istoria*** (from a conversation with a geography teacher);

(9) *Ya, naprimer, nikogda ne hotela byt'* < ... > *direktorom medicinskogo centra, no eto vot lichno,* ***eto ne moya istoria*** (from an interview with a venereologist);

(10) *Posle etoj, pyatoj, pary s vami u menya eshchyo aspiranty.* ***Mozgodrobitel'naya istoria****!* (from a conversation);

(11) *Obidchivost' – eto tozhe* ***istoria*** *pro nashe zhelanie kontrolya* (from a TV show);

(12) *U nego* ***tol'ko odna istoria****: biohimiya. Bol'she ego nichego ne interesuet* (from a conversation).

3.2 Results of the Pilot Experiment

The results of the translation experiment are given in the Table 1. Color designations are deciphered as follows. Black cell (32 cases, 26%)—translation not given at all. Gray cell (8 cases, 7%)—an incomplete translation is given, namely, only a fragment that does not contain the studied word is translated (for example, T3 translated only first part of the context (2), which says that someone is allergic to cats). Green cell (10 cases, 8%)—a desemanticized analogue of the word under study was found during translation. Red cell (20 cases, 17%)—the word under study was translated by its full-fledged, non-desemanticized counterpart. Yellow cell (6 cases, 5%)—the word under study was translated by a non-desemanticized contextual analogue. Blue cell (44 cases, 37%)—the word under study is omitted, the meaning is conveyed by other lexical and grammatical means. The vertical division of the cell into 2 parts (for example, the translation of contexts (1), (2), (4), (5) in T4) means that the translator gave 2 translation options.

According to the results of the experiment, it can be seen that there are four possible solutions for translating phrases with a problematic desemanticized element, three of which do not raise doubts in terms of correctness: (1) a desemanticized analogue is found, (2) a non-desemanticized contextual analogue is found, (3) the desemanticized word is omitted, the message is conveyed by lexical and grammatical means that differ from the structure of the original.

The fourth solution (4)—the translation of the desemanticized word through its usual full-valued counterparts—is doubtful. For example, such full-meaning Buryat words as *tüükhe* (7 cases) and *ushar* (12 cases) became analogues for the word *istoria*, cf:

Table 1 Translations made by the participants of the experiment

Context \ Translator		1	2	3	4	5	6	7	8
1	*tema*								
2	*istoria*								
3	*moment*								
4	*istoria*								
5	*istoria*								
	delo								
	moment								
6	*istoria*								
7	*fakt*								
8	*istoria*								
9	*istoria*								
10	*istoria*								
11	*istoria*								
12	*istoria*								

- *Ene beye makhabadai bolon ene tamkhi tatalgatai namda oryoo* ***tüükhe*** *daa… = S etim organizmom i kureniem u menya slozhnaya* ***istoria****…* ("I have a complicated history with the body and smoking…") (context 4, T5);
- *Mashina soo dorohoo dulaasuulga – ene tiimesheg* ***ushar****, dulaasabal bolikho kheregtei = Podogrev snizu v mashine – eto takoj* ***sluchaj****, kak razogreesh'sya, nado prekrashchat'* ("Heating from below in the car is such a case, when you warm up, you need to stop") (context 6, T1);
- *Gomdodog zan geeshe bahal kontrolirovalkha gezhe oroldohonoimnai* ***tukhai ushar*** *yum = Manera obizhat'sya – eto tozhe* ***sluchaj pro*** *nashe staranie kontrolirovat'* ("The manner of being offended is also a case of our attempt to control") (context 11, T2).

If we refer to the Buryat-Russian dictionary [27], it turns out that *tüükhe* is an analogue of the word *istoria* only in the following meanings—"reality in the process of development", "the past", "historical narrative", "legend", and the word *ushar* can be an analogue for the word *istoria* only in the meaning "case, incident". Thus, the above translations sound strange, and the first of them is a calque from the Russian original. The decision to translate the desemanticized word with a full-fledged analogue was also made in relation to the word *fakt*, but only once: *Khudal dokumentaar pensi abadag beshe gy gehen* ***barimta medeneb*** (context 7, T4), where *barimta medeneb* literally means "I know the fact" and *barimta* means "argument, reason, proof", i.e. corresponds to the Russian *fakt* only in its regular, "dictionary" meanings.

As for the first three methods mentioned, as part of method (1), the translators were able to determine the specifics of problematic uses and find the corresponding Buryat counterparts. The most frequent one (6 cases) is the word *yuumen* "something, anything", which is regularly used in Buryat speech as a substitute word for the object or phenomenon in question. *Yuumen* was used to translate the words *istoria, tema, fakt*, cf:

- … ***Zhegtei yuumen*** *baina daa* = ***Chto-to strannoe/udivitel'noe*** ("It's weird") (context 10, T2);
- … ***iime yuumen*** *baha Amerikahaa garaltai* … = … ***eto chto-to*** *tozhe prishlo iz Ameriki* ("this also came from America") (context 1, T7);
- *Bi* ***nege yuume*** *medeneb, teresh khuurmag barimtaar pensiyaa abadag beze gezhe* = *Ya znayu* ***koe-chto****, ona po fal'shivym dokumentam pensiyu poluchaet* ("I know something, she receives a pension under false documents") (context 7, T7).

In two cases concerning the translation of the same context (*chto ty mne rasskazyvaesh' tut istorii*), the word *yuu(n)* was used as an analogue of the word *istoria*—it is an interrogative pronoun "*what*", and this choice is due to the presence of an interrogative construction:

- … *shi* ***yuugee*** *khelenesh, khöörenesh?* = ***Chto*** *ty govorish', rasskazyvaesh'?* ('What are you saying, what are you talking about?') (context 2, T1);
- … *shi namda* ***yuugee****, khara zolig, khöörenebshi daa*?! = ***Chto*** *ty mne, chort etakij, rasskazyvaesh'?!* ("What the hell are you telling me?!") (context 2, T2).

The "non-dictionary" idiomatic expression *rasskazyvat' istorii* (cf.: a "dictionary" expression *rasskazyvat' skazki/basni* "to tell tall tales, to tell a lie") in both cases is conveyed by non-idiomatized combinations, but it is noteworthy that T2, through the insertion of *khara zolig* (an expletive word), seeks to convey the expressiveness and emotionality inherent in the original idiomatic expression.

The third possible desemanticized analogue—the word *ene* "this, it"—was used once when translating the word *tema*: ***Ene*** *khadaa Amerika kha yum…* = ***Eto*** *Amerika…* ("This is America…") (context 1, T4).

As for the translation of the word *moment*, the word *züil* "grade, kind, class" was once used. This word is ranked by researchers among a number of such full-valued units, which, "used as semi-affixes, almost completely lose their lexical meaning" [28: 245]: *Enen' almalgyn nege* ***züil*** *bolono* = *Eto nekotoryj* ***rod*** *ekonomii/Eto* ***v nekotorom rode*** *ekonomiya* ("It's a kind of economy") (context 3, T8).

The second (2) of the mentioned solutions is interesting in that the translator also uses full-valued analogues in translation, however, these analogues are contextual. For example, to translate the word *tema* in context 1, the words *üge* "word" and *zanshal* "habit, custom, tradition" were used: … *tendehee garahan* ***üge*** = … *ottuda [iz Ameriki] poshlo* ***slovo*** ("the word came from there [from America]") (context 1, T1); …*ene* ***zanshal*** *Amerikahaal ekhitei* = …*etot* ***obychaj*** *beret nachalo v Amerike*

("…this custom originates in America") (context 1, T5). The use of these analogues does not violate the meaning of the statement, although the colloquial nature of the fragment is not preserved. However, the stylistic component is maintained, for example, in another case, when the *istoria* is translated as *honin* "news", "interesting", as part of the already mentioned phraseological unit *rasskazyvat' istorii*: *Yamar honin khöörene yum shi*? = *Chto za* ***novosti*** (*mne tut*) *rasskazyvaesh'*? ('What are you talking about?') (context 2, T6). Within the framework of the method (2), two more contextual full-valued analogues, selected for the word *istoria*, are also interesting, – *khööröön* "conversation, chat, talk" and *ermelzel* "pursuit, ambition, aspiration": *Tarkhiin ühen dorokhi arhanda toho türkhihen tushaa amindaa* ***khööröön*** = *Po povodu naneseniya masla na kozhu golovy – otdel'nyj* ***razgovor*** ("Regarding the application of oil on the scalp—a separate conversation") (context 5, T5); *Tere khünde gansal* ***ermelzel***… = *U etogo cheloveka tol'ko odno* ***stremlenie*** ("This man has only one aspiration") (context 12, T1 and T5).

Finally, solution (3), which translators have used most often, is characterized by the fact that the problematic word is not translated in any way, and the meaning of the fragment is conveyed by other means. The arsenal of these means is not limited, and it is difficult to systematize the translations received within the framework of this technique, although individual contexts may require certain solutions. For example, T3, T7, T8 translated context 8 (*Bilety za poltory tysyachi – vpolne* ***pod"yomnaya istoria***) identically, namely with the help of a special verb form that includes the affix *aar/oor/eer* and has the modal meaning of the assumption or possibility of some action: *Myanga taban zuun solkhoobto bilet* ***daakhaar*** *baina* = *Bilet za poltory tysyachi* ***mozhno snesti/vyderzhat'*** ("A ticket for one and a half thousand can be afforded'); *Myanga taban zuugaar tahalbari* ***abakhaar*** *bajna*; *1500 sentei bileduudye khudaldazha* ***abakhaar*** = *Bilety za poltory tysyachi* ***kupit' mozhno*** ("It's okay/possible to buy tickets for one and a half thousand").

The same form is used in the translation of another context with the expressive unit *mozgodrobitel'naya istoria*: *Tabadakhi khoyorolzhon khesheelei hüülde namda üshöö aspirantnuud erekhe.* ***Tarkhyaa er'ekheer****!* = *Posle etoj pyatoj pary ko mne eshche aspiranty pridut.* ***Golova mozhet krugom poekhat'****!* ("My head's going to spin around!") (context 10, T4). It is noteworthy how the same fragment was translated by T5: *Uurag tarkhimnai urdakha* = *Mozgi potekut* ("Brains will leak").

A large number of black cells attracts attention – the translation was not performed at all in 26% of cases. It is difficult to interpret this unambiguously, but this may be due to the large volume of the task (although the time was not limited), and in the future it is possible to reduce the burden on translators without shortening the contexts, but, for example, by offering to translate only the problematic fragments highlighted in them.

In conclusion, it is important to consider the question of what may be the reason for the choice of a translation method. At the stage of the experiment, 3 main factors can be distinguished: (1) the degree and nature of semantic bleaching; (2) speaker's linguistic "flair"; (3) the specifics of the context.

The importance of the first factor can be demonstrated by context 4 (*Slozhnaya istoria u menya s etim zdorov'em…*): the fact that almost all translators translated this context using a full-valued analogue of the desemanticized word, apparently indicates its vaguely expressed desemanticization.

The second factor is obvious if we take a look at context 2. T4 and T5 translated the unit *rasskazyvat' istorii* as *usharnuudye/tüükhenüüdye khöörekhe*, not taking into account either the desemanticization of the element or the idiomatic nature of the whole unit, but, for example, T7 took into account the peculiarities of the discourse and the intention of the speaker, whose response he translated. In the original context, this remark implies that the speaker does not take seriously the interlocutor's complaints about their allergy and the answer to the complaint sounds surprised and condescending. T7 conveys this in two ways: (1) *Ööryngöö khelezhe baihan yuumeye shagna = Poslushaj sam, chto govorish'* "Listen to yourself"; (2) *Khelezhel baigaarai* = (*Nu-nu*) *govori* (*mne tut*) "(Well, well) go on".

Finally, the importance of the third factor can be seen in contexts 3 and 7. When working with these contexts most translators did not translate desemanticized words, and this, apparently, is the most successful solution for the words *moment* and *fakt* in these contexts, since in the original these words can be extracted from the statement almost without modification.

4 Conclusion

Everyday "relaxed" Russian speech cannot be neglected by lexicographers and, especially, translators and specialists in comparative studies. An attempt to consider the problem of translating desemanticized words was implemented in a pilot translation experiment which allows us to formulate some preliminary observations. The results of the experiment show that in most cases (37%) the semantically bleached word is ignored in translation and the meaning of the utterance is conveyed by other lexical and grammatical means. The translation depends on at least 3 main factors, but the formula for the most successful translation consists of a thorough analysis of the discourse—the conditions of the communicative situation, the intentions of the author of the message and some other elements. The results of this work may have practical significance both in the field of Russian colloquial language study and in the field of Buryat studies.

Acknowledgements The presented research was supported by a grant from the Russian Science Foundation (project #22-18-00189 "Structure and Functionality of Stable Multiword Units in Russian Everyday Speech"). I also express my gratitude to all the enthusiasts who took part in the experiment, which could not have taken place without the help of L.D. Radnaeva (Doctor of Sciences in Philology, Professor of Buryat State University) and N.V. Bogdanova-Beglarian (Doctor of Sciences in Philology, Professor of St. Petersburg State University).

References

1. Luo, Y., Jurafsky, D., Levin, B.: From insanely jealous to insanely delicious: computational models for the semantic bleaching of English intensifiers. In: Proceedings of the 1st International Workshop on Computational Approaches to Historical Language Change, 1–13 (2019)
2. Sweetser, E.: Grammaticalization and semantic bleaching. In: Proceedings of the 14th Annual Meeting of the Berkeley Linguistics Society, pp. 389–405 (1988).
3. Traugott, E.C.: Semantic change: bleaching, strengthening, narrowing, extension. In: Brown, K. (ed.) Proceedings of the Encyclopedia of Language and Linguistics, pp. 124–131. Elsevier Science, Oxford (2006)
4. Vinogradov, V.V.: Russian language. Grammatical Doctrine of a Word. State Educational and Pedagogical Publishing House, Moscow, Leningrad (1947) (in Russian)
5. Zemskaya, E.A.: Semantically bleached words. In: Russian as a Foreign Language. Russian Colloquial Speech. Linguistic Analysis and Learning Problems. Textbook, 4th ed., Revised & Enlarged Edition, pp. 37–39. Flinta, Nauka, Moscow (2011) (in Russian)
6. Sokolova, S.V.: Dynamic processes in the system of pronominal words in the modern Russian language: Ph.D. Thesis, Lomonosov Moscow State University (2007) (in Russian)
7. Gak, V.G.: Limits of the semantic evolution of words. In: Krysin, L.P. (ed.) Russian Language Today, vol. 2, pp. 88–97. V.V. Vinogradov Russian Language Institute, Moscow (2003) (in Russian)
8. Bogdanova-Beglarian, N., Sherstinova, T., Blinova, O., Martynenko, G.: An exploratory study on sociolinguistic variation of spoken Russian. In: SPECOM 2016. Lecture Notes in Artificial Intelligence, LNAI, vol. 9811, pp. 100–107. Springer, Switzerland (2016)
9. Bazarzhapova, A.D.: Verevochnaya or Covidnaya Istoria: Desemantization of the Word *Istoria* in Different Discourse Types. In: Russkaya Rech', vol. 1, pp. 7–20 (2023) (in Russian)
10. Evgenieva, A.P. (ed.): Dictionary of the Russian Language: in 4 vols. Vol. 1. A–J, 4th ed., ster. Russian language, Polygraphic resources, Moscow (1999) (in Russian)
11. Gorbachevich, K.S. (ed.): Dictionary of the Modern Russian Literary Language: in 27 volumes, vol. 7. Nauka, Moscow (2007) (in Russian)
12. Kuznetsov, S.A. (ed.): Big Explanatory Dictionary of the Russian Language. Norint, St. Petersburg (2000) (in Russian)
13. Ozhegov, S.I., Shvedova, N.Y.: Explanatory Dictionary of the Russian Language, 4th Revised & Enlarged Edition. LTD «A Temp», Moscow (2006) (in Russian)
14. Sklyarevskaya, G.N. (ed.): Explanatory Dictionary of the Russian Language at the Beginning of the 21st Century: Current Vocabulary. Eksmo, Moscow (2006) (in Russian)
15. Khimik, V.V.: Explanatory Dictionary of Russian Colloquial Everyday Speech. In 2 Volumes, vol. 1, 528 p.; vol. 2, 532 p. Zlatoust, St. Petersburg (2017) (in Russian)
16. Bogdanova-Beglarian, N.V. (ed.): Everyday Russian Language: Functioning Features in Different Social Groups. Collective Monograph. LAIKA, St. Petersburg (2016) (in Russian)
17. Dictionary of Modern Vocabulary, Jargon and Slang (2014) (in Russian). http://argo.academic.ru/. Accessed 1 July 2023
18. Bazarzhapova, A.D., Bogdanova-Beglarian, N.V.: Idiomatic potential of word Istoria in modern everyday discourse: cognitive research on the communicative behavior of the word. In: Languages and Cultures in the Digital Age: Collection of articles based on the materials of the International Scientific Conference, pp. 35–41. N.I. Lobachevsky Nizhny Novgorod State University, Nizhny Novgorod (2022) (in Russian)
19. Fyodorov, A.I.: Phraseological Dictionary of the Russian Literary Language, 3rd ed., rev. Astrel, ACT, Moscow (2008) (in Russian)
20. Bazarzhapova, A.D.: *To Chto, Tot Fakt Chto* and *Istoria* as cohesive means: Lexico-grammatic excessions in everyday speech. In: Radnaeva, L.D. (eds.) Speech Analysis (Theoretical and Applied Aspects), pp. 23–35. Publishing House of the Buryat State University, Ulan-Ude (2023) (in Russian)

21. Dressler, W.U.: Syntax of a text. In: New in Foreign Linguistics, vol. 8, pp. 111–137. Progress, Moscow (1981) (in Russian translation)
22. Komissarov, V.N.: Modern Translation Studies, 2nd ed., corrected. R. Valent, Moscow (2011) (in Russian)
23. Muller, V.K.: Complete English–Russian Russian-English Dictionary. 300,000 Words and Expressions. Eksmo, Moscow (2013) (in Russian)
24. Large English–Russian and Russian-English dictionary. https://dic.academic.ru/contents.nsf/eng_rus. Accessed 2 July 2023
25. Vakhtin, N.B.: Languages of the Peoples of the North in the Twentieth Century. Essays on Language Shift. Dmitry Bulanin, St Petersburg (2001) (in Russian)
26. Grosjean, F.: Myths About Bilingualism. On: University of Neuchâtel, Switzerland (website) (2000). https://www.francoisgrosjean.ch/myths_en.html. Accessed 2 July 2023
27. Shagdarov, L.D., Cheremisov, K.M.: Buryad-Orod Toli. Buryat-Russian Dictionary. In 2 vols. Vol. 1, 636 p.; Vol. 2, 708 p. Respublikanskaya Tipografiya, Ulan-Ude (2010) (in Buryat and Russian)
28. Buraev, I.D., Shagdarov, L.D.: Buryat Language and Its Dialects. In: Abaeva, L.L., Zhukovskaya, N.L. (eds.) Buryats, pp. 227–251. N.N. Miklukho-Maclay Institute of Ethnology and Anthropology, Nauka, Moscow (2004) (in Russian)

A Comparative Analysis of Significant Thematic Lexis Based on the Corpus of Liturgical Texts in German

Mikhail Koryshev and Maria Khokhlova

Abstract Church hymns in German did not gain much attention from linguists and were typically studied by theologians or musicologists. The project is related to the study of the genesis of the church hymn genre from the philological viewpoint. The authors dwell on the history of German liturgical tradition and present the developed corpus of liturgical texts in German. The aim of the study is to correlate thematically significant lexical items with the matrix of fundamental theological ideologemes. For this task, the authors compared frequency lists extracted from the corpus with the ones from the Gutenberg corpus evaluating them the values of keyness score. Further work involved selecting theologically significant concepts (ideologemes) and subsequent annotation of the identified lexical units by experts. The results include such important thematic lexis as *Gott* "God", *Mensch* "Human", and *Engel und Heilige* "Angel and Saints". The emergence of *Gott* "God" as the central ideologeme indicates that the Catholic Church preserves the ideals of the Middle Ages. The peripheral position of ideologemes such as *Heilige/Engel—Kirche—Maria* "Saints/Angel—Church—Mary" can be also seen in contrast to the *Mensch* "Human" ideologeme that goes back to the Reformation.

Keywords Hymnography · Text corpus · Liturgical texts · Church ideologemes · German language

1 Introduction

The German hymnographic tradition itself has rarely been the focus of philology. Church hymns in German were typically studied by theologians or musicologists.

M. Koryshev · M. Khokhlova (✉)
St. Petersburg State University, Universitetskaya Emb. 7-9-11, 199034 Saint-Petersburg, Russia
e-mail: m.khokhlova@spbu.ru

M. Koryshev
e-mail: m.koryshev@spbu.ru

P. Eismont et al. (eds.), *Literature, Language and Computing*,
https://doi.org/10.1007/978-981-96-0990-1_19

Liturgy, as one of the theological disciplines, has been closest to the theme of interest. The studies of hymn texts' history were predominantly carried out by theologians, as they undertook the initial attempts at systematizing the extensive hymnographic material, using a historical principle as the basis. As a result, the hymnographic heritage was distributed across traditionally mentioned periods in church history. The resulting periodization served as an auxiliary tool without claiming objectivity. Thus, liturgy aligns the history of the genre's development with the conceptual framework established by church history. There is no justification for the appropriation of the heuristic system of one theological discipline for the analysis of material considered by another discipline. However, this borrowing, as reiterated, serves auxiliary purposes and is sufficient for the current tasks of liturgics.

2 Research Background

The hymnographic material, for literary studies, holds a peripheral nature, as demonstrated by the "Handbuch der literarischen Gattungen" published in 2009 [1], where essays on each genre are written by leading literary scholars and narrow specialists. Notably, the remarkable essay on the German-language church hymn (geistliches Lied, Kirchenlied) by I. Schaitler [2] occupies the same volume as the essay on comics. For Russian philology, educated in the traditions of D.S. Likhachev, it is clear that the significance of these genres for the history of literature is incomparable. Additionally, it is noteworthy that I. Schaitler's bibliography predominantly provides information on comprehensive editions of textual and only partially musical material. The works of theologians and musicologists are included, but there are no strictly literary studies. German academic literary studies only discover German-language church hymns. The interest of Russian literary studies in hymnographic heritage is sporadic and peculiar, but this peculiarity is entirely understandable: individual studies in Russia focus on the intersection of the tradition of German-language church hymnography and German hymn-odical poetry. It is evident that Russian literary scholars are developing the idea of W. Kayser regarding the substantive specificity of hymn-odical literature in German literature during the Klopstock era, prompting poets to seek new expressive forms. Thus, literary studies move away from solving the question of the genre's genesis and the driving forces behind its development.

It is important to understand that the doctrinal component does not contribute to finding an answer since the truth of faith has an absolute, timeless character. What we find in the history of the Church regarding forms of church life can be attributed not to doctrinal but disciplinary provisions. This thought leads to the conclusion that church history operates more with categories borrowed from the Western European tradition of political historiography. An example is the periodization of the history of Catholicism based on key political formations, subsequently focusing on periods associated with the papacy of each pope individually. The development of church life resists this categorization: for example, we commonly contrast the medieval church with the Reformation churches of early modern times, but Luther's figure cannot be understood outside the context of the Middle Ages (medieval *evotion moderna* as the foundation of his views). In the twentieth century, Pius XII is conventionally contrasted as a "retrograde" with the "progressive reformer" John XXIII, while in reality, John XXIII's steps are prepared by the teachings of Pius XII.

In the context of hymnography history, it turns out that liturgics, relying on the conceptual framework of church history, does not provide a solid foundation for understanding the patterns of development of church hymn as a genre. Considering the timeless nature of doctrinal content that reveals the absolute, it is necessary to acknowledge that studying historically changeable aspects must be grounded in the categories of culture as a fundamental anthropological category, correlated with the Church existing both in the transcendent-timeless and the immanent-historical dimensions. Consequently, understanding the history of hymnography, the church hymn as a literary genre, is possible in the context of the history of church culture.

Supporting this perspective is the fact that in liturgics, the cultural-historical approach possesses greater explanatory power than the traditional abstract-dogmatic approach, which relegates history to the background. It's worth noting in passing that the "*history of the development of theological thought*" unfolds within this approach as the history of theological intellectual culture, motivated by the culture in which *ecclesia peregrinans* exists in a specific place and time.

3 Aim of the Study

The above leads to the assumption that the stages in the history of the development of the German-language church hymn as a genre correspond to the stages in the history of German culture. However, with some adjustments that highlight the stages of development of church culture, the following periods can be distinguished:

- Medieval period;
- Reformation;
- Baroque (comparable with Catholic Counter-Reformation and gallant absolutism);
- Enlightenment (comparable with enlightened absolutism);
- Historicism (comparable with Gründerzeit);
- Liturgical renewal;
- Neo-Gründerzeit of the 1950s to the early 1970s;
- Postmodernism of the contemporary era (second half of the 1970s – present).

It is important to note that given the practical vastness of hymnographic material, it is necessary to distinguish between two approaches – the thesaurus approach, attempting to consider the entire body of texts, and the actualizing approach, focusing on material that lives in cultural memory and setting aside what only has museum value. The thesaurus approach is not only labor-intensive but also seemingly objective: firstly, different periods have different amounts of surviving material, meaning not everything that existed has reached us, as some periods are better documented by chance, while others are not; secondly, different periods produce varying amounts of texts, and these periods can be drastically different. On the other hand, the actualizing approach allows for a focus on what is of interest, on the living cultural tradition. This choice is determined by the sources of the studied material, which will be further characterized.

The Middle Ages and the Modern Era are the two main stages, with the Reformation period serving as a bridge connecting them. However, not all eras in the hymnographic tradition are equally represented: a small number of texts from the eighteenth century have been preserved in cultural memory (the Enlightenment era practically contributed nothing to the tradition, and only a few texts from this period are used in worship, albeit having exceptional significance, such as "Großer Gott, wir loben dich"). Similarly, there are few texts from the first half of the nineteenth century (which is why there is no Romantic period in the above proposed list). On the other hand, there are many texts from the period of Historicism (the Gründerzeit era), the period of the "invention of the German nation", culminating in the official Wilhelminism that preserved the cultural spirit of the Gründerzeit in what we now perceive as the cultural modernism at the turn of the centuries.

This cultural modernism was decisively rejected by church culture (we are not talking about theological modernism), so we do not refer to modernism in the context of hymnographic material. The liturgical renewal, drawing on both the anti-modernism of church culture and the emerging existentialist motives within modernism, took place in the 1920s-1930s. The contemporary postmodern stage is characterized by steps toward popular culture, consistently taken by a movement in contemporary hymnography known as *Neues Geistliches Lied*.

The objective of this research is to correlate thematically significant lexicon with the matrix of fundamental theological ideologemes and thus to indirectly test the research hypothesis. The research hypothesis, the logic of which has been demonstrated earlier, can be formulated as follows: the hymnographic heritage should be considered not from the perspective of the "history of the development of theological thought" but from the standpoint of the development of the culture and art of individuals and communities (primarily, in this case, church communities) that gave rise to it.

4 Research Data

The chosen approach for studying hymnographic material, which focuses on actualization, has determined the selection of sources. Since the primary focus is on the living hymnographic tradition, i.e., textual material spanning different historical periods that remains relevant in cultural memory, a source containing texts of German-language church hymns from various epochs is required. These hymns should have been used over a significant period and on a considerable territory, collectively serving as a living testimony to this tradition.

Such a collection is the Gotteslob 1975 [3]. It is the first unified hymnal for Catholic German-speaking dioceses. While there were preceding hymnals, they were primarily intended for specialists rather than the broader religious community. In this post-war project, German-speaking dioceses from Germany, Austria, France (Strasbourg, Metz), Belgium (Liège), and Luxembourg (where the Gotteslob is known as Magnificat)[1] participated. The hymnal consists of two parts—a basic part and a regional part, with the regional section varying from diocese to diocese—totaling 32 editions. There is no separate edition of the "basic Gotteslob". For 38 years, the Gotteslob 1975 remained the sole hymnal in use, pushing all other hymnals out of common usage (with the exception of a hymnal for the armed forces, which aimed to remind military personnel of the civilian Gotteslob). Thus, for four generations of believers, the Gotteslob 1975 embodied the hymnographic tradition, and the texts from this hymnal essentially constituted their church hymns, and nothing more.

Nevertheless, since 2013, the use of the Gotteslob 2013 [4] has become mandatory. However, until 2020, this hymnal had not been fully adopted, and the period of the COVID-19 pandemic led to a temporary abandonment of liturgical singing for hygiene reasons. The distinctive features of this source lie in its historical approach, as the authors aimed to restore the original form of the texts and eliminate later accretions. Additionally, it includes a sub-genre of new spiritual songs (Neues Geistliches Lied), which was not present in earlier hymnals. Based on the above, the decision was made to include in our corpus the material from this hymnal that is absent in the basic part of the Gotteslob 1975. The material present in the Gotteslob 1975 but not covered in the Gotteslob 2013 is considered regional.

Concluding the discussion on the research material, it is essential to address potential concerns regarding the limited number of texts contained in the Gotteslob 1975, considering the vastness of the hymnographic heritage, which raises questions about the representativeness of the selected material. Another question that may arise is: What grounds are there to claim that the Gotteslob 1975 genuinely provides an accurate representation of contemporary hymnographic practice? In our view, the Gotteslob 1975 adequately captures the living hymnographic tradition we are interested in, rather than a museum-like representation. Otherwise, it would not have "endured" in liturgical practice for such a long time. Furthermore, the Gotteslob 2013 aligns with this living tradition without breaking away from it.

5 The Corpus of Liturgical Texts

We developed a corpus of liturgical texts that at this stage has been supplemented with materials from the basic part of the Gotteslob 1975, which is common to all dioceses in Germany. The total size of the corpus is about 27,000 words (see Table 1).

---

[1] However, for various reasons, other German speaking contries such as Switzerland and Liechtenstein did not participate in the project.

Table 1 The corpus of liturgical texts: characteristics

Item	Number
tokens	33,266
words	27,191
sentences	2,011
hymns	232
stanzas	1,149

The hymns from the Gotteslob 1975 have been categorized in the corpus into the following seven temporal periods:

- before the sixteenth century (14 hymns);
- sixteenth century (30 hymns);
- seventeenth century (46 hymns);
- eighteenth century (5 hymns);
- nineteenth century (13 hymns);
- twentieth century: up to 1950 (26 hymns);
- twentieth century: after 1950 and up to 1975 (98 hymns).

The proposed division corresponds to the historical periods outlined in Sect. 3 above. The texts were provided with metatextual annotation, which include the following characteristics: (1) temporal periods; (2) year of hymn composition; (3) presence of musical accompaniment from the same era; (4) presence of a hymn ancestor; (5) stanza number; (6) year of stanza composition (if applicable); (7) indication of whether the stanza is original. In the future, we plan additional literary analysis based on the principles laid out in the development of the poetic corpus within the framework of the Russian National Corpus [5].

6 Methodology

The research methodology involved two steps. The first one implied comparing the developed corpus of liturgical texts with a reference corpus of substantial volume, specifically the German-language Gutenberg German corpus comprising 74.7 million words. To extract lexical items that can be significant, the keyness score coefficient [6] was utilized. The coefficient values were employed to rank keywords and phrases that are more characteristic of the given thematic (focus) corpus or subcorpus compared to the neutral (reference) corpus or the entire corpus as a whole. The formula for calculating the keyness score coefficient is as follows:

$$keynessscore = \frac{fpmf + n}{fpmr + n}, \quad (1)$$

where:

- f_{pmf} is the relative frequency in the focus corpus in items per million (ipm),
- f_{pmr} is the relative frequency in the reference corpus in items per million (ipm),
- n is a smoothing coefficient.

This coefficient helps to rank keywords and phrases based on their significance in the focus corpus compared to the reference corpus (see Table 2). The value of n in the keyness score formula is a smoothing factor, and we chose the following values: $n = 0.001$, $n = 1$, and $n = 10$. These values influence the sensitivity of the keyness score and can affect the significance of certain terms in the analysis. A smaller n value tends to emphasize rare terms, while a larger n value may give more weight to common terms. We explored different values of n to trace how the results change based on the smoothing factor and to find the most suitable value for our analysis.

The second step involved selecting theologically significant concepts (ideologemes) and, consequently, subsequent expert annotation of the identified lexical units (see Table 3).

At this stage, a manual verification of the automatic morphological analysis was performed, and the results were corrected as necessary. Additionally, collocations with the examined lexemes were considered, and the analysis helped to specify the semantic features of the ideologemes.

Table 2 Keyness score values and frequencies for lexical items

Word form	Relative frequency (Corpus of Liturgical Texts)	Relative frequency (Gutenberg German corpus)	Keyness score values
haileluja	270,53836	0	270539,344
krippelein	120,23927	0	120240,266
christkönig	120,23927	0	120240,266
befehln	90,17946	0	90180,453
erzeig	90,17946	0	90180,453
kerubim	60,11964	0	60120,633
zebaot	60,11964	0	60120,633
begehrn	60,11964	0	60120,633
entzünd	60,11964	0	60120,633
unerschaffne	60,11964	0	60120,633

Table 3 An example of the expert annotation for lexical items

Word form	Lemma	Ideologeme
krippelein	Krippe	Gott
christkönig	Christkönig	Gott
befehln	befehlen	göttliches
erzeig	erzeigen	göttliches
kerubim	Cherubim	Engel und Heilige

7 Results

Experimentally, it was established that the value n = 0.001 allows for the identification of lexical units present in our corpus of liturgical texts but absent in the Gutenberg corpus. The main theological and culturological ideologemes identified through the analysis of our data can be correlated with the following cultural-historical epochs (for culturally significant ideologemes) and the following main sections of theological knowledge:

- Cultural and historical epochs correlated with culturally significant ideologemes (cf. [7, 8]):
  - Ideal of the Middle Ages – Dimension of fundamental/the basic theology: *Gott* 'God' (e.g. ***O Lebensfürst**, o starker **Held*** [GL1975, Nr.226]).
  - Ideal of the Modern Era – Dimension of pastoral theology: *Mensch* 'Human' (e.g. *Nun **lobet** Gott im hohen Thron, ihr **Menschen** aller Nation, hochpreiset ihn mit **Freudenschalle**, ihr **Völker** auf der Erden alle* [GL1975, Nr.265]).
- Main sections of theology:
  - Eschatological dimension: *Himmel* 'Heaven' (e.g. *Aus seinen Wunden fließen her, Halleluja, fünf **Freudenseen**, fünf **Freudenmeer**.* [GL1975, Nr.585]), *Hölle* 'Hell' (e.g. *Du bist das Siegeszeichen, davor **der Feind erschricket**, wenn er es nur **anblicket*** [GL1975, Nr.182]), *Fegefeuer* 'Purgatory'.[2]
  - Mariological dimension: *Maria* 'Mary' (e.g. *Ave **Maria klare**, du **lichter Morgenstern**!* [GL1975, Nr.581]).
- Ecclesiological dimension: *Kirche* 'Church as community' (e.g. *Stimmt die Saiten **der Kitara** und laßt die süße **Musica** ganz freudenreich **erschallen*** [GL1975, Nr.554]); three images of the Church, stemming from the teachings of Robert of Melun (cf. [9, 10]):

  o triumphant Church – *Engel und Heilige* 'Angel and Saints' (e.g. martyrs: *Ihr Leben haben sie verloren, zur Erde ander **samengleich**; aus ihrem Blute sind geboren die neuen **Zeugen für dein Reich*** [GL1975, Nr.611]);

  p pilgrim / militant Church – *Erde / Erdenreich* 'Earth / Earth realm' (e.g. *Ihr **Tiefen des Meeres, Gelaich** und **Gewürme**, **Schnee**, **Hagel** und **Regen**, ihr brausenden **Stürme*** [GL1975, Nr.259]), *Mensch* 'Human' (e.g. *Und wie zu zwei und zweien **der Mensch** den Weg **durchmisst**, wenn er **zum Ende ander*** < ... > [GL1975, Nr.74]);

  q suffering Church – *Fegefeuer* 'Purgatory'[2].

Quantitative representation of ideologemes allows us to state that they are organized into a field structure. At the center of this field are both culturally and theologically significant ideologemes *Gott* "God" (45 occurrences) and *Mensch* "Human" (20 occurrences), confirming the priority of historical and cultural over theological

[2] There are no examples for the given ideologeme in the corpus.

with an emphasis on the worldview of the Modern Era. Ideologemes such as *Heilige / Engel* "Saints / Angel" (9 occurrences), *Kirche* "Church" (9 occurrences), *Maria* "Mary" (6 occurrences), *Erde / Erdenreich* "Earth / Earth realm" (6 occurrences), *Himmel* "Heaven" (3 occurrences), and *Hölle* "Hell" (2 occurrences) are peripheral. These ideologemes lead us to two thoughts: firstly, the idea of the reality of the transcendent, lost by modern culture, which is predictably represented in church culture; secondly, the idea of optimism in church culture, as negatively charged ideologemes (for example, *Hölle* "Hell") are almost absent in the examined material, which generally corresponds to the optimistic main mood of the Modern Era, despite the cultural pessimism of modernism and our time.

8 Discussion

The analysis conducted led to the following preliminary conclusions. Firstly, the emergence of *Gott* "God" as the central ideologeme indicates that the Catholic Church preserves the ideals of the Middle Ages (medieval culture). At the same time, the influence of the Reformation is evident, as indicated by the appearance of the *Mensch* "Human" ideologeme in the center as a transitional stage from the Middle Ages to the Modern Era. This influence can also be seen in the peripheral position of ideologemes such as *Heilige / Engel—Kirche—Maria* "Saints / Angel—Church—Mary", in contrast to the *Mensch* "Human" ideologeme. It is worth noting that in other hymnographic cultures, the field structure formed by the identified ideologemes may be different. For example, in Poland, one can find a large number of hymns mentioning the Virgin Mary, so the place of the *Maria* "Mary" ideologeme in Polish hymnographic culture would be quite different.

As a second conclusion, it is noted that hymnography does not directly reflect official church doctrine but mirrors specific stages in the cultural development of society, placing corresponding emphases. Thus, hymnography is not the history of theology but the history of culture.

Thirdly, despite analyzing Catholic hymnographic material, it is based on the worldview of people from the Modern Era, shaped by the Reformation. Figuratively speaking, Martin Luther can be considered the father of German hymnography for both Protestant and Catholic traditions.

9 Conclusion

In the face of the vastness of the hymnographic heritage, both diatopic and diachronic, there is an obvious need for the application of statistical methods that would allow for evidence-based conclusions in a situation of knowingly incomplete coverage of material regarding the internal regularities of the development of this genre. The attempt made in this work to analyze ideologemes using computational linguistics tools supports the hypothesis that the dynamics of the development of the genre under study are determined by the dynamics of the development of church culture, rather than the dynamics of the development of systematic theological ideas.

The plan for further research involves continuing the exploration of trends in the development of the genre through indirect means convincing the theory of science. The proposed classification of periods in the development of German Catholic hymnography, as suggested in this work, requires further verification. The next step will be to construct an evidence-based model of the dynamics of the genre's development, identifying culturally conditioned relationships between periods recorded in the texts of hymnographic monuments and uncovered through indirect research methods offered by methods used in computational linguistics.

References

1. Handbuch der literarischen Gattungen.: Hrsg. von Lamping, Dieter. Stuttgart: Alfred Kröner Verlag. 772 S (2009)
2. Scheitler, I.: Geistliches Lied, Kirchenlied. Handbuch der literarischen Gattungen. Hrsg. von Lamping, Dieter. Stuttgart: Alfred Kröner Verlag. S. 316–324 (2009)
3. Gotteslob.: Katholisches Gebet- und Gesangbuch. Ausgabe für das Bistum Trier. Trier: Paulinus Verlag. 1054 S (1975)
4. Gotteslob.: Katholisches Gebet- und Gesangbuch. Ausgabe für das Bistum Trier. Trier. 1296 S (2013)
5. Russian National Corpus, http://ruscorpora.ru, Last accessed 2023/12/01
6. Statistics used in the Sketch Engine. https://www.sketchengine.eu/wp-content/uploads/ske-statistics.pdf, Last accessed 2023/12/01
7. Kraus, W.: Die Spuren des Paradieses. Verlag Paul Zsolnay, Über Ideale, Wien, Hamburg (1985)
8. Friedell, E.: Kulturgeschichte der Neuzeit. Ausgabe in einem Band. Beck, München (1996)
9. Lexikon für Theologie und Kirche.: Hrsg. von Kasper, W. u.a. Freiburg, Basel, Wien: Herder. Bd. 3, Sp. 437–438 (1995)
10. Lexikon für Theologie und Kirche.: Hrsg. von Kasper, W. u.a. Freiburg, Basel, Wien: Herder. Bd. 8, Sp. 1221–1222 (2006)

Transformations of Precedent Phenomena in the Polycode Internet Meme (Based on the Cats and Fishes Meme)

K. A. Shchukina and T. V. Smirnova

Abstract The article deals with the polycode Internet meme about cats and fish and its constituent precedent phenomena, on the basis of which subsequent transformations are made. One of the components of an Internet meme as a polycode text (visual or verbal) or both components can be transformed simultaneously. Mostly, substitution or contamination techniques are used while preserving the spelling, punctuation, syntactic, and graphic features of the original meme. In addition to the traditional precedent name, statement, text, and situation, precedent visual phenomena are distinguished in a polycode Internet meme, which are markers of either a stereotypical or precedent situation. Visual phenomena can refer the viewer to the iconic part of other polycode Internet memes, and thus it becomes possible to speak of visual precedent phenomena. Precedent statements from Internet memes can not only undergo transformation within the Internet discourse, but also go beyond it: to function offline in advertising discourse as memes proper.

Keywords Precedent phenomena · Polycode Internet meme · Polycode text

1 Introduction

An Internet meme is a special way of Internet communication, a humorous polycode text containing verbal and iconic components. This term first appeared in the first decade of the twenty-first century, although the concept of "meme" was used by Professor R. Dawkins as early as 1976.

The problems of precedent phenomena are actively discussed in the publications of Russian scholars: I. V. Vysotskaya, D. B. Gudkov, I. V. Zakharenko, Yu. N. Karaulov, V. V. Krasnykh. The essence of the transformation of precedent phenomena lies in

K. A. Shchukina (✉) · T. V. Smirnova
St. Petersburg State University, Saint-Petersburg, Russia
e-mail: k.shukina@spbu.ru

T. V. Smirnova
e-mail: smyrnanova2.0@gmail.com

P. Eismont et al. (eds.), *Literature, Language and Computing*,
https://doi.org/10.1007/978-981-96-0990-1_20

intentional changes in order to achieve a certain communicative effect. The transformations of precedent phenomena in Internet memes, which are a polycode text, and especially their non-verbal component, have not received enough attention, which determines the relevance of this work.

In addition, it is worth noting that the understanding of written texts, oral speech and of the language of Internet memes is ensured by the presence of a certain cultural experience—the knowledge of current events, feature films and literature, stereotypical and precedent situations characteristic of a given society, as well as the coincidence of the cultural background of communicants and the commonality of relevant presuppositions [13], that is, everything that underlies the precedent phenomena. According to N. G. Asmus, "the phenomenon of precedence implies the presence of common background knowledge of communicants" [1], therefore, Internet memes can be recognizable and popular in certain social groups or cultural communities, but be partially or completely incomprehensible to representatives of other cultures, which indicates the practical significance of this study, in particular, for students studying Russian as a foreign language. Currently, the need to modernize the educational process in accordance with modern trends and the interests of students has become obvious; Internet memes can also be used to improve didactic tools as an additional way to visualize the material.

The purpose of our study was to identify the composition of the precedent phenomena in the polycode Internet meme "about cats and fish" and the possibilities of transforming the precedent phenomena that make up the Internet meme.

2 Literature Review

As a rule, memes reflect the peculiarities of culture, stereotypes, and current phenomena of modern reality that are of interest to participants in Internet communication.

S. V. Kanashina writes that the Internet meme itself "is a precedent phenomenon, since it is a unit of Internet communication transmitted from user to user, replicated and reproduced in the Internet space" [7]. L. S. Gutorenko adheres to the same point of view, since, in her opinion, the Internet meme "is based on a text or graphic image that is repeatedly reproduced in various contexts" [5]. Without knowledge of precedent phenomena characteristic of a given linguistic culture, as well as without knowledge of memes, it is quite difficult to build communication that ensures mutual understanding between its participants.

S. V. Kanashina also notes that the use of precedent phenomena in Internet memes differs from the use of precedence in other types of texts and has its own characteristics. The researcher refers to the features of using a precedent phenomenon in Internet memes: the transformation of a precedent phenomenon in Internet memes, the intertextuality of a precedent phenomenon in Internet memes, the reinterpretability of precedent phenomena in Internet memes, the semiotic nature of precedent phenomena in Internet memes [7].

O.S. Issers considers the Internet meme from the point of view of the transformation of the original text. In the article "Potential of transformations in polycode internet meme within the event-related context of 2020", several stages of transformation of the source text were identified: deployment of the visual range in combination with the addition of a verbal component; convolution of the visual range with the preservation / transformation of the verbal component; context reframing, which ensures the use of the meme in a wide range of relevant situations; pragmatic transformation, leading to a change in the illocutionary force of the statement; intertextual transformation, including the effect of metacommunication; reduction / transformation of the image with the preservation of visual markers; reframing with a change in the verbal and visual components; adaptation of the meme in texts of other spheres and genres [6].

Since a polycode text (like a polycode meme) consists of two parts: verbal and non-verbal, it is important to recall that precedent phenomena can also be verbal (texts as products of speech activity) and non-verbal (works of architecture, painting, various musical works). Therefore, precedent phenomena can function both in the verbal part of the Internet meme and in its non-verbal part. In our article, we consider Internet memes from the point of view of precedence and transformation of the precedent polycode text—both its verbal and visual components.

A number of studies have been devoted to the transformation of precedent phenomena. So, D.B. Gudkov speaks about the main types of transformations of precedent statements [3]. B.V. Krivenko distinguishes two main types of transformations:

- semantic—the technique of combining two semantic plans - phraseological and literal, i.e. "during semantic transformation, the composition of the precedent phenomenon itself remains unchanged, but at the same time, new shades of meaning are introduced into it, or a play on words arises as a result of combining direct and figurative meanings, and then a certain expressive effect is achieved"
- analytical—in contrast to the semantic, it makes changes to the verbal composition of the precedent phenomenon. This variety is more diverse in its techniques and comes down to several main types: lexical and syntactic [10].

At the same time, the mentioned researchers mainly pay their attention to verbal precedent phenomena. If we are talking about a polycode text, which is an Internet meme, we also need to consider non-vebral phenomena. Precedence is usually understood as a reflection of information about the cultural space that is significant for society, which is not only linguistic, but also **extralinguistic** (highlighted by us—K.Shch.). Yu. N. Karaulov attributed quotations, names of characters, authors, as well as texts of a non-verbal nature to precedent phenomena [8]. Therefore, here we rely on L. A. Mardieva, who singles out the precedent visual phenomenon as a material way of embodying a mental image, separating it from the "precedent visual image" as a mental formation. Under the precedent visual image of L. A. Mardieva understands "visual images of cultural space stored in the memory of representatives of a certain socio-cultural community (the term "image" is understood by us as a unit of mental code, the substrate of such an internal formation can be different; speaking of precedent visual images, we mean those images of consciousness that have visual nature, or at least a visual substratum is mandatory for them)" [11].

Thus, in the article we intend to consider both verbal and non-verbal precedent phenomena.

3 Materials and Methods

The theoretical basis of this study was made up of works in the field of the theory of precedence (Yu. N. Karaulov, V. V. Krasnykh, D. B. Gudkov, Zakharov, and others). In the analysis of precedent phenomena, we rely on the classification of precedent phenomena, following Gudkov, where texts, statements, situations, and names are singled out [4]. At the same time, it seems appropriate, since we are talking about the visual component of the Internet meme, to use the idea of L. A. Mardieva, which highlights a precedent visual phenomenon [11].

In addition, it is necessary to clarify that we distinguish between a precedent situation and a stereotypical situation. The precedent situation, following D. B. Gudkov, is a "real single situation, the minimized invariant of perception of which, including the idea of the action itself, its participants, the main connotations and evaluation, is included in the cognitive base of the cultural community and is familiar to almost all socialized representatives of this community." [2]. It is important that the precedent situation is actualized by the precedent name and the precedent statement.

By a stereotypical situation, we mean a situation that regularly arises in the course of everyday interaction, but does not carry a reference to any precedents. We are talking about a stereotype that creates the basis for a given communicative situation and exists in the cultural consciousness as a "typical" fragment of the real world, "a certain invariant of a certain part of the picture of the world" [9].

Research methods and techniques: descriptive method, method of analysis and classification of research material, method of linguistic and cultural analysis, methods of directed and partial sampling of research material.

The material of the study was a popular Internet meme, which acts as a precedent phenomenon in the Internet discourse and serves as the basis for further transformations. During the selection of material, a number of transformed Internet memes were collected, based on the Internet meme about "cats and fishes" (Fig. 1).

The visual code of the Internet meme "about cats and fish" (Fig. 1) is a photograph in which a man, presumably at the market, is selling fish, and two cats are sitting in front of the fish laid out on fabric. The verbal code contains a supposed dialogue between the participants in the situation—the cats and the seller of fish: *–vy prodoyote rybov—net prosto pokazyvayu—krasivoe… / are you selling fish—no I'm just showing—beautiful…* In the text of the meme, there are intentional spelling, grammatical (*prodoyote* instead of *prodayote*, *rybov* instead of *ryb*) and punctuation (*net prosto pokazyvayu*) errors necessary to express the characteristics of speech and behavior of the characters, as well as corresponding to modern trends observed in the verbal code of the Internet memes of recent years.

Fig. 1 Original meme about cats and fish

4 Results

In the course of our work, we, following D.B. Gudkov and L.A. Mardiyeva, identified 5 types of precedent phenomena:

precedent texts,

precedent statements,

precedent situations,

precedent names [4]

and precedent visual phenomena [11].

Let's see which of the precedent phenomena can be transformed within one (with variations) Internet meme.

By transformation we mean a deliberate change in the construction of a precedent phenomenon, leading to a variation in its semantic structure and functional meaning. Transformation is "the intentional introduction of changes by the author in order to achieve a certain communicative effect" [12].

The original polycode text consists of two components, visual and verbal.

The precedent visual phenomenon of this meme includes the following: an image of a fish and cats, an image of a cat or cats, an image of a fish, an image of a buying and selling situation.

The precedent statements present in the meme in question include the following: *Vy prodoyote rybov?/are you selling fish, Net tol'ko pokazyvayu/no I'm just showing, Krasivoe/beautiful*, with specific grammatical and syntactic constructions, as well as spelling, grammatical, and punctuation features.

Neither precedent statements nor precedent visual phenomena are markers of a precedent situation; here we are talking about a stereotypical situation: the purchase of goods on the market and the dialogue between the buyer and the seller.

Let us consider in more detail what precedent phenomena can be transformed in the context of this meme.

The first and most obvious thing that can happen with the transformation of a precedent phenomenon is the transformation of a precedent statement. The precedent visual image remains the same, the precedent statement changes.

In the first example of a transformed meme the iconic part of the original meme "about cats and fishes" does not change, and in the first part of the verbal code, a transformation is observed: *Vy dollarov prodayote/Are you selling dollars?* The rest of the text remains unchanged. In this case, according to D. B. Gudkov, there is a "substitution" [4]: instead of the original word *rybov*, the word *dollarov* is used, repeating the morphological features of the first and being in the same syntactic position. This transformation shifts the semantic focus to the transformed word, which is explained by the interest in the current situation – the growth of the dollar against the ruble.

In another example, the verbal part of the meme is also transformed. Recognizable by a precedent visual phenomenon, the dialogue between cats and the salesman is reimagined by creating a new humorous level. The precedent statement *Vy prodoyote rybov?/are you selling fish* is transformed into *skol'ko stoit posmotret' na rybov / how much does it cost to see fish* with the grammatical distortion in the word *rybov* preserved and the lack of punctuation. The seller's response is also designed with an attempt to imitate the style of the original Internet meme and the designation is not a specific currency, but a generalization: *5 deneg/5 money*. Also, the characteristic lack of punctuation and erroneous spelling are also displayed in the following remark: *spasibo nenado/no, thanks*. In this example, a textual transformation is observed due to the placement of a part of the precedent statement in a distorted context. The subject of irony in this case is the cats' lack of money and their desire to *look* at the *rybov* for free, and the reference to a precedent visual phenomenon (and, therefore, an Internet meme) serves as the basis for understanding the interaction between the original and new situations.

Further, in all the examples we have considered, both the precedent statement (depending on the context) and the visual image of the meme are transformed, while the visual image can refer the reader/viewer to a stereotypical situation, a precedent situation, or a precedent text.

The third variant of the meme we are considering shows the variant of combining elements of two Internet memes to enhance expressiveness when conveying the current situation. The iconic part is a medieval image of heads, reminiscent of the Zoom video conferencing program. The reference to the real situation is related to the coronavirus pandemic and the need to switch to an online format for learning and working under quarantine. As a rule, the massive use of video communication platforms was accompanied by numerous technical difficulties (an unstable Internet connection, a microphone turned on at the wrong time, unsuccessful screen sharing during a presentation), as evidenced by the following statements, some of which are precedent: *Da che u vas so svyaz'yu, Oleg, vyklyuchi zvuk/What's wrong with your connection, Oleg, turn off the sound, A vy videli mem pro rybov?/Have you seen the meme about fish?, A chto s prezentaciej delaem?/What are we doing with the presentation?, Da prosto pokazyvaem/We're just showing it, Dajte mne zarplatu!/ Give me a salary!* Here, with the help of naming the precedent name *rybov*, the meme "about cats and fish" is mentioned, the reference to which continues in the phrase *Da prosto pokazyvaem/Yes, we're just showing*. And also in the picture there is an image of the head of a lion, pronouncing the phrase *Dajte mne zarplatu!/Give me a salary!*, which is an allusion to the meme "about a lion and a branch" (which we do not consider in this article), the elements of which, obviously, also become precedent.

The fourth variation of the meme we are considering depicting a long line at the Mausoleum of V. I. Lenin on Red Square refers to the stereotypical situation for Russians "to go to the mausoleum to look at Lenin", while the precedent statement of the original meme *нет, показываем* is actualized. Further in the text, a lexical transformation is observed—the replacement of the original *rybov* with (*Vy prodoyote rybov?|are you selling fish—Vy prodoete leninov?|Are you selling lenins?*) with the preservation of morphological characteristics and syntactic position in the sentence.

At the same time, we can say that the visual images used in the memes discussed above are not precedent, but they mark a stereotypical situation.

There are other options for transforming the original meme, where the visual phenomenon is precedent and marks an already precedent situation.

In the fifth example we are considering, the visual precedent phenomenon is the image of the fresco of the Fraternal refectory of the Holy Trinity Sergius Lavra. In the center of the image is the figure of Jesus Christ, who spreads his arms to the sides, and next to him are people and tubs filled with fish. In this case, there is a reference to the precedent biblical situations "The Miracle of Five Loaves and Two Fishes" and "The Miracle of Seven Loaves and Fishes". The verbal component remains unchanged and is a dialogue:—*Vy prodoyote rybov?/are you selling fish—Net tol'ko pokazyvayu/no I'm just showing—Krasivoe/beautiful.*

In the seventh example frames from the famous Soviet film by Eldar Ryazanov "*The Irony of Fate, or Enjoy Your Bath!*!", which has become a precedent text for Russian culture, are used as a visual component, and a frame from the film is obviously a visual precedent phenomenon. Recall that one of the heroes is offered fish in aspic, after which he utters the famous precedent statement: *Kakaya gadost', kakaya gadost' eta vasha zalivnaya ryba!/What disgusting, what disgusting, this jellied fish of yours!* In this case, the first utterance of the original meme about cats and fish is transformed by placing it in a new context: *vy zalivaete rybov?| do you gel the fish?* With the preservation of the grammatical form of the word *rybov*, and the second utterance—in *zalivayu/I gel*, due to which there is a reference to the situation presented in the film. The transformation of the last line of the original meme is the substitution of the word *Krasivoe/beautiful* for a similarly grammatical *gadostnoe/ disgusting*.

That is, in the memes discussed above, the visual precedent phenomenon marks the precedent situation.

In addition, visual phenomena can also refer the viewer to the iconic part of polycode Internet memes, and thus we can also talk about their precedence: for example, the visual part of the meme about a lion and a branch became the basis for the transformation of the verbal part of the meme about cats and fish:

The image of the original meme about a lion and a branch is used as a precedent visual phenomenon, and the precedent statement of the meme about cats and fish forms the basis for the verbal code. However, there is a lexical transformation "contamination" (*Vy vydayote zarplatov?/Do you issue salaries?*) with the preservation of the morphological features of the original word *rybov*. Thus, here we see not only contamination at the lexical level, but also at the visual one.

We see the same kind of contamination of precedent phenomena and in another case the Internet meme about cats and fishes and the Internet meme about cats and Natasha are combined. The phrases *Nam rybov ne prodayut /They don't sell us fish, Prosto pokazyvayut/it just shows, No krasivoe/but it's beautiful* lexically refer to the precedent statement of the meme about cats and fish, and the visual location of the cats refers to the precedent visual phenomenon of the meme about cats and Natasha.

Transformed precedent Internet memes often go beyond the Internet discourse. You can see various transformed memes not only on the Web, but also in stores or organizations, on banners, they are used as an advertisement for a particular product. According to E. M. Zabalueva, memes are used in the marketing strategies of companies operating in various fields—commercial, tourism, financial, etc. [14: 280]. It should be noted that in this case, the precedent statement is transformed, but the visual part can be anything: it can address the needs of advertisers or can be absent altogether.

So, for example, one version of the meme was placed in printed form in one of the DNS stores in 2021 in Nizhny Novgorod. The iconic part depicts a sales consultant and a buyer. The syntactic structure of the text of the meme and the language game with the use of a characteristic grammatical form (*vy prodaete videokartov/do you sell video cards)* refer the reader to the meme about cats and fish—a source of precedence. The use of such techniques draws the attention of buyers to the product and encourages them to seek help from sales consultants. So, going beyond the Net, the Internet meme becomes an advertising text and performs some of the functions of this genre, primarily two fundamental ones: attractive and phatic.

The following examples could be found several years ago in St. Petersburg in Apraksin Dvor, in a store of fake branded items, the stairs to which were decorated with such inscriptions. In one version, the viewer could see an image of a cat as a reference to a meme about cats and fish, but the main allusion is presented in the text, which is designed in the same font to enhance the effect. Visually, the steps of the stairs are used to separate the lines: *Vy prodoyote rybov?/are you selling fish вы продоёте рыбов?, net, no est' lyuks, krasivoe/ no, but we have lux, something beautiful.* In another version, on the steps of a store in Apraksin Dvor was placed a similarly transformed precedent statement: *tut ne prodayut rybov, no prodayut lyuks brendy /they don't sell fish here, they sell luxury brands.* Thus, the original meme continues to exist outside the Internet space, and in this case, the reference is freely read due to the visual, graphic, syntactic, punctuation design of the text and the precedent words *rybov* and *krasivoe.*

We found another prime example of using the precedent statement of an Internet meme about cats and fish as an advertisement for a product. In one of the malls, on the advertising banner of the Reebok sportswear chain, there is a poster, the iconic part of which is an image of sports shoes; it interacts with a verbal component, obviously referring the reader to the meme-source of precedence. The text, consisting of three lines (*Vi prodoyote Reebok?, Da!, Krosivoe/Are you sell Reebok?, Yes!, Beautiful*), reflects the transformation. The language game is based on the consonance of the brand name "Reebok" (*Ribok*) and the precedent *rybov* or possible in this context *rybok* (*Vy prodaete rybok?/Are you sell small fish?*). The original *vy* is deliberately garbled to *vi* in order to give the lines a cute "cat" tone and probably partly explain the distortion in the word *ribok* and the last line. An advertising banner that takes into account the needs and interests of the target audience of the product attracts the attention of young people who are fond of sports and are familiar with the Internet meme about cats and fish. Here, the effectiveness of the advertising text is ensured precisely by the precedent of the original Internet meme, and it is the recognition of precedent phenomena that ensures going beyond the Internet. So the Internet meme about cats and fish becomes not only an advertising text, but also a meme itself, defined by R. Dawkins as a "unit of cultural information transmission".

5 Discussion

In the polycode Internet memes discussed above, we have identified several types of precedent phenomena. In this case, as a rule, one of the components of an Internet meme as a polycode text (visual or verbal), both components can be transformed simultaneously, or different Internet memes can be contaminated. Basically, methods of substitution or contamination are used while preserving the spelling, punctuation, syntactic, and graphic features of the original memes.

The visual images used in the transformed memes may or may not be precedent. In the case when the visual image is not a precedent, it marks a stereotypical situation; when a visual image is precedent, it marks an already precedent situation.

Visual phenomena can also refer the viewer to the iconic part of other polycode Internet memes, and thus we can speak of visual precedent phenomena here. D. B. Gudkov said that a precedent name and a precedent statement can be markers of a precedent situation, but, from our point of view, a visual precedent phenomenon is also such a marker.

In addition, due to the "acquisition" of the precedence of an Internet meme, and, in particular, precedent statements, it gains the ability to go beyond the Internet discourse, function in an area unusual for it and acquire the features of a meme itself as an actively distributed unit of information significant for a given linguistic culture.

6 Conclusions

In the course of the study, an attempt was made to identify the composition of precedent phenomena in the polycode Internet meme "about cats and fish", as well as the possibility of their transformation.

In addition to the traditional precedent name, statement, text, and situation, we also identified precedent visual phenomena in Internet memes as markers of either a stereotypical or precedent situation, which are addressed in the process of perception and decoding of precedent phenomena in the mind of the reader / viewer. Precedent statements from Internet memes are able to go beyond the Internet discourse and function in offline advertising discourse already as memes as such.

To decode precedent phenomena, one must have sufficient knowledge of culture, history, art, politics, economics, religion, as well as current events in the country and the world. With insufficient awareness of the reader, decoding is possible only with an explanation, which often leads to the loss of the comic effect. The results obtained in the course of the study provide an opportunity to improve the cultural competence of students, since the precedence of Internet memes is easily recognized by native speakers, but for foreign students it presents a certain difficulty.

References

1. Asmus, N.G.: Precedentnost internet-memov. Slovo, vyskazyvanie, tekst v kognitivnom, pragmaticheskom i kul'turologicheskom aspektah: materialy VIII Mezhdunar. nauch. Konf. In: Precedent of Internet memes. Word, Statement, Text in Cognitive, Pragmatic and Linguocultural Aspects: Materials of the 8th International Scientific Conference. Chelyabinsk: Enciklopediya, (2016). S. 165–168. (in Russian)
2. Gudkov, D.B.: Precedentnaya situaciya i sposoby ee aktualizacii. D. B. Gudkov. Yazyk. Soznanie. Kommunikaciya. Precedent situation and ways of updating it. Gudkov, D.V. Language. Consciousness. Communication. M., (2000). Vyp. 11. S. 40–46. (in Russian)
3. Gudkov, D.B.: Teoriya i praktika mezhkul'turnoj kommunikacii. Theory and practice of intercultural communication. M., (2003). 288 s. S. 209–210. (in Russian)
4. Gudkov, D.B., Krasnyh, V.V., Zaharenko, I.V., Bagaeva, D.V.: Nekotorye osobennosti funkcionirovaniya precedentnyh vyskazyvanij. Vestnik Moskovskogo universiteta. Some features of the functioning of precedent statements. Bulletin of Moscow University. (1997). 4. - Seriya 9. Filologiya. - S. 12–19. (in Russian)
5. Gutorenko, L.S.: Precedentnost' v kreolizovannyh tekstah komicheskogo haraktera v sovremennoj internet-kommunikacii (na materiale anglijskogo yazyka). Filol. nauki. Voprosy teorii i praktiki. Precedent in creolized texts of a comic nature in modern Internet communication (based on the material of the English language). Philological Sciences. Questions of theory and practice. (2017). 3–3. S. 82–85. (in Russian)
6. Issers, O.S.: Potencial transformacij polikodovogo internet-mema v sobytijnom kontekste 2020 goda. Vestnik VolGU. Seriya 2: Yazykoznanie. The potential for transformation of a polycode Internet meme in the event context of 2020. Bulletin VolSU. Series 2: Linguistics. (2021). URL: https://cyberleninka.ru/article/n/potentsial-transformatsiy-polikodovogo-internet-mema-v-sobytiynom-kontekste-2020-goda (Last accessed: 09.07.2023). (in Russian)

7. Kanashina, S.V.: Internet-mem i precedentnyj fenomen. Vestnik Tomskogo gos. ped. Un-ta. Internet meme and precedent phenomenon. Bulletin of Tomsk State Pedagogical University. (2018). 4 (193). S. 122–127. (in Russian)
8. Karaulov, Y.N.: Russkij yazyk i yazykovaya lichnost. Russian language and linguistic personality. - M.: Editorial URSS, 2004. - 264s.
9. Krasnyh, V.V.: Etnopsiholingvistika i lingvokul'turologiya: Kurs lekcij. Ethnopsycholinguistics and linguoculturology: Course of lectures. M., (2002). 284 s. S.177–178 (in Russian)
10. Krivenko, B.V.: Frazeologiya i gazetnaya rech. Rus. rech Phraseology and newspaper speech. Russian speech. (1993). 3. S. 44–49. (in Russian)
11. Mardieva, L.A.: Kollektivnaya kul'turnaya pamyat' obshchestva (precedentnye vizual'nye obrazy i fenomeny). Vestnik Permskogo universiteta. Rossijskaya i zarubezhnaya filologiya. [Collective cultural memory of society (precedent visual images and phenomena)//Bulletin of Perm University. Russian and foreign philology. (2011). 3. URL: https://cyberleninka.ru/article/n/kollektivnaya-kulturnaya-pamyat-obschestva-pretsedentnye-vizualnye-obrazy-i-fenomeny (Last accessed: 05.07.2023). (in Russian)
12. Mironova, D.A.: Transformaciya precedentnyh vyskazyvanij v perevodah zagolovkov mediatekstov onlajn-formata: Avtoref. dis. ... kand. filol. nauk. Transformation of precedent statements in translations of titles of online media texts. Abstract of the dissertation of a candidate of philological sciences. Tyumen', (2013). 24 s. (in Russian)
13. Shshurina Yu. V.: Internet-memy kak fenomen internet-kommunikacii. Nauchnyj dialog. Internet memes as a phenomenon of Internet communication. Scientific dialogue. 2012. №3. URL: https://cyberleninka.ru/article/n/internet-memy-kak-fenomen-internet-kommunikatsii. Last accessed: 09.07.2023. (in Russian)
14. Zabalueva, E.: Internet-mem kak social'noe yavlenie. Psihologo-pedagogicheskaya deyatel'nost': sfery sotrudnichestva i vzaimodejstviya : materialy IV Mezhregion. zaoch. internet-konf. s mezhdunar. Uchastiem. Internet meme as a social phenomenon. Psychological and pedagogical activity: areas of cooperation and interaction: materials of IV Interregion. in absentia Internet conf. with international participation. Kostroma: Izd-vo Kostrom. gos. un-ta. S. 278–281 (2018). (in Russian)
15. Zaharenko, I.V., Krasnyh, V.V., Gudkov, D.B., Bagaeva, D.V.: Precedentnoe imya i precedentnoe vyskazyvanie kak simvoly precedentnyh fenomenov. Yazyk, soznanie, kommunikaciya: Sb. statej [Precedent name and precedent statement as symbols of precedent phenomena. Language, consciousness, communication: Sat. articles. Otv. red. Krasnyh, V.V., Izotov, A.I., M.: Filologiya, (1997). Vyp. 1. S. 82–103. (in Russian)

The manufacturer's authorised representative in the EU is Springer Nature Customer Service Centre GmbH, Europaplatz 3, 69115 Heidelberg, Germany. If you have any concerns regarding our products, please contact ProductSafety@springernature.com

Printed and bound by CPI Group (UK) Ltd, Croydon, CR0 4YY
08/10/2026
02229819-0001